DATE DUE

MAR 1 2 2010			

JUl 0 6 2009

Fostering Creativity

PERSPECTIVES ON CREATIVITY RESEARCH
Mark A. Runco, *Series Editor*

Expanding Visions of Creative Intelligence: An Interdisciplinary Exploration
Donald Ambrose

Creative Intelligence: Toward Theoretic Integration
Donald Ambrose et al. (eds.)

Fostering Creativity: A Diagnostic Approach for Higher Education
and Organizations
Arthur Cropley and David Cropley

Critical Thinking and Reasoning: Current Research, Theory and Practice
Daniel Fasko, Jr.

Investigating Creativity in Youth: A Book of Readings on Research and
Methods
Anne S. Fishkin et al. (eds.)

Quantum Creativity: Waking Up to Our Creative Potential
Amit Goswami

The Educational Psychology of Creativity
John C. Houtz (ed.)

Educating Creativity: A Primer
John C. Houtz

Enhancing Creativity of Gifted Children: A Guide for Parents
Joe Khatena

Social Creativity Volumes One and Two
Alfonso Montuori and Ronald Purser (eds.)

My Teeming Brain: Understanding Creative Writers
Jane Piirto

The Dancing Self: Creativity, Modern Dance, Self Psychology and
Transforming Education
Carol M. Press

Creativity Research Handbook Volume One
Mark A. Runco (ed.)

Critical Creative Processes
Mark A. Runco (ed.)

Creating Conversations: Improvisation in Everyday Discourse
R. Keith Sawyer

The Young Gifted Child: Potential and Promise—An Anthology
Joan Smutny (ed.)

Underserved Gifted Populations: Responding to Their Needs and Abilities
Joan Smutny (ed.)

Fostering Creativity

A Diagnostic Approach for
Higher Education and Organizations

ARTHUR CROPLEY

University of Hamburg

and

DAVID CROPLEY

University of South Australia

HAMPTON PRESS, INC.
CRESSKILL, NJ 07626

Printed in the United States of America

Library of Congress Cataloging-in-Publication Data

Cropley, A. J.
    Fostering creativity : a diagnostic approach for higher education and organizations / Arthur Cropley and David Cropley.
       p. cm. — (Perspectives on creativity research)
    Includes bibliographical references and index.
    ISBN 978-1-57273-888-1 (hardbound) — ISBN 978-1-57273-889-8 (paperbound)
    1. College teaching. 2. Creative thinking. 3. Creative teaching. 4. Creative ability in business. 5. Universities and colleges—Aims and objectives. 6. Universities and colleges—Administration. I. Cropley, David. II. Title.
    LB2331.C75 2009
    370.11'8—dc22   2008053704

Hampton Press, Inc.
23 Broadway
Cresskill, NJ 07626

Contents

Foreword   ix

1 The Need for Creativity in Education and Business   1
    The Call for Innovation   1
    The Problem   6
    The Contents of This Book   10
    What Is Special About Our Approach?   15
    Stocktaking   19
    Practical Guidelines   20

2 Creativity of Products   23
    What Is Creativity?   23
    Creativity of Products   28
    Applying These Criteria   37
    Stocktaking   38
    Practical Guidelines   40

3 Novelty-Generating Thinking   43
    Effortless Creativity   43
    Systematic Production of Novelty   46
    Thinking Tactics That Generate Variability   51
    Self-Direction in Thinking—Meta-Cognition   59
    Stocktaking   61
    Practical Guidelines   61

4 Conventional Thinking and Creativity   67
    Effortful Creativity: The Prepared Mind   67
    Knowledge and Creativity   72
    The Interaction of Divergent and Convergent Thinking   79
    How Do Divergent and Convergent Thinking Work Together?   84
    Innovation: The Extended Phase Model   87
    Stocktaking   91
    Practical Guidelines   92

5 Intrapersonal Factors in Creativity   95
    The Search for the Creative Personality   95
    Studying Personality and Creativity: Methods   100
    Studying Creativity and Personality: Results   102
    Dynamics of Personality and Creativity   106
    Motivation and Creativity   110
    A Dynamic System   118
    Stocktaking   119
    Practical Guidelines   119

6 Creativity and the Social Environment   123
    A Social Approach to Creativity   123
    The Social Dimensions of Creativity   126
    The Social Nature of the Creative Impulse   135
    Society's Mechanisms of Suppression/Support of Creativity   137
    Stocktaking   146
    Practical Guidelines   147

7 The Institutional Environment and Creativity   151
    Organizations as the Site of Creativity   151
    Management for Innovation   158
    Creativity and Gender   162
    Groups and Creativity   166
    Stocktaking   169
    Practical Guidelines   169

8 Diagnosing Creativity of Products and People   175
    The Need to Diagnose Creativity   175
    Specifying the Creativity of Products   178
    Recognizing Creative Potential in People   181
    A Creativity Quotient?   188
    Creativity-Facilitating Aspects of Organizations   197
    Stocktaking   201
    Practical Guidelines   201

9 Techniques, Packages, and Programs for Fostering Creativity   207
    Fostering Creativity   207
    Fostering Creativity in Individual People   212
    Specific Creativity-Facilitating Techniques   216
    Popular and Commercial Procedures   223
    The Effectiveness of Creativity Training   224

10 A Case Study of Creative Instruction in Higher Education   227
    A Creativity-Facilitating Engineering Class   227
    Organization of the Class   228
    Instructional Aspects of the Class   229
    Creativity Counseling   234
    The Assignments   235
    The Evaluative Phase   237
    What Happened?   238
    What Does This All Mean?   242
    Generalization to Other Classes and Disciplines   243
    Stocktaking   247

11 Assessment and Creativity: A Problem-Solving Approach   249
    Problem Solving and Creativity   249
    The Effect of the Problem on Creativity   256
    Preference for Overdefined Problems—A Case Study   258
    Setting Assignments   260
    Evaluating Assignments   261
    Applying These Guidelines   263

References   275

Author Index   291

Subject Index   297

Foreword

e is widespread agreement nowadays that creativity is a vital element in the organizations—not only business, manufacturing, commerce, and market- ell as the military, law enforcement, and similar organizations, but also organized education (our particular interest here is higher education). Despite this idea, it is also apparent that many managers and teachers are hostile to creativity, apathetic to it, or, at best, theoretically willing but uncertain what to do in practice. We believe that this state of affairs is largely the result, not of ill will, but a lack of understanding of what creativity is in a practical sense, how it can add value to the solution of real problems, and what needs to be done to foster it. This misunderstanding in turn results from the fact that creativity is usually conceptualized too broadly as a general, all-or-nothing property, and yet at the same time too narrowly, as mainly to do with aesthetics. It is also regarded too narrowly in a second way—being treated as mainly a matter of thinking and especially unfettered thinking. As a result, it is not infrequently linked with lack of rigor, pandering to impulses, free expression of ideas without regard to quality or even sense, and similar factors. We refute some of these ideas. We have been strongly influenced by the application of creativity in fields such as engineering, where the focus is on solving practical problems and satisfying customer needs, with the result that there is little room for aesthetics, and discussions must, of necessity, focus on concrete results.

We see creativity as having three key aspects: (a) *generation*; (b) *evaluation*; and (c) *exploitation* of novelty. The last step involves the actual insertion of effective novelty into a functioning system. When all three steps occur, the result is often referred to as *innovation*. These aspects of creativity need to be looked at in terms not only of the traditional four **P**s (**P**erson, **P**rocess, **P**roduct, **P**ress), but of the *six* **P**s *of creativity*: **P**erson, **P**rocess, **P**roduct, **P**ress (environment), **P**hase, and **P**roblem. In existing discussions, **P**erson is typically looked at from the point of view of thinking processes, personality, and motivation; **P**rocess in terms of cognition; and **P**ress in terms of social factors such as roles, models, norms, and the like. In education, especially school-level education, **P**roduct has received the least attention, for instance, because a focus on products might seem to imply that school creativity is aimed at producing great works or because of the difficulty of saying just what is creative (as against, for instance, plain wrong, stupid, socially maladapted, or crazy).

Our purpose in this book is to show that all the elements involved in creativity need to be looked at in a highly differentiated way. We do this by mapping **P**erson, **P**rocess, **P**roduct and **P**ress onto the two additional **P**s that we introduce here: **P**hase and **P**roblem. Our **P**hase concept is based on Wallas' (1926) traditional four-phase model (Preparation, Incubation, Inspiration, and Verification), but we expand this by adding phases of Activation, Communication and Validation, seven phases in all. **P**roduct is looked at in a more differentiated way with the help of four criteria: (a) relevance and effectiveness, (b) novelty, (c) elegance, and (d) generalizability.

Discussions of creativity are confronted by a number of apparent paradoxes: Aspects of the processes of creativity, the personal properties associated with it, the conditions that foster its emergence, and the products it yields seem to be mutually incompatible. For instance, lack of structure in the environment may encourage creativity some of the time, but inhibit it at other times, whereas different properties of the individual and environment may be important at different times in the process. As a result, to foster creativity, it is necessary to say in a differentiated way what part of the process is to be fostered in whom and when, what personal strengths and weaknesses relate to particular components of creativity, when a particular environmental property is facilitatory or inhibitory, what kind of product is being sought, and so on. The purpose of this book is to develop a differentiated conceptualization of creativity that makes this possible. A phase approach helps greatly in doing this.

1

The Need for Creativity in Education and Business

Innovation is vital in all kinds of organizations, including higher education. The foundation of innovation is effective novelty, which is generated via creativity. However, in both higher education and business, industry, and the like, insufficient effort is being made to encourage and develop creativity. This book aims at promoting deep, functioning knowledge of the six **P**s of creativity in both "creativity thought leaders" (professors in higher education and policymakers and senior management in business and industry), "creativity technicians" (junior managers, research and development team members, etc.), and "apprentices" (students, beginners in a profession or occupation, etc.). The purpose of this book is to provide a solid basis for the development of behaviors that foster the generation of effective novelty (creativity) and its insertion into functioning systems (innovation).

THE CALL FOR INNOVATION

At their meeting in Cologne in June 1999, the members of the Group of Eight (Britain, Canada, France, Germany, Italy, Japan, Russia, and the United States)— essentially the world's biggest economies—identified "entrepreneurship" as the key property that needs to be developed in human beings. This call has been repeated in other countries too: In a newspaper interview a few days before his election on May 23, 2004, for instance, the incoming president of the Federal Republic of Germany called for "a new spirit of initiative" to enable Germany to deal with problems of contemporary life in innovative ways.

Knapper and Cropley (2000) identified change as the motor driving society's need for innovation. According to these authors, modern processes of change are:

- more rapid (changes that once took several generations to be completed now occur during the lifetime of a single individual);

1

- more pervasive (change affects more aspects of life and is global, affecting more societies); and

- more intimate (change affects day-to-day life, as well as the way people understand the world, their place in it, and their communication with other people) than in the past.

Competition between businesses is another driver of change. Commercial innovation is the response to competitive pressure and is evident in statistics typical of First World economies. In Australia, for example, for the 3 years ending in December 2003, 61% of businesses employing more than 100 employees were "innovating" businesses (Australian Bureau of Statistics, 2003).

One of the most obvious areas of change that exemplifies these phenomena, one that scarcely needs further elaboration, is that of information and communication technologies. Other emerging technologies, notably biotechnology and nanotechnology, add to the pressure for change and further drive innovation. Other social issues are demographic (e.g., ageing of the population, changing family patterns), social (e.g., inequality, adaptation of labor migrants and refugees), environmental (e.g., global warming, gene-modified crops), political (e.g., terrorism, achieving fairness in international relations), and industrial (e.g., off-shore manufacturing, globalization). The fear is that societies will stagnate, even deteriorate, unless their leaders and thinkers find innovative ways of dealing with changes of the kind just outlined.

> There is widespread agreement that the world needs novelty, change, and innovation.

Innovation and Creativity

Innovation involves the introduction of effective novelty into a functioning system. The first step is the generation of the effective novelty; this is the task of creativity. Creativity (production of effective novelty) is thus a prerequisite for innovation. From the point of view of organizations, when looked at in this way, creativity is a source of organizational change and development. From the point of view of societies, it is an instrument of renewal and development, as well as an approach to solving problems of equity, human welfare, peaceful coexistence, and stability. Cropley, Kaufman, and Cropley (2008) demonstrated the pervasiveness of creativity as a factor in modern society by discussing the "malevolent creativity" of terrorists and the need for a creative response on the part of law enforcement agencies. Such considerations mean that creativity is no longer purely the domain of aesthetes and intellectuals wrestling with questions of truth and beauty (as important as these issues may be), but is also the pathway to individual and national prosperity, just and fair societies, and strong and safe nations.

> Creativity is the first step in the development of innovative solutions to society's problems.

Who Are the Creative People?

The focus until now has been creativity. But what about creative people? The bulk of this book is not concerned with describing and defining creativity (although we do not ignore this issue; see e.g., chap. 2), but with encouraging people to *be* more creative. Who and where are the creative people? Florida (2002) answered this question in an eloquent summary. According to him, creative people are involved in the production of "meaningful new forms"—we call this *effective novelty*. He went on to point out that these new forms involve products that are useful, such as objects that can be made, sold, and used; theorems or strategies that can be applied in many cases; systems for understanding the world; music that can be performed again and again; and so on.

We see the people involved as falling into three groups: The *core group* consists of scientists and engineers, architects and designers, philosophers and psychologists, but also poets and novelists, artists, entertainers, and actors, and many more. The most outstanding of these people generate "sublime" new forms that are widely acknowledged, possibly for centuries, and lead to Nobel Prizes and the like. These people are the actual producers of acknowledged creativity. In addition, to borrow a term from Florida, there are *thought leaders*: university professors, nonfiction writers, editors, cultural figures, think-tank researchers, analysts, and other opinion-makers who contribute to the production of effective novelty at a more abstract level and in a more general way. For instance, they may, produce no definable products that exist as entities in themselves (i.e., they are not necessarily producers), but may encourage in other people the belief in the importance of creativity, foster openness for innovation in both individuals and organizations, indicate the directions in which effective novelty can go, develop approaches to generating effective novelty, and so on. Thus, as shown in Fig. 1.1, the core group consists of actual producers of creative products, on the one hand, and those who encourage them, establish a favorable climate, and so on, on the other hand.

Florida goes beyond this core group, however. Some people who can also be regarded as creative solve specific, relatively concrete problems. This group includes those who work in the high-tech sector, engineering, financial services, legal and health care professions, business management, and so on. These people differ from those listed above in that, although they may sometimes generate effective novelty that changes existing paradigms or turns out to be more widely

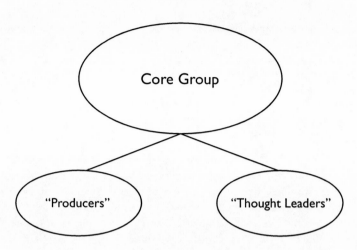

FIG. I.I.   Creative people—the core group.

useful than expected, this is not their basic job. Their primary job is to apply a high level of specialized knowledge and experience of standard approaches, typically acquired through formal education and focused training, in novel or unexpected ways, to solve particular, specific problems. They exercise a great deal of independent judgment, and from time to time they may achieve something radically new. Florida sees these people as "creativity technicians."

Florida goes further and sees creativity in work that is often regarded as everyday. He gives the example of the creative secretary who makes decisions, interprets work, channels information, and devises new operating systems. Thus, he introduces a differentiated structure of creativity ranging from the creativity of those who generate effective novelty at the coal face in the course of specific, everyday work for a highly defined, concrete purpose, and those who develop effectively novel general principles (that may later be transferred to specific situations), create sublime works of great beauty, and so on. Finally come people who help develop the ability and willingness of coal-face creatives to generate effective novelty and who establish in organizations conditions that are conducive to generation, exploration, and exploitation of effective novelty. (We do not mean to imply a hierarchical relationship, simply different roles in a differentiated examination of creative people and their contribution to creativity.) These three groups are shown in Fig. 1.2.

This distinction is helpful for, among others, professors: It is not uncommon for education professors to be asked why they simply talk about how to teach, let us say, Grade 5 mathematics better, instead of actually doing it, or for engineering professors to be asked why they do not actually design and build a better mousetrap (so to speak). Our answer would be that the professors are functioning as creative thought leaders, whereas teaching Grade 5 or building the better mousetrap is a task at the coal face. There is an important role for both these groups in the process of creativity.

Our focus of interest in this book is not the producers of sublime creativity, but in **coal-face creatives** and **thought leaders** (see Fig. 1.2). We chose this focus, not because we believe that developing new paradigms, winning Nobel Prizes, or producing immortal works does not involve creativity, but because we do not want to focus on the small group of outstanding people who function at the sublime level (and who have already proved that they know how to generate effective novelty, anyway), but on the large group of people who are the backbone of organizations and education and make a contribution to generating effective novelty on a day-to-day basis. Thus, we focus here on those who set the tone in organizations (thought leaders: professors, top managers, policymakers, etc.), and those who carry out the concrete work (coal-face creatives: students, middle managers, team leaders, technicians, etc.).

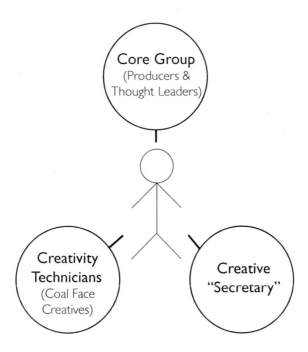

FIG. 1.2. Creative people—three types.

THE PROBLEM

The Educational Problem

The 1996 report of the Alliance of Artists' Communities concluded that "American creativity" is "at risk." The problem is not confined to the United States and goes beyond artistic/aesthetic areas. Employers surveyed in Australia in 1999 complained that three quarters of new university graduates there show skill deficiencies in creativity, problem solving, and independent and critical thinking and are therefore largely unemployable. Tilbury, Reid, and Podger (2003) also reported on an employer survey in Australia which concluded that Australian graduates lack creativity. Cooper, Altman, and Garner (2002) concluded that in the United Kingdom the system discourages innovation—the British General Medical Council, for instance, recognized that medical education is overloaded with factual material that discourages higher order cognitive functions such as evaluation, synthesis, and problem solving, and engenders an attitude of passivity. Thus, it would seem that the creative thought leaders and coal-face creatives that a society needs do not appear spontaneously.

Cropley and Cropley (2005) reviewed findings on fostering creativity in engineering education in the United States and concluded that there is little support for creative students. It is true that there has been some effort in recent years to encourage creativity in colleges and universities. For instance, in 1990, the National Science Foundation (NSF) established the Engineering Coalition of Schools for Excellence and Leadership (ECSEL), whose goal is transforming undergraduate engineering education. However, a recent review of current practice throughout higher education in the United States (Fasko, 2000–2001) pointed out that the available information indicates that deliberate training in creativity is rare.

Although the European Union (EU) has established programs bearing the names of famous innovators such as SOCRATES or LEONARDO, it is astonishing that in the guidelines for the development of education in the community, concepts like *innovation* or *creativity* simply do not exist. At least until recently, the Max-Planck-Institute for Human Development, Germany's leading research institute for the development of talent in research in the social sciences, had never supported a project on the topics of creativity or innovation. Most recently, in a letter dated April 26, 2006, the office of the President of the Max-Planck Society confirmed that the organization does not see creativity as a significant area of research. It seems that creativity continues to be neglected.

It is worth noting that the situation is much the same in schools. Although research more than 25 years ago showed that then most teachers claimed to have a positive attitude to creativity, even today in classrooms in many different countries, properties and behaviors actually associated with creativity are frequently frowned upon. The evidence summarized by Cropley (2001) is that teachers discourage traits such as boldness and a desire for novelty or originality or even actively dislike children who display such characteristics. Thus, although there are calls for creativity, there may be limited effort to foster its emergence, or even dislike of people who display it.

> The problem in a nutshell:
>
> Despite its acknowledged importance, creativity is not being encouraged in education.

The Place of Creativity in Higher Education

The term *creativity* may seem out of place in a discussion of higher education or to have relevance only for fine art, theatre, music, literature, dance, and the like. Indeed, although creativity has been a topic of interest for many years, stretching back to antiquity, earlier discussions focused mainly on the areas just mentioned, what we refer to later as *aesthetic* or *artistic* creativity. The situation changed dramatically about 50 years ago. The turning point was the successful launching in October 1957 by the then-Soviet Union of the first artificial earth satellite, Sputnik I, an event that caused the so-called "Sputnik shock." In the United States and most North American/Western European societies, Sputnik led to a wave of self-criticism centering mainly on the argument that the Western world's engineers and scientists were not as good as their Soviet counterparts.

At first it was not clear what American graduates lacked. However, the 1949 address of the incoming president of the American Psychological Association (Guilford, 1950) had already laid the groundwork for an answer that was quickly seized on when the crisis occurred. Guilford argued that psychologists, teachers, educational theorists, parents, and even politicians had, in their definitions of human intellectual functioning, focused on "convergent thinking": Schoolchildren, students, employees, and even managers are said to be trained to apply their intelligence in a way that leads mainly to preservation of the status quo (see chaps. 3 and 4 for more details). This outcome results from the models they observe, the way in which new material is presented to them, the assessment tasks they are required to complete, the kind of activity for which they are rewarded or promoted, and so on.

> Higher education concentrates excessively on uncreative forms of thinking.

However, Guilford (1950) argued that people are capable of applying their intellect in a different way, involving branching out from the given to envisage previously unknown possibilities and arrive at unexpected or even surprising answers: divergent thinking. By the time of the Sputnik shock, the idea that convergent thinking usually leads to conventional products (even if they are useful in a limited way), whereas divergent thinking is involved in creativity, was well established—indeed, Guilford's paper was entitled "Creativity." Following the line of argument developed by Guilford, the failure of American graduates to make the breakthrough that the Soviets had achieved in the space race was quickly attributed to defects in their "creativity," and these defects were argued to be a result of their education. Thus, from the beginning of the modern era, lack of creativity was seen as a practical problem centering on higher education.

> What is needed in higher education is encouragement of creativity.

The Problem of Organizations

Turning to business, Higgins (1994) described 10 challenges that he anticipated organizations would have to master with the help of innovation in the first decade of the 21st century. These challenges present problems, it is true, but they also offer opportunities. The challenges include accelerating rate of change, increasing competition, globalization, and the transformation of First World economies from industrial to knowledge-based economies. These mean that business is operating in an environment that is not only highly competitive, but also unpredictable. Indeed, economic theory suggests that returns on investments in rich countries should have been lower during the second half of the 20th century than during the first half, because the stock of capital was rising faster than the workforce. However, the fact is that they were considerably higher. How was this possible? The decisive factor that defeated the law of diminishing returns was the addition to the system of new knowledge and technology (i.e., innovation). In fact, innovation currently accounts for more than half of economic growth ("Thanksgiving for Innovation," 2002, p. 13).

Pilzer (1991, p. 2) describes this phenomenon through the concept of *economic alchemy*. He argues that a society's wealth is not limited by the availability of physical resources, but that "technology controls both the definition and the supply of physical resources." It follows, therefore, that "In fact, for the past few decades, it has been the backlog of unimplemented technological advances, rather than unused physical resources, that has been the determinant of real growth." We would turn this around and stress that it is the lack of innovation (the implementation of creative ideas), or poor implementation, that has prevented growth from reaching its real potential. Looking to business in the future, writers such as Oldham and Cummings (1996) concluded that innovation is a key factor in the prosperity of organizations exposed to the conditions that exist today.

> Business too is not producing effective novelty to the extent that is now necessary.

Unfortunately, psychological analyses of organizations show that they resist introduction of novelty (e.g., Katz & Kahn, 1978), even minor change. Florida (2002) refers back to the work of Olson (1982), who discussed the way organizations resist change. Adapted for our purposes, Olson was referring to the problem that, once an organization has prospered as a result of functioning in a certain way, it is difficult or even impossible for it to adopt novelty no matter how effective it might be. Olson called this "institutional sclerosis"—a kind of organizational hardening of the arteries. Cultural and attitudinal norms become so powerfully ingrained that the organization rejects new ways of doing things, which stamps on creative people and stamps out introduction of effective novelty. Thus, we are concerned here with breaking down organizations' resistance to change and promoting what we call openness in chapter 5.

CASE STUDY: Resistance to Change

A student in a program aimed at training German graduates to become business advisers did her practicum in the shoe department of the Hamburg branch of a large department store with branches in many other German cities and its headquarters in Cologne. She was puzzled that the Hamburg shoe sales staff often had to send customers away empty-handed, because the shoes the customers wanted were sold out and the assistants did not know when (or if) new supplies would become available. She soon discovered that ordering of shoes was done centrally in Cologne. The shoes ordered by the Cologne commercial buyers to restock the shoe department shelves matched the tastes of customers in Cologne, but often were not what customers in Hamburg wanted to buy. She suggested that the manager of the Hamburg shoe department should be allowed to send a monthly report to Cologne, recommending what shoes should be ordered for Hamburg. This idea was greeted with anger, along the lines: "This business has been built up for the last 100 years without any help from you, thank you. When we want a beginner's advice we will ask for it." A few years later, the store went bankrupt after a century in business!

We divide the processes involved in change into three steps: generation of novelty, exploration of the novelty (including evaluation of effectiveness), and exploitation of the novelty by inserting it into a functioning system. Organizational sclerosis discourages generation of novelty, uses the process of exploration to discredit and belittle the novelty, and blocks exploitation. Of course, as we show in chapter 4 (see Fig. 4.1), not all change is good, so that even in an open organization the exploration phase is of great importance: It might be asked, for instance, how well the Coca-Cola Company explored its own decision to introduce "new" Coke. Ultimately, the company had to back down in the face of consumer resistance and reintroduce "classic" Coke.[1] Unexplored (blind) change or incorrectly explored change can cause problems, although even successful change involves risks such as overconfidence. Thus, we are not pleading for unreflected, ill-considered, excessively hasty change, but for institutions that are open for considered change. In this book, we show how this can be achieved.

> Organizations need to become more open. However, this idea must not be confused with blind change, which we call *unexplored*.

THE CONTENTS OF THIS BOOK

This book provides a set of research-based concepts that will help teachers in higher education and managers in business, industry, and other organizations, including the military, understand creativity in a systematic way, crystallize out its key aspects, develop it in themselves, foster its development in students and coworkers, and acknowledge and reward it appropriately. Our aim is to:

- demystify the concept of creativity (i.e., help educators, managers, students, and colleagues understand it in a practical, realistic way);

- show that there is a common core to creativity in all disciplines;

- help people acquire a foundation of creative skills, motives, attitudes, and values, from the beginning;

- show educators and managers how to facilitate the development of these through their leadership; and

- show educators and managers how to evaluate other people's work in ways that foster creativity.

The emphasis of the book is on: (a) the thinking skills and strategies people need for creativity (cognitive factors); (b) the personal and motivational properties

---

[1] Of course this decision may have been simply an innovative approach to marketing. If that is the case, then the example still serves as an important case study of creativity in a particular domain.

that permit and activate these skills and strategies (non-cognitive factors); and (c) the characteristics of the environment (social and organizational factors) that influence the whole process.

The basic questions asked in this book are:

What are the characteristics of creative behavior and the products it yields?

What is it inside a person that makes it possible for him or her to exhibit such behaviors?

What are the characteristics of the environment outside the people that encourage such behaviors?

How can teachers and managers facilitate the emergence of these behaviors/ facilitate the development of the internal factors mentioned?

The practical question is not what it is that people possess that enables them to *be* creative, but how to change the environment so they can *become* creative?

The Differentiated Model of Creativity

There is a tendency to speak of creativity in a global way. However, from early in the modern era, it was broken into the "three Ps" (e.g., Barron, 1969): **Person**, **Product**, and **Process**. Rhodes (1961) added the *fourth* "P" (**Press**; i.e., the *press*ure exerted by the environment—see chaps. 6 and 7). Numbers of psychologically oriented authors have discussed the **Process**, usually, however, from the point of view of thinking processes within creative individuals (see chaps. 3 and 4, as well as the earlier remarks about convergent and divergent thinking). Viewed in this way, **Process** overlaps with **Person**. We go beyond this view of **Process** by considering more closely its relationship to **Product**—for instance, different kinds of process may be needed for different aspects of a product (or different *sub*-products). There have also been numerous discussions of the creative **Person** involving issues such as personality and creativity or motivation for creativity (see chap. 5). However, even divided into the four **Ps**, the existing concept of creativity is still too diffuse to provide relatively concrete hints on how to recognize and foster creativity.

In an earlier publication (Cropley & Cropley, 2005), we began to develop a more differentiated concept of creativity by examining the idea of **Product** more closely. This emphasized: (a) novelty; (b) effectiveness and relevance; (c) elegance; and (d) generalizability of products (see chap. 2). In this book, we make a further differentiation of the concept of creativity by looking more closely at **P**rocess, which we examine not only from the point of view of mental processes within the person, but also in terms of the actual steps leading to the emergence of a creative product. Our approach is based on Wallas' (1926) well-known four-phase model: In the *Preparation* phase, a person becomes thoroughly familiar with a content area; in the *Incubation* phase, the person "churns through" or "stews over" the information obtained in the previous phase; in the *Illumination* phase, a solution emerges, not infrequently seeming to the person involved to come like a bolt from the blue; and in the *Verification* phase the person tests the solution thrown up in the phases of *Incubation* and *Illumination*. However, for reasons discussed more fully in later chapters (e.g., chap. 4), we further differentiate Wallas' system by adding three additional phases (*Activation*, *Communication*, and *Validation*), thus conceptualizing creativity as involving seven consecutive **P**hases. The idea of **P**hase constitutes the fifth **P** of creativity (see Fig. 1.3).

With the help of the phase approach, **P**roducts can be differentiated into subproducts, which are intermediate steps in the process of emergence of a creative

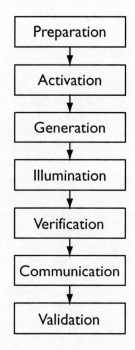

FIG. 1.3. The extended phase model of the creative process.

product. The subproducts can, in turn, be mapped onto the **P**hases, different phases involving different subproducts. **P**erson and **P**rocess (in the sense of thinking processes within the person) can also be mapped onto **P**hases, different phases not only yielding different subproducts, as just mentioned, but also depending on different combinations of personal properties and thinking processes. Finally, we treat **P**roblem separately as one of the factors influencing the emergence of effective novelty. It constitutes the sixth **P** of creativity.

    This differentiated model of creativity permits an analysis of the interactions among the six **P**s—that is, among (a) the task (**P**roblem); (b) the setting in which it is to be dealt with creatively (**P**ress); (c) the knowledge, thinking skills, and personal characteristics of the person or people solving the problem (**P**erson and intrapersonal **P**rocesses); and (d) the **P**hases in developing a **P**roduct. The differentiated analysis, in turn, permits a differential diagnosis of creativity in individuals and more systematic approaches to fostering creativity at the level of the individual and organization.

The six **P**s of creativity with which this book is concerned:

    Problem (the task to be accomplished)

    Press (the environment)

    Person (the individual actor in the process)

    Process (the mental and actual steps in realizing a product)

    Product (the result/output of the creative process)

    Phase (the stages involved in realizing a product)

What Do We Hope to Achieve With This Book?

We believe that the model of creativity that we present is sufficiently general to be applicable in a wide variety of areas and not, for instance, solely in education. In particular, we believe that the principles for fostering creativity that we enunciate here apply in all organizations, business and education alike. Although the book is intended for a wider audience, there is a certain degree of focus on engineering and higher education in our discussions, especially in the practical examples provided, because our practical experience in fostering creativity has been in these areas. It is also the case that certain issues that we wish to emphasize (e.g., the problem of effectiveness) are more obvious in engineering than in, let us say, literature: If a bridge falls down, it is fairly obvious that this is a serious defect, whereas defects in an essay on imagery in Shakespeare's sonnets may be harder to pin down or may arouse less public dismay or anger. Examples of engineering products are also easier to depict in the text. For instance, several variants of an innovative model of a wheeled vehicle can be presented side by side as diagrams, whereas several essays would require a number of pages and could not be so easily compared. Despite this tendency, we believe that our arguments can be applied in many content areas.

We assume that it is not necessary to convince our readers that creativity is a good thing. We are writing for people who already acknowledge its vital role in business, science, engineering, and, above all, education, and who see the value of attempting to foster creativity both in themselves and in other people, such as coworkers, team members, and students. In making this assumption, we run the risk of simply preaching to the converted about something in which we and they already believe. However, we are convinced that there is a need for a text that helps even those whose attitude to creativity is positive to articulate the concept clearly, and above all, to apply it better in their day-to-day work.

The audience we have in mind consists both of those who lead others and help to develop and train them (already referred to earlier as thought leaders) and those whose main role is to acquire and apply knowledge and skills under the guidance of the leaders (the coal-face creatives). Examples of what is in effect a master and an apprentice relationship include:

- faculty members and students;

- managers and staff;

- decision makers and followers;

- team leaders and team members; and

- project managers and engineers.

Our own special interest is higher education. Thus, in the first instance, this book is for teachers in universities and colleges who want to improve their teaching by displaying and fostering creativity and for students who want to understand creativity better and be more creative in their learning. However, much of what we say can be transferred to other settings such as science, engineering, technology, industry, commerce, and even the armed forces. We do not see creativity as something for artists and aesthetes, but as a matter of great importance for people working in practical settings. Later we refer to this as involving "functional" creativity.

> The audience envisaged for this book consists of both masters and apprentices in all organizational contexts.

WHAT IS SPECIAL ABOUT OUR APPROACH?

Much of what has been written about creativity in practical settings is in our view unsatisfactory because it is, on the one hand, too dependent upon shallow, factual knowledge, often in the form of fixed techniques imparted via catchy phrases, and, on the other hand, because it is acquired without any deep analysis of creativity itself or of its psychological basis. This involves what we call *fast food creativity*. In the context of our food analogy, it is attractively packaged, can be consumed directly without the need for laborious preparation, tastes good or is even habit-forming, and leads to a quick feeling of satisfaction without too much effort on anybody's part. Despite these apparent advantages, however, it contains very little healthy nourishment and, indeed, seduces the unwary away from such nourishment. Continuing with the food analogy, what we are interested in is *spinach* creativity: It is not particularly good to look at and requires considerable preparation before it can be consumed, although many people think that it smells bad, tastes terrible (unless it is skillfully prepared), and can only be swallowed with effort. Nonetheless, it is good for you, and making the effort to consume it brings many lasting benefits.

> *Fast-food creativity*: attractively packaged, quick and easy, and makes you feel good, but provides little lasting mental nourishment.
>
> *Spinach creativity*: needs careful preparation, does not look appealing, does not taste very good, but is full of creative nourishment.

This point can be made in a more scholarly way with the help of Biggs' (2003) analysis of learning in higher education. He distinguished among four kinds of knowledge:

- Knowledge of thing or facts (declarative or propositional knowledge—"what?");
- Knowledge in the form of competencies or skills (procedural knowledge—"how?");
- Knowledge of the applicability of facts and skills (conditional knowledge—"when?" and "why?"); and
- Knowledge as an ability to apply facts and skills in an appropriate manner (functioning knowledge—"application" and "performance").

Biggs also emphasized the relationship among the four kinds of knowledge and the range of levels of understanding that are possible for that knowledge. In simple terms, we can speak of the difference between *surface* and *deep* understanding of any given body of knowledge. Biggs describes five levels of understanding (see Table 1.1), each of which can be characterized by learning verbs.

In this book, we want to go beyond a quantitative approach to creativity, focused on accumulating large amounts of theoretical knowledge of facts and processes (declarative and/or procedural knowledge), often at a shallow (uni- or multistructural) level of understanding, and instead steer the reader toward a qualitative knowledge of creativity, focused instead on deepening understanding of all facets of knowledge, leading to an ability to apply the concepts elaborated in this book. Biggs labels this contrast *university knowledge* versus *professional knowledge*. We have already labeled the same contrast *fast food* versus *spinach*.

In emphasizing the development of conditional and functioning knowledge, we are not abandoning declarative and procedural knowledge. Deep conditional and functioning knowledge includes all the underlying knowledge of facts and processes (declarative and procedural knowledge), but goes beyond these. It leads to understanding of the material being learned that differs not just quantitatively, but also qualitatively, from the understanding resulting from mere declarative or procedural knowledge. A fairly recent striking example involves the mathematics performance of Japanese secondary school students in the now almost infamous TIMSS study (Stigler & Hiebert, 1997).

CASE STUDY: Two Contrasting Ways of Teaching Mathematics

Typical German and American teachers, when teaching mathematics, first demonstrated standard solutions to problems and then gave the students further problems of the given type and required them to reapply the solution just learned in a cookbook manner. By contrast, Japanese teachers started by giving the students problems they had not seen before, and challenged them to work out their own understanding of the problem, specify what was needed for a solution, and then develop a solution. Japanese children were the third best mathematics achievers of 41 countries in the project, whereas the Germans reached place 23 and the Americans place 28.

Table 1.1
Levels of Understanding in Education

Level of Understanding	Learning Verbs
Prestructural	Misses the point
Unistructural	Identify, name, memorize
Multistructural	Enumerate, describe, comprehend
Relational	Explain, apply, relate
Extended abstract	Theorize, generalize, reflect

Analysis of videotapes showed that the American and German teachers concentrated on surface declarative and procedural knowledge—everything standardized, sanitized, and made tasty (like fast food). In our terms, the teachers denied their students the *Preparation* and *Activation* phases. This action has serious consequences for *Generation* and *Illumination*, although it leads to homogenized solutions and thus increases the likelihood of relevant solutions (at the expense of novelty). The Japanese teachers' approach required the students to work through the *Preparation* and *Activation* phases before attempting the *Generation* and *Illumination* phases. After this teachers and students discussed the solutions and then investigated possible wider application of these solutions to new problems (*Verification, Communication,* and *Validation*).

This example also raises a second point. The highly successful Japanese teaching started with a problem, not with a solution. The students had to work out their own solutions, and then explore how these could be applied in other concrete situations. Teaching was based on problem solving, not on solution learning. Furthermore, when teachers and students moved from the more general solutions they had worked out and applied these to new problems they were engaging in a form of top–down learning: starting with a specific solution and working out how to apply it in new settings, modified as needed. Biggs would say that this requires an extended abstract level of understanding, characterized by learning verbs such as *generalize, hypothesize,* and *reflect.* This standard procedure is found in many scientific disciplines, where the general principles of a known corpus of knowledge are reapplied in new settings, being selected and modified as necessary. Indeed, we show that one of the characteristics of creative solutions is their ability to be generalized from one domain to another.

Our goal is to help students, professors, and practitioners move from shallow declarative knowledge of creativity (the stereotypical new university student), shallow functioning knowledge (stereotypical junior practitioner or "apprentice"), or deep declarative knowledge (stereotypical professor) to possession of deep functioning knowledge (the fully effective professional). This goal is presented diagrammatically in Fig. 1.4. Biggs referred to deep functioning knowledge as professional knowledge, and for this reason we have labeled the upper right-hand quadrant *professional.* This quadrant represents our idealized goal. In this respect, the present book differs from publications on creativity that focus on nothing more than techniques for idea production (i.e., fast-food creativity). We have nothing against such techniques, and indeed we discuss them in detail in a later chapter, but we do not see them as providing, on their own, an adequate basis for acquiring deep functioning knowledge of creativity.

A second feature of our approach is that we adopt a problem-solving approach. Furthermore, we work in a top–down way by starting with a particular problem and proceeding from there to a review of the functioning knowledge required to solve this problem and to be capable of solving related problems in

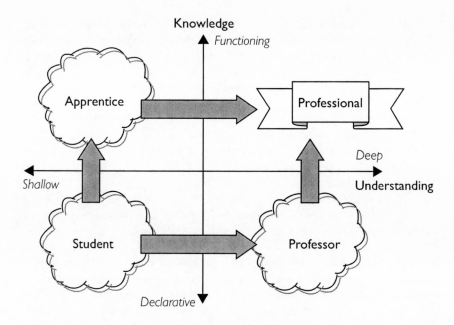

FIG. 1.4. The goal of this book.

the future. We also speak, in the main, of problems and solutions rather than, for instance, products.

> The educational philosophy of this book:
>   It aims at developing conditional and functioning knowledge.
>   It aims at developing deep understanding.
>   It does this through problem-based learning.
>   It adopts a top–down approach.

The Didactic Approach of This Book

We emphasize building up step by step throughout the book a map of the domain *fostering creativity*. At the end of each chapter, we present successively more complex summaries in the form of tables based on the seven **P**hases of the process of production of a creative product and four central dimensions of a creative product: relevance and effectiveness, novelty, elegance, and generalizability. These tables map aspects of **P**rocess, **P**erson, and **P**ress (environment) onto the **P**hases, thus differentiating the concept of creativity and showing *what* needs to be fostered, *when* (during the course of the process of generating effective novelty), and *where*. As we show in chapters 10 and 11, it also provides guidelines for (a) stating problems/tasks in such a way as to encourage creativity, and (b) assessing/scoring solutions in such a way as to identify both level and also kind of creativity.

Essentially the book has two parts: Chapters 2 to 8 are concerned with building the psychological framework for a differentiated model of creativity based on the six **P**s, and chapters 9 to 11 are concerned with applying this knowledge to the question of how to foster innovation in organizations, using the practical example of higher education. At the end of each of the first eight chapters, we offer broad guidelines for applying the theory. In chapters 9 to 11, we review practice directly, including the practical issues of detecting and identifying creativity in products, people, and organizations; training creativity; teaching creatively; and assessing students' assignments from the point of view of creativity.

However, the guidelines offered in this book remain fairly general and abstract. We do not spell out patent blueprints that can be followed word for word and applied mechanically. We hope that the principles enunciated will activate the creativity of our readers. Our map of creativity is initially simple (because it involves only the material presented in early sections of the book), but becomes increasingly comprehensive and differentiated as more of the **P**s are considered. The aim is to develop a detailed model from which it is possible to infer practical hints on how to foster creativity. The later chapters of the book will then use this model to illustrate how to foster creativity—for instance, through a case study (chap. 10) and a schema for assessing student assignments, designs, new product suggestions, and the like (chap. 11).

The book aims at providing a scholarly, research-based introduction to innovation and creativity. It is extended by summaries at the end of many chapters of the practical consequences of the theory for higher education and organizational management. This material does not, however, consist of formulae or paint-by-numbers advice. The practical advice is given in the form of guiding principles that each individual reader can apply in a concrete way in a particular setting. Thus, the advice, "Be open for way-out or apparently irrelevant or even crazy ideas from students and colleagues," might mean that a professor accepts and takes seriously unexpected or apparently irrelevant questions in a seminar, whereas for a manager it might mean looking carefully at a proposal for a change in, let us say, marketing procedures that appears, at first sight, to be absurd or unfeasible.

STOCKTAKING

The first summary table is to be found below. It is of necessity simple because only a few rudimentary ideas in the study of creativity have been introduced to this point. This table, like all that follow, focuses on the differentiated model of creativity. It maps onto the sixth **P**—Phase—the other five **P**s (**P**erson, **P**roduct, **P**rocess, **P**ress [environment], **P**roblem).

Summary Table I
Relationship Between **P**erson, **P**rocess, **P**roduct, **P**roblem, and **P**hase

Phase	**P**erson	**P**rocess	**P**roblem	**P**roduct	**P**ress
Preparation	+				
Activation	+		+		
Generation	+	+	+		+
Illumination		+	+	+	
Verification				+	
Communication	+			+	+
Validation				+	+

In keeping with the desire to present a differentiated analysis of the process of generation of effective novelty, Summary Table 1 shows which of the Ps are of predominant importance in the various phases: A plus sign in a cell indicates that a special creativity-favoring aspect of this **P** is of particular importance in this **P**hase. The absence of a plus sign does not imply that the **P** in question is unimportant, but that it is not the dominant factor (in a creativity-favoring form) in this **P**hase. To take one example, **P**ress (environmental circumstances) is important in some way or another in all **P**hases, but is dominant in *Communication* and *Validation*. To extend the example, we argue that in the **P**hases of *Preparation* and *Activation*, special characteristics of the person (such as problem awareness, curiosity, dissatisfaction, and openness; see chap. 5) as well as of the problem (loosely defined problem, open solution pathway, loosely defined solution) are the key factors, whereas in the *Verification* phase, it is the product and in the *Validation* phase the product plus the reaction of the social environment that are decisive. The arguments on which the assessments in Summary Table 1 are based are presented in following chapters, especially chapters 2 to 7. The main purpose of this first summary is to begin the process of differentiating the discussion of creativity and how to foster it. It should not be regarded as a definitive overview.

PRACTICAL GUIDELINES

General guidelines for practice can be worked out from the theory in the first eight chapters. As is the case in all eight chapters, implications of the material in this chapter are summarized in Box 1 as a set of practical, everyday prescriptive heuristics (hints or tips) to be used in a variety of social and cognitive contexts. They are divided up into guidelines for "creativity thought leaders," on the one hand, and those for "creativity technicians" and "coal-face creatives," on the other hand. Each chapter presents a set of guidelines specific to that chapter's content. The guidelines in later boxes are not meant to replace the contents of earlier boxes, but to supplement them.

Box 1. Practical Advice Based on Chapter 1

Who? (For whom is this advice intended?)	When? (To what activities should it be applied?)	What? (What is the advice?)
Teachers and managers (Thought leaders)	Interactions with students and colleagues	Remember that students and colleagues are working on different phases of creativity (e.g., preparation, generation, communication, etc.) at different times.
		Accept that people will often not be good at all Ps in all phases.
		Identify people's special strengths—different Ps in different phases.
	Instructional and leadership strategies	Regard creativity as divided into phases and Ps: Do not accept a single, global view.
		Help students and colleagues to understand creativity in a differentiated way.
		Identify which phase and which P you are dealing with at any particular time.
		Seek to fuse or merge the results of differing phases and Ps, possibly from different people.
	Evaluating other people's work	Identify the phases and Ps in people's work; if necessary, evaluate them separately.
		Recognize and/or reward creativity in particular phases and Ps.
Students and colleagues (Coal-face creatives)	Self-image	Identify the Ps and phases where you have particular strengths.
		Do not necessarily expect yourself to make great achievements in all phases and with all Ps.
	Learning and work strategies	Be aware of the phase and P you are working on at any particular time.
		Be aware of the place of your work in the whole set of phases and Ps related to a particular problem.
	Learning and work assignments	Set tasks that focus on identifiable phases.
		Provide phase-specific feedback on work assignments.

2

Creativity of Products

Creativity is not simply a matter of thinking or behaving in ways that differ from the customary—it involves effective, novel, elegant, and generalizable products. These range from ideas, principles, and procedures (mental objects) to tangible products such as works of art, structures, or machines (physical objects). The criteria of creativity of products form a hierarchy, in which effectiveness and novelty are necessary elements, whereas elegance and generalizability add value. The criteria interact in a system involving thinking, properties of the persons involved, and aspects of the settings in which novelty is produced or into which it is to be introduced. Understanding of this system makes it possible to foster creativity in individuals and organizations, including institutions of higher education.

WHAT IS CREATIVITY?

Vielot's Conundrum

University students complained about experiencing discomfort in the classroom because the desks—even the large ones—were too small for some of them.[1] However, simply increasing the desks' size was not the answer because large desks would be too large for smaller students. A special team was formed to solve the problem. The team's members concluded that there were three issues:

1. The desks needed to fit both small and large people;

2. They needed to be able to prevent pencils rolling off onto the floor; and

3. A cup holder was needed on the desks.

---

[1] This case was posted on the website (www.ijee.dit.ie/forum/forum1.html) by Jacques Vielot in 2001. The site is dedicated to the "Forum on Creativity in Engineering Education" of the *International Journal of Engineering Education*.

After a brainstorming session, the team designed an expanding desk that could be adjusted according to the size of the user. The top had grooves for pencils and a hole bored in it as a cup holder. When the desk was built, it was found to work so well that the team began the process of obtaining a patent.

In discussing this case study, Vielot (2001) posed a series of important questions. Modified for our purposes, these were:

1. Where did the creativity lie? Was it in (a) the desk (the *product*), (b) the *processes* that led to the development of the product, or (c) the *people* who designed the product?

2. What factors enabled the creativity?

3. Just because the desk proved to be useful, can it be said that the ideas involved in designing it were creative?

4. Are other desks that may well have involved a good idea nonetheless not creative because they did not get built?

Vielot made a number of interesting points. If the desk is the creativity, what is it about it that is creative? The individual parts are not new: Sliding mechanisms are not new, nor are grooves for pencils or holes for holding cups. The whole desk is not new either, nor is its function, because we are perfectly familiar with sitting at desks. Unusual is that the desk is adjustable, but the basic idea of adjustability is not new. The following sections lay down principles that lead to answers to these and similar questions.[2]

We need to be able to answer this question: What is creativity in higher education and in practice in organizations?

Creativity and Usefulness

Creativity involves a deliberate challenge to the status quo. It involves an intention to bring about change so that it differs from introduction of novelty that results simply from natural evolution with the passage of time, by accident, or through misunderstandings—it is revolutionary, rather than simply evolutionary. Creativity has sometimes been seen as involving simply novelty without regard to usefulness. An extreme position of this kind is to be found in the art-for-art's-sake movement in 19th century Paris; As the novelist Gautier (1836) put in the preface to his novel, *Mademoiselle de Maupin,* "Nothing is truly beautiful unless it is *useless*" (italics added).

---

[2]We answer the questions later in the chapter.

However, as we argue in more detail later in agreement with King (1992), creativity in the sense that we use the term always involves introduction of novelty with the aim of benefiting the system into which it is introduced. Nonetheless, as Cropley, Kaufman, and Cropley (2008) pointed out, "benefit" is a subjective concept—one person's benefit may be another's curse. The novelty of new weapons of war or unusual ways of using technology to steal money may well benefit one group, but will be reviled by another. Despite this, creativity is not simply good for its own sake. It must have a purpose. The novelty must be capable of being applied in some setting even if what is meant by *application* differs sharply from, let us say, fine art to engineering. Novelty that can be applied and actually solves a problem of some kind is relevant (to the problem it solves) and effective.

The idea of novelty that is relevant to some problem and leads to a solution that is effective in solving it is perhaps most obvious in business, manufacturing, marketing, and trade, as well as other areas such as health care, social services, and the like. In such areas, failure to introduce effective novelty, or introduction of novelty that is not effective, can have obviously disastrous results, such as patients dying, businesses going bankrupt, or bridges falling down. However, we do not regard the idea of usefulness as confined to these areas. It also encompasses aesthetic/artistic creativity: Here too creative people seek to bring into existence novel products that effectively solve some problem even if the problem is not so much that of getting traffic across a river or increasing the sales of a product, but that of, let us say, transmitting a feeling about a landscape to other people.

> Creativity is important because it is the basis of the ability to generate and implement useful (i.e., relevant and effective) novelty.

Creativity as a System

Treffinger, Sortore, and Cross (1993) stressed the importance of what they called the *full ecological system of creativity*. This system involves recognition of interactions among psychological properties of the individual, aspects of the creative process, effects of the situation, characteristics of the task, and the nature of the desired product. Creativity involves:

- thinking, personality, and motivation (intrapersonal factors);
- interactions with other people (interpersonal factors);
- supportive or destructive aspects of the social and physical environment, including places of learning and workplaces.

These factors interact to form a system encompassing characteristics of the field in which effective novelty is to be generated, the person and the environment. Thus, some of them are psychological, others social, some even physical, whereas they sometimes include aspects of the setting or of the historical age. They even include lucky breaks or other aspects of opportunity. In later chapters, we give more emphasis to the full system of factors involved in the production of novelty, and we argue for a more socially defined concept of creativity (see especially chaps. 6 and 7).

Innovation thus results from this system of interacting factors, some of them located within the individual person, some in the knowledge and skills of the field, and some in the practical setting. Its two components—production of relevant, effective novelty (creativity) and insertion of the novelty into a functioning setting—involve subsystems of cognitive factors (thinking, knowledge and skills), intrapersonal factors (personality, motivation, and self-image) and interpersonal factors (action of the group on the former two sets of factors, management and leadership, and teaching and learning activities). The way these work together is depicted in Fig. 2.1.

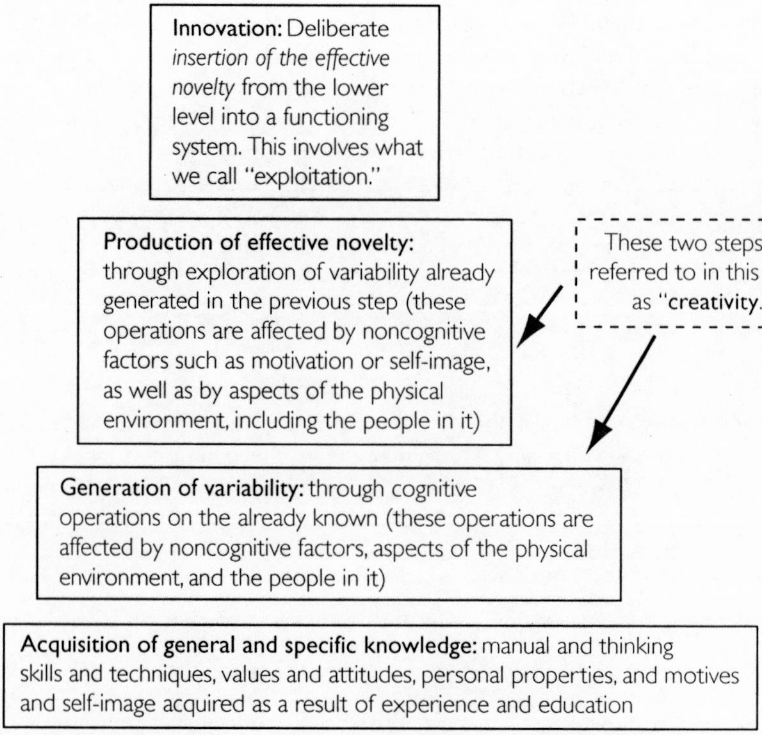

Innovation: Deliberate *insertion of the effective novelty* from the lower level into a functioning system. This involves what we call "exploitation."

Production of effective novelty: through exploration of variability already generated in the previous step (these operations are affected by noncognitive factors such as motivation or self-image, as well as by aspects of the physical environment, including the people in it)

These two steps are referred to in this book as "creativity."

Generation of variability: through cognitive operations on the already known (these operations are affected by noncognitive factors, aspects of the physical environment, and the people in it)

Acquisition of general and specific knowledge: manual and thinking skills and techniques, values and attitudes, personal properties, and motives and self-image acquired as a result of experience and education

FIG. 2.1. The innovation pyramid.

The relationship among innovation, insertion of novelty, effective novelty, creativity, generation of variability, and exploration of variability (see Fig. 2.1) may not be immediately apparent, especially because some of these terms may appear to be used more or less interchangeably in some places. We see innovation as the pinnacle of a hierarchical structure. Innovation is the process of deliberate insertion of beneficial novelty into a functioning system. It thus happens more or less suddenly as the result of a conscious intervention and is not simply the result of natural development of the system, which would occur on its own given enough time. At the next level lower in the hierarchy comes production of the effective novelty, in order that it can be inserted. This process of production of effective novelty is often referred to as *creativity*: Thus, *creativity* and *production of effective novelty* are almost synonyms.

Creativity (or production of effective novelty) rests on processes that come lower in the hierarchy. In the first instance, novelty (regardless of whether it is effective) has to be produced. We refer to this as *generation of variability*. Generation of variability offers novel ways of looking at things, to be sure, but on its own is not sufficient; what is needed is effective novelty. Thus, when variability is generated, it must be checked out from the point of view of workability, acceptability, or similar criteria to determine if it is effective. The latter step (checking out novelty once it has been generated) is discussed in more detail in chapter 4.

Creativity has two components: *generation* of novelty and *evaluation* of the relevance and effectiveness of the novelty. These two components require cognitive skills (thinking, etc.), personality properties (openness, willingness to take risks, etc.), and appropriate social conditions (tolerance of deviation, etc.).

Creativity in Different Fields

Creativity in science or engineering clearly differs from creativity in, for instance, fine art. Despite this notion, there seem to be common elements to creativity in all domains. There has been disagreement among researchers for many years about whether a unified model of creativity can be developed. Baer (1998) and Plucker (1998) reviewed much of the discussion, coming to contradictory conclusions: Creativity is domain-specific (Baer) versus creativity is general (Plucker). Ludwig (1998) analyzed creativity in different fields and concluded that there are differences between fields based on the demands of the field, but that a general approach is also possible. We examine this issue in greater detail in chapter 9. Later in this chapter, we present a schema for recognizing products that we believe can be applied to all kinds of creativity—from what we call *functional* creativity to *aesthetic* creativity while allowing for differences across domains.

For the purposes of the present chapter, we take the position that, although there are differences among higher education disciplines and among different areas of practice such as engineering, advertising, finance, commerce, the armed forces, fine arts, literature, dance, and so on, these do not mean that there are fundamental differences in either the need for creativity or in what is meant by creativity. The basic principle of deliberate introduction of effective novelty always applies. This process also always involves cognitive, personal, motivational, and social aspects, although the precise details of what is meant by *novelty* and *usefulness*, as well as the details of cognition, personality, motivation, and social aspects, may differ across fields. As a result, we believe that a general discussion of creativity and of how to foster it is possible.

> Despite obvious differences between domains, creativity has elements common to all domains, so that a general discussion is possible.

CREATIVITY OF PRODUCTS

From the point of view of this book, the most striking aspect of creativity is its practical, useful products, which are exploited by being inserted into a functioning setting to achieve innovation. MacKinnon (1978) concluded that "analysis of creative products" is "the bedrock of all studies of creativity." Nonetheless, in recent years, products have not received as much attention in discussions of creativity as might be expected perhaps because modern research has been dominated by psychologists and educators. Some writers have even concluded that it is too difficult to define creative products in a practical, objective way because the concept is so subjective, and have recommended focusing on creative processes and characteristics of the creative person. Bailin (1988) was a strong advocate of the opposite view. She strongly criticized the tendency to look at creativity purely in terms of psychological processes and urged writers to focus on products, labeling efforts to foster creativity without reference to products *misleading* and *dangerous*. Indeed, we show here that the creativity of products is not as diffuse a concept as might at first appear to be the case.

The idea of useful products is probably more obvious when it is applied to tangible, functioning, physically useful objects such as a structure, a machine, or an effective, complex system of some kind (such as a jet aircraft or a business information system), or, in contrast, a process in the sense of a service, technique, or method (a manufacturing process, a control process, a logistics service). In the domain of engineering, we speak of solutions to the needs of society as encompassing products, processes, systems, and services. However, paintings, musical compositions, poems or novels, or even systems of ideas as in, let us say,

Table 2.1
Typical Creative Products in Contrasting Fields

Artistic/Philosophical Products Consist of:	Applied/Functional Products Consist of:
• interesting, exciting, or provocative ideas • beautiful or otherwise interesting objects that did not exist before • systems of ideas that cast new light on some issue • novel techniques for producing the above	• objects that perform existing tasks more effectively (such as machines, buildings, or systems) • objects that perform new tasks effectively (such as machines, buildings, or systems) • objects, processes, or systems that reveal new tasks • novel technologies

philosophy or mathematics are also mental products that perform tasks or solve problems of their own kind, such as capturing the essence of beauty or order or communicating a feeling to another person, and such products can also be more or less effective. Nonetheless, the decisive characteristics of creative products may differ across fields, and can be considered in terms of two contrasting idealized types—artistic/philosophical versus applied/functional. The most obvious differences between these two types of product are summarized in Table 2.1.

The Fundamental Criteria of the Creativity of Products

It seems more or less self-evident that the first characteristic of a creative product is novelty—creativity always leads to something new. However, there is a limit to the amount of deviation from the already known (surprise/novelty) that an individual or a society can tolerate. When a person is confronted by excessive novelty, thinking may become disorganized or the person may cling rigidly to the already known, the reverse effect from the one we desire. In a similar way, when a product is so surprising that it surpasses the society's capacity to tolerate novelty, the product is rejected or—from our point of view, even worse—the person generating the surprise may be rejected, persecuted, declared insane, or even imprisoned (see, e.g., the case studies of Galileo and Semmelweiss). This point is developed more fully in chapter 6, where creativity is discussed in terms of society's ability to tolerate surprise, not as a property of products.

Despite its importance, novelty is not sufficient on its own. If it were, every crazy idea or absurd suggestion would be creative. Amabile and Tighe

(1993) emphasized that products must be appropriate, correct, useful, or valuable. Thus, creative products must not only be novel, but also socially tolerable and capable of doing that for which they were designed. Critically, therefore, they must be relevant and effective. Cattell and Butcher (1968) popularized the term *pseudocreativity* to refer to variability whose novelty derives only from nonconformity, lack of discipline, blind rejection of what already exists, and simply letting oneself go. To this can be added *quasicreativity* (Cropley, 1997a, translating Heinelt, 1974), which has many of the elements of genuine creativity—such as a high level of fantasy—but only a tenuous connection with reality. An example would be the novelty generated in daydreams. Other writers also emphasized the importance of distinguishing between relevant and effective creativity and mere facileness, glibness or slickness. These characteristics may be observed in some genuinely creative people, and thus confused with creativity, but they are not actually part of it.

The order of these criteria is not arbitrary. Although novelty seems intuitively to take precedence over effectiveness, our view is that, at the least in certain fields, there can be no discussion of creativity without first dealing with the issue of effectiveness. To take a simple example, a bridge must first solve the problem of getting traffic across a river. If it does not do what the engineers were hired to build it for, it is a bad product no matter how beautiful or surprising it is. Higgins (1994, p. 9) reiterated this idea in a more general business sense when he stated that, "to be a true creative product it must have value and not just be original. To be innovative, it must have *significant* value" (italics added). It is conceivable that in other fields, such as aesthetic creativity, novelty may have precedence.

Even in artistic domains, however, effectiveness is often important. Emile Zola displayed extraordinary imagination and poetic fantasy (novelty) in his novels, it is true, but without his mastery of the French language, painstaking research, and detailed drafting of plot, his manuscripts may well have been surprising, even shocking, but would have lacked effectiveness and may well have produced no more than quasicreativity—surprisingness unaccompanied by effectiveness. A further striking example is to be seen in the case of Vincent Van Gogh. He lacked technical knowledge and had to return at the age of 32 to the Academy of Art in Antwerp, where he learned in the course of technical training to express his flair for color and light (novelty) in an effective way. He did not have to learn how to generate novelty, but how to convey it effectively to others.

Novelty alone is not sufficient: Creative products must also be adapted to reality and effective. Be on guard against pseudocreativity and quasicreativity, especially in your own work.

Further Criteria of the Creativity of Products

We propose two additional criteria of the creativity of products. The first additional criterion is elegance. Einstein argued that it is not difficult to find novel solutions to problems: The difficult part is finding solutions that are elegant (see Miller, 1992). Grudin (1990) reinforced this idea when he referred to "the *grace* of great things" (italics added). Such solutions not infrequently cause a more or less instantaneous "shock of recognition" when they occur and provoke a "Why didn't I think of that?" reaction. Indeed, an elegant solution may look so simple and obvious—after the fact—that viewers may underrate its creativity or denigrate it as "banal." The second additional criterion is generalizability. In 1605, Francis Bacon developed a binary cipher using only "five-bit" combinations of the letters a and b, thus showing that complex messages could be represented without loss of information using only two values. Gottfried Leibnitz built on this to invent the binary number system late in the same century. The two could scarcely have conceived of modern computers, but they laid the foundation for modern digital computing. This descripton is a dramatic example of *generalizability*.

The special quality of generalizability as a criterion of creativity is that it not only offers new possibilities for the situation for which the novelty was generated, but also:

1. is applicable in other apparently unrelated situations (i.e., it is transferable to other situations regardless of whether the creative person intended this at the time);

2. introduces a new way of conceptualizing a whole area or opens up new approaches to existing problems, possibly in many areas (i.e., it is *germinal*);

3. demonstrates the existence of previously unnoticed problems and suggests the need for new work (i.e., it is *seminal*); and

4. lays a foundation for later innovations for which the original novelty is necessary, although the original innovator may have had no idea of the future innovation (i.e., it is *foundational*).

The Hierarchical Organization of Creative Products

One way of classifying products is to use the four dimensions just listed to arrange them in a hierarchy ranging from the *routine* product (characterized by effectiveness alone) at one pole to the *innovative* product (characterized by effectiveness, novelty, elegance, and generalizability) at the other pole, with original and elegant products between these poles. This relationship is shown in Table 2.2, where a plus sign means that a property is necessary for this kind of product and a minus sign means that it is not. The schematic in Table 2.2 can also be used to demonstrate the position of pseudo- and quasicreativity, where the only necessary property of products seems to be novelty. The table shows that each product higher in the hierarchy incorporates all the properties of products at lower levels, but adds something to them. According to our criteria, routine products are not creative because the second necessary criterion (novelty) is missing. However, this notion does not mean that such products are useless. In areas such as engineering, for example, a large number of products perform important functions that benefit humankind and contribute to the advancement of society, yet are devoid of creativity. They are effective, but that is all. Rather than representing creativity, improvement to these products are instead simply evolutionary changes that exploit existing technologies. Moving beyond routine products is to enter the realm of revolutionary change.

The hierarchical organization of products shown in Table 2.2 introduces an important principle into the discussion of creativity: Creativity is not an all-or-nothing quality of a product, but there are levels or kinds of creativity. It is not something that products either have or do not have. Different products can have creativity to greater or lesser degrees or they can display different kinds of it. We have already suggested different labels for different kinds of creativity (original, elegant, innovative), whereas the hierarchical organization of these kinds of creativity means that there are also levels of creativity (innovative is more creative than elegant, whereas elegant is more creative than original). The practical usefulness of this approach is demonstrated by the answers to Vielot's questions which follow.

Table 2.2
The Hierarchical Organization of Products

	Kind of Product				
Criterion	Routine	Original	Elegant	Innovative	Pseudo- or quasicreativity
Effectiveness	+	+	+	+	?
Novelty	−	+	+	+	+
Elegance	−	−	+	+	?
Generalizability	−	−	−	+	?

Not all creativity leads to sublime products that are universally acclaimed. There are levels and kinds of creativity in products.

Situation Versus Domain Relevance of Creative Products

Another way of distinguishing between kinds of creativity involves a distinction between what we call *situation-relevant* and *domain-relevant* creativity. Situation-relevant creativity solves a specific, concrete problem (e.g., how to get traffic across a particular river at a particular spot). The effectiveness of the solution is judged according to specific criteria related to the particular situation. In the bridge example, these may include cost, speed with which traffic is collected and transported, durability, attractiveness of appearance, environmental impact, and the like. A creative solution would satisfy these constraints in a novel and effective way, and the constraints would normally be specified by the customer. This situation is what we previously called a *novel* product.

Domain-relevant creativity, by contrast, (a) expands the way the domain is conceptualized, (b) emphasizes new issues not previously noticed, and (c) suggests new ways of solving problems in the area. It involves what we called *elegant* and *generalizable* products. Ideally, domain-relevant creativity also leads to solutions that are situation-relevant (i.e., the solution would also do what it was supposed to do, such as getting the traffic across the river). However, it is possible for the two kinds of creativity to exist separately—a product could involve situation-relevant creativity without domain relevance (what we call *merely novel* creativity) or domain relevance without situational relevance.

Domain-relevant creativity unaccompanied by situation-relevant creativity is probably more acceptable in aesthetic and philosophical domains, where the opening of new perspectives, the developing of new ways of attacking problems, and the like may have at least equal status with utilitarian issues such as getting traffic across a river. However, in engineering, situation-relevant creativity may be an absolutely indispensable prerequisite before we can even think about domain relevance. Some disciplines, such as architecture, may occupy a middle position, in which it may not be clear which kind of creativity takes precedence. As a result, controversy about a particular product may become almost violent.

Consider the case of the Sydney Opera House. Despite being built ostensibly as a venue for the staging of large-scale operas, some argue that the building is not ideally suited to this purpose (e.g., because of questions regarding the quality of the acoustics and the suitability of seating arrangements). At a more down-to-earth level, relevant stage machinery already specially constructed and purchased prior to the building's completion had to be sold off before the theatre was opened because the stage, as actually built, did not have the proportions agreed on between customer and architect. The degree to which the building is situation-relevant is thus, at the least, questionable (is it an effective venue for staging grand opera?). However, it is now widely recognized that the building transformed construction techniques (prefabricated concrete, the roof was built first) and opened up new perspectives on building design (the sail-like roof shape), that is, it possesses domain-relevant creativity of a high order, even if situation-relevant creativity left something to be desired. The Opera House has also become a national icon in Australian public consciousness and has increased the nation's openness for innovation. Whether the architect, Jørn Utzon, is judged to have been highly creative (the view of those who emphasize domain relevance) or a charlatan (the position of those who emphasize situation relevance) thus depends on the kind of creativity emphasized by the observer. A more differentiated understanding of creativity makes it possible to sort out the issues involved in this and similar situations and deal with problems in judging creativity that would otherwise remain intractable.

Product Creativity as a System

For our purposes, the most important aspect of the four-dimensional model of creativity is that the dimensions form a hierarchy. Effectiveness, on the one hand, and novelty, on the other hand, are fundamental and necessary conditions for a creative product, but neither is sufficient on its own. Only when both are present is it possible to talk about creativity. Elegance and generalizability come lower in the hierarchy:[3] It is possible and perfectly reasonable to talk about creativity without them, and, in the normal course of events, they are only interesting when the first two criteria have been met.

The relationship among the criteria is also dynamic. To put this slightly differently, addition of the criteria higher in the hierarchy adds value to those below them. To take the most obvious example, novelty increases effectiveness. Elegance adds to both novelty and effectiveness, and generalizability adds to novelty as well as increasing relevance and effectiveness. Thus, although elegance and generalizability are not absolutely indispensable for creativity, they add value to the creativity of a product. A change in the context or particular purpose can also have the opposite effect, destroying the relevance and effectiveness of a product. Thus, in a sense, creativity is not an aspect of the product at all, but of the context: The context determines creativity by defining a product's relevance and effectiveness. The role of the context as part of a system is discussed in more detail in chapter 7.

---

[3]In this description, we assume that elements at the top of a hierarchy are the most important, mandatory elements, whereas those lower in the hierarchy are either less important or optional.

CASE STUDY: The Relationship Between Novelty and Effectiveness in Creative Products

The acts of terror on September 11, 2001, are a stark example of the interaction between novelty and effectiveness in a creative *product* (in this case, the product must be seen as the terrorist attack). The initial, successful attacks benefited from the element of surprise and were entirely effective. The attempt to repeat the act on United Airlines Flight 93, however, was markedly less successful. What was the main difference between the first three attacks and UA93? We argue that the key factor in foiling the terrorists, apart from the bravery of the passengers and crew, was a decline in the novelty of the terrorist attack. We call this *creative decay*. The novelty of hijacking a plane and crashing it into a building had already decayed sufficiently by the time the passengers on UA 93 heard about the morning's events that they were able to compete against that terrorist *product* to the point that their response succeeded in foiling the terrorists' main aim. We can extend the decay analogy further. On the morning of September 11, 2001, the half-life of the novelty of using passenger aircraft as suicide bombs was a matter of minutes, and a lack of novelty on UA93 rendered that terrorist product far less effective than the first three attacks. In this case, because the novelty of the attacks decayed rapidly, the effectiveness also declined quickly.

Cropley, Kaufman, and Cropley (2008) explore this issue, and the concept of malevolent creativity, in more detail.

This issue becomes particularly important in a situation where a product is forced to compete with a rival. A novel product may have its effectiveness, and thus its creativity, destroyed by its rival in the way that, to take a single example, the vacuum tube's relevance was destroyed by the silicon chip. Nonetheless, the vacuum tube continues to have been creative in its day, although it is no longer in general use because of the existence of a more effective rival. The need to make a product robust in the face of a rival product or even capable of subtracting value from the rival supports the importance of loading new products with novelty, and suggests several reasons for doing this:

1. Novelty may add so much value to a product that it is immune to value subtractions resulting from a rival's novelty;

2. The product's novelty may also give it the capacity to subtract value from a rival product (i.e., to nullify the rival's effectiveness); and

3. "Extra" novelty may add to a product's generalizability.

However, because the nature of the rival may be unknown at the time a product is being developed, added value resulting from novelty may initially be only latent.

Latent Functional Creativity

In Table 2.2, we touched on the possibility that aesthetic products, while displaying novelty, may or may not involve other criteria such as effectiveness. This idea raises the possibility that, despite our earlier insistence on the necessity of effectiveness in creativity, there may be two kinds of novelty that are worth taking seriously; one kind that is actually observed to be effective in a particular setting, and another kind that has not yet been seen to do this, but may eventually do so, if and when an appropriate context is encountered—a kind of abstract novelty that yields potential or latent creativity. We cannot dismiss large numbers of products as lacking creativity simply because they cannot be used to solve a particular problem in a given situation (e.g., because necessary technology must first "catch up" before the usefulness of the novelty can become apparent). Thus, even seemingly ineffective novelty could possess hidden or latent effectiveness. A discussion on the website (www.u-sit.net) puts the point succinctly: "... it behooves the creative thinker to go the extra mile and find a new vantage point *solely for the potential value of the new perspective*" (italics added).

CASE STUDY: Latent Creativity

In 1832, the mathematician Evariste Galois was killed at the age of 20 in a duel so uneven that he knew that he was doomed. (See Rothman [1982], for a description of Galois' life.) Galois left a body of mathematical writings that were so important to him that he worked on them even on the night before his death. After his death, these were examined and pronounced to be defective—despite the importance that he had attached to them—on the grounds that the mathematical arguments had gaps in them. They were novel, to be sure, but they were judged to have no basis in current mathematical knowledge and to lead nowhere (i.e., to be lacking in effectiveness). Galois was aware of the missing steps, as he indicated in his notes that more detail was needed to flesh out arguments. Unfortunately, he did not have time to do this. It was only after the passage of several years, during which mathematics advanced enough for the relevance and effectiveness of Galois' work to become apparent, that their functional creativity was recognized.

Galois is now famous as the founder of group theory, known today as "Galois Theory," and is regarded as one of the most creative mathematicians who ever lived, despite this lack of recognition in his own time. The inability of his contemporaries to recognize the creativity of his ideas does not mean that the ideas were uncreative, but simply that their creativity was at first latent. This latency was at least partly due to Galois' own chaotic work style and the fact that he carried many of his results more or less entirely in his head or wrote them down in a disorganized way (i.e., to a weakness in the *Communication* phase) (for a discussion of the importance of communication in creativity, see chap. 4). Once again, a differentiated approach makes it possible to be more specific about Galois' creativity.

> The creativity of a product may not be immediately apparent, but may remain latent for shorter or longer periods of time.

APPLYING THESE CRITERIA

We return now to the case study of the universal student's desk at the beginning of the chapter and to Vielot's conundrum. How was creativity involved in the design and construction of the adjustable desk?

1. *The product*: The desk was effective—it did what its designers wanted it to do. However, effectiveness alone does not produce creativity. In the sense of Vielot's third question, simply being built and proving useful did not make the desk creative. Fortunately, the desk displayed an additional property—it was adjustable. Adjustable desks are not commonplace. Thus, the design went beyond usefulness and displayed novelty. The minimum requirements for a creative product were met, and it is possible to say that the desk was an original product in the sense of Table 2.2. An adjustable desk may even possess a certain degree of elegance—it would probably be "neater" than a device with, let us say, several different seats and footrests in some kind of staircase arrangement: The desk earns a "?" in this category. The presence of generalizability is highly questionable: Does the design help us to see desks in a new light? What new lines of attack are offered by the adjustable desk (germinality)? What new problems or issues did it reveal (seminality)? Does it suggest spinoffs in other areas (was it foundational)? We argue that the product's creativity is limited to originality—a low level of creativity. Its greatest weakness, according to our criteria—is that it has no visible added value or latent creativity. In analyzing their own product, the students in Vielot's case study would be advised to attempt to increase its elegance and generalizability—for instance, to avoid it being rendered obsolete almost at once by the appearance of a competitor with more added value (such as generalizability). An example of what this competitor might be is a desk suitable for physically handicapped individuals. From the point of view of fostering creativity in organizations, whether other designs

that did not get built would also be creative depends on the task set for the team. If this taste had merely been to produce a design, unbuilt products might well also be regarded as creative. However, if the task were to build a functioning desk, unbuilt designs would be restricted to latent creativity. This example shows the way in which, in the case of functional creativity, to some degree the task (the context) defines the product's creativity, which is one of the paradoxes of creativity.

2. *The process*: Novelty was generated and inserted. This process involved transfer of the already known (adjustability, pencil grooves, hole for coffee cups) to a new setting in a process of conceptual replication or analogy and synthesis. Once again, a low level of creativity was involved in the process. The basis of this creativity was knowledge of existing ways of changing the size of objects, containing pencils, and holding coffee cups. The creative process was the transfer of these to a new setting.

Vielot's final question involved the factors that enabled whatever creativity occurred. Answering this question goes beyond the contents of the present chapter, but we can say here that it was a mixture of aspects of the environment (such as rewards for generating variability) and of the students involved (such as motivation or courage).

STOCKTAKING

Summary Table 2 maps criteria of the creativity of a product onto phases in the product's process of production. A plus sign in a cell indicates that a particular phase is especially closely connected with a particular criterion. The task in the *Preparation* and *Activation* phases is to grasp the nature of the problem at least sufficiently well to be in a position to start the process of developing a relevant solution. In the *Generation* phase, the task is to generate novelty, and so on. If the process stops after a particular phase has been completed (from our point of view, prematurely), the resulting product could be expected to fulfill at least the criterion/criteria indicated with a plus sign for phases up to and including the one where the process was broken off. For instance, when the process has gone no further than successful completion of the *Activation* phase, it could be expected that the results of the deliberations to date would at least satisfy the criterion of relevance, but perhaps no more than that. *Generation* yields novelty, but does not guarantee relevance, effectiveness, elegance, or generalizability.

We have also introduced in Summary Table 2 the idea of *subproduct*. This idea has been introduced to make it easier to grasp the sequential, differentiated understanding of the production of effective novel products that is at the heart of our thinking. A solution, to use the more general term for a product, can be thought of as a sequence of partial solutions, each a step in the pathway to the ultimate effectively novel product. We call these partial solutions *subproducts*.

Summary Table 2

Relationship Between **P**hases and Criteria of Creativity of **P**roducts

Phase	Subproduct	Relevance	Effectiveness	Novelty	Elegance	Generalizability
Preparation	Necessary knowledge	+	+			
Activation	Understanding of the problem	+	+			
Generation	Combinations of ideas (configurations)	+	+	+		
Illumination	A few special configurations of ideas (novelty)	+	+	+	+	
Verification	Explored novelty (privately)	+	+	+	+	
Communication	"Published" novelty	+	+	+	+	
Validation	Publicly explored novelty: A "truly" creative product	+	+	+	+	+

The idea of a creative solution emerging as a sequence of partial solutions has been proposed by creativity theorists for much of the modern era (e.g., Campbell, 1960; Olken, 1964; Sternberg & Davidson, 1999) and is discussed in more detail in later chapters. Successive subproducts incorporate earlier subproducts and build on them; they do not replace them. A creative solution fuses subproducts to produce a result that is more than the sum of the subproducts. The plus sign indicates the phase where a particular criterion of creativity is of central importance in the production of a creative product.

The purpose of these considerations is not simply to construct an abstract model of creativity. Their practical value is that they emphasize that:

- the process can be blocked at various points, not just at the beginning;
- an incomplete process may nonetheless yield useful results;
- different kinds of work are required in different phases (e.g., *Preparation* vs. *Generation*);
- different subproducts can be produced by different people;
- different people may have strengths relevant to different phases; and
- different kinds of support may be needed in different phases.

In education, in particular, the *Preparation* and possibly also *Activation* phases are often carried out by the professor, who defines what is required (relevance) and what is accepted as a solution (effectiveness). Indeed, short-circuiting these phases may well be one of the most serious problems in the failure of higher education to promote creativity, something that is difficult to spot without a differentiated model. The PISA and TIMSS studies of school achievement, although admittedly school-based, videoed mathematics teachers in a number of countries and found that, in our terms, a minimum of *Preparation* and *Activation* was carried out by students in the United States and Germany (most of the work in these phases was done by teachers), whereas in Japan students did a great deal of work in these two phases. When it came to achievement in mathematics, the United States and Germany were in the lower group, whereas Japanese students were near the top.

PRACTICAL GUIDELINES

The question that now arises is: What advice do we have for higher education and other organizations? It is already possible to offer some preliminary suggestions, and these are summarized in Box 2. Our conclusions are offered in the form of hints or guidelines for innovation-friendly teachers and managers, students, and colleagues. The guidelines in Box 2 refer only to the contents of the present chapter, but they are extended and expanded on in successive chapters.

Box 2. Practical Advice Based on Chapter 2

Who?	When?	What?
Teachers and managers (Thought leaders)	Interactions with students and colleagues	Regard students and colleagues as capable of at least some aspects of creativity
		Assume that one of your major tasks is to foster this creativity
		Remember that ineffective novelty in the present setting might be effective elsewhere
	Instructional and leadership strategies	Help students and colleagues to understand creativity in a "down-to-earth" manner; emphasize effectiveness
		Foster understanding of the criteria of a creative solution
		Encourage a differentiated understanding of the production of creativity, especially the phases
		Give examples of phases of creativity in your discipline
		Encourage understanding of subproducts
		Encourage people to do the work of Preparation and Activation themselves
	Evaluating other people's work	Recognize that creativity is not an all-or-nothing phenomenon: A solution can be creative in some ways, or more or less creative
		Identify latent creativity in people's work
		Identify subproducts relevant to creativity in people's work
		Give credit for novel work in the phases of Preparation and Activation
Who?	When?	What?
Students and colleagues (Coal-face creatives)	Self-image	Understand the usefulness of creativity to you as a professional qualification
		See yourself as capable of creativity, but do not expect it to come of its own accord
	Learning and work strategies	Accept that you are learning and working (in part) in order to be creative
		Understand that creativity involves products and not just thoughts
		Appreciate the importance of effectiveness in creativity, and not just deviation from the known
		Understand the role of subproducts in the production of effective novelty
	Learning and work assignments	Try to produce something effectively surprising, remembering the above points
		Strive for seminality, germinality, and so on in your solutions

3

Novelty-Generating Thinking

The first thing needed for creativity is *generation* of novelty. Although this novelty may sometimes derive from blind combinations, luck, intuition, or simply letting ideas flow unchecked (we call this unfettered thinking), it usually results from *special kinds of thinking* that systematically generate novelty. These kinds of thinking can loosely be labeled as belonging to the family of divergent thinking. Such thinking involves *special processes and strategies for processing information*, including constructing remote associates, building unusual categories, building broad networks, assimilating rather than accommodating, and using creativity-facilitating cognitive styles. To produce relevant and effective ideas (and not just plentiful and surprising ones), such thinking has to be steered by meta-cognitive *heuristics* that filter out in advance unpromising lines of attack or help to recognize possible solutions. All of these can be trained.

EFFORTLESS CREATIVITY

The development of the self-adhesive "Post-it" notepad by 3M occurred without any systematic plan. The idea grew from the actions of staff members who stuck brief notes in places where they would be noticed, without any intention of developing a new product. Eventually someone saw the commercial possibilities, and a new product was born. James Goodyear is said to have discovered how to vulcanize rubber by accident, when he unintentionally dropped a mixture of rubber and sulfur onto a hot stove. In fact, there are many examples of apparently lucky combinations of events that led to effective novelty. For instance, Pasteur, Fleming, Roentgen, Becquerel, Edison, Galvani, and Nobel all described chance events that led them to breakthroughs. What mechanisms could produce creativity without effort?

Blind Combinations

Some writers seem to suggest that the main way of achieving effective novelty is to stumble on it more or less by accident. Without advocating blind guessing,

Sir Harold Kroto (1996 Nobel Prize for Chemistry) drew attention to the importance of being open for the unexpected or for something that you were not actually seeking at the moment of discovery: "If it interests you . . . explore it, because something unexpected often turns up, *just when you least expect it*" (Frängsmyr, 1997; italics added). The flow approach to creativity (e.g., Csikszent-mihalyi, 1996) also seems to advocate unfettered production of ideas. Indeed, some writers argue that novel ideas evolve through what Sternberg and Davidson (1999) called *haphazard recombinations*. According to the evolutionary view of creativity (e.g., Campbell, 1960), a process of blind variation generates novelty, and selective retention leads to preservation of effective elements of the novelty, thus yielding creativity.

Simonton (1988a) refined this approach through what he called the *chance configuration* model. He concluded—somewhat adapted for present purposes—that generation of effective novelty starts with acquisition of a large number of mental elements (pieces of information, memories, ideas, and concepts). We would say that these are gathered in the *Preparation* phase and organized to some extent in the *Activation* phase. Unfettered associations are then made, more or less randomly or blindly (in the *Generation* phase), until the chance occurrence of a happy combination that is just what is needed to solve the problem in question—a configuration. In its extreme form, the blind-variation-and-survival-of-whatever-proves-effective approach to creativity interprets generation of effective novelty in a way similar to Charles Darwin's position on the origin of species. Indeed, Simonton (1999) made this link explicit by referring to "the origins of genius" in the title of his book. Dasgupta (2004) pointed out that more philosophically oriented writers coined the term *evolutionary epistemology* to describe this model of creativity.

In art, the chance–configuration model would involve daubing paint on canvas and hoping that an effective work would emerge; in music, it implies simply stringing notes together in the hope of achieving something worth listening to. Such forms of music have existed for some time. *Aleatoric music*, or *aleatory*, was first identified by Werner Meyer-Eppler at the Darmstadt Summer School in the early 1950s and has been utilized, for example, by Stockhausen in his composition Klavierstück XI. Aleatoric music leaves either some component of the musical composition to chance or leaves elements of the performance to the decision of the performer. The origins of this musical form can even be linked to Mozart, who is thought to have indulged in the so-called *Musikalische Würfelspiele* (Musical Dice Games), popular at the time. These games involved creating sequences of music whose variations were selected literally by the throw of a dice. The general form of *chance music* is also linked to John Cage, who used a variety of methods, including coin tossing, to compose some works.

In fact, despite the fact that some daubers may succeed, there are well-known cases of famous artists (e.g., Vincent van Gogh) who had to learn technical skill before their work was accepted, whereas even improvisation in jazz music, where combinations appear to be random, is actually not blind variation at all, but is highly disciplined. The chance-configuration approach would see only a limited role for efforts to foster creativity. Presumably creativity training would be confined to encouraging people to accumulate large numbers of mental elements (*Preparation, Activation*), combine them in an unfettered way (*Generation*), and recognize configurations if and when they occurred (*Illumination*).

> Effectively novel ideas sometimes seem to result from uninhibited combinations of pieces of information—we will argue below, however, that this is rare and cannot provide a basis for systematic fostering of creativity.

Luck

Cropley (1992a) cited several well-known writers from differing societies and with different scientific backgrounds who emphasized the role of luck in creativity. The German physicist, Ernst Mach, referred to "die Rolle des Zufalls bei Erfindungen und Entdeckungen" [the role of chance in inventions and discoveries], the French philosopher of aesthetics, Etienne Souriau, concluded that "le princip de l'invention est le hasard" [the basis of creativity is chance], and the Scottish philosopher and educator, Alexander Bain, acknowledged the importance of hard work in creativity, but saw this work as "energy put forth . . . on the chance of making lucky hits."

Austin (1978) identified four kinds of happy chance leading to creativity: *blind chance* (the individual creator plays no role except that of being there at the relevant moment); *serendipity* (a person stumbles on something novel and effective when not actually looking for it); the *luck of the diligent* (a hard-working person finds in an unexpected setting something that is being sought; Diaz de Chumaceiro [1999] called this *pseudoserendipity* because in genuine serendipity the person would not be looking for what was found), and *self-induced luck* (special qualifications of a person, such as knowledge, close attention to detail, or willingness to work long hours, create the circumstances for a lucky breakthrough). Case studies suggest, however, that genuinely creative people enjoy a combination of all four kinds of luck, which raises the question of whether it is a matter of luck at all, because at least the luck of the diligent and also self-induced luck clearly contain elements of hard work and the like. We show in chapter 4 that the seeds of creative luck usually germinate and blossom where knowledge, personality factors, motivation, and the like provide fertile soil.

> It is a matter of debate whether creativity can result from pure luck. We take the position that, as a rule, it does not.

Intuition

In his now classical stage model, Wallas (1926) identified an *Incubation* stage during which ideas seem to churn and work in a person's head without the person being aware of them until—apparently out of the blue—an answer pops up. The classical definition of intuition is: A process of fermentation until an idea is suddenly there, even seeming to come from nowhere. The eminent French mathematician, Jacques Hadamard, who is famous for, among other things, the Hadamard matrices wrote about his own creativity (Hadamard, 1945), arguing that he did not think in words, construct categories, and so on (i.e., he argued against a strict cognitive approach to creativity), but depended more on intuitions that seemed to pop up at just the right moment.

Hadamard believed that this also happened in other fields and gave the example of Mozart, who reported that complete musical compositions just came into his head (e.g., during sleepless periods at night) and only the details had to be tidied up later. There is, however, considerable doubt about the accuracy of Mozart's description of how he composed. For instance, corrected trial versions of Mozart compositions have been found that, according to his account, never existed. Indeed, as we argue in chapter 4, intuition may well not be the product of blind or haphazard events at all, but of experience, learning, and knowledge.

> Generation of novelty derives not from ideas just popping up, but is the result of special kinds of thinking. Even intuitions may well result from prior learning.

SYSTEMATIC PRODUCTION OF NOVELTY

The idea of creativity through unfettered production of ideas is attractive. It seems to hold out the prospect of creativity without the necessity of making much effort, an idea that is no doubt attractive to many undergraduates. However, our position here is that, although effective novelty may indeed sometimes come like a bolt from the blue, it cannot be purposely and systematically fostered by simply sitting back and waiting for it to happen. The first thing that is needed is an understanding of how novel ideas come into existence.

Generating Variability

Thinking uses ideas to produce further ideas, including, among other things:

- *selecting* from among the masses of information available at any moment (perception is not simply a passive acceptance of everything that impinges on the senses or is already stored in the mind),

- *relating* elements of information to each other,

- *combining* elements of new and old information,

- *evaluating* these combinations,

- *selectively retaining* combinations (which may then function as new information, returning the process to the phase of relating elements of information), and

- *communicating* the results to others.

In the present context, these processes are most interesting when they lead to generation of variability. Examples of processes that are likely to do this are: (a) adapting the general to special circumstances in *unexpected* ways; (b) recognizing opportunities to *transfer* specific knowledge to settings that do not at first seem similar; (c) building broad categories; (d) crossing boundaries; and (e) working with *uncertainty*. Other writers have extended the list to include: (a) *uniting disparate ideas* by putting them into a common context; (b) imagining almost anything, at least as a theoretical possibility; (c) *fantasizing* and thus enriching one's own thinking; and (d) using humor to spice up thinking.

All of these cognitive processes are favorable to generation of variability, the first step in production of effective novelty. They can be thought of not as random or isolated processes, but as constituent elements of broader systematic patterns of thinking (thinking strategies) that generate variability. What then is special about such thinking? Various writers have described it in various ways.

> In the main, effective novelty is generated via special thinking processes, although other factors are also important, as is shown in later chapters.

Divergent Thinking

The earliest modern discussions of this topic focused on Guilford's distinction between *convergent* thinking—quickly equated with conventional intelligence—and *divergent* thinking, which was seen as the cognitive basis of creativity. How do the two differ? Convergent thinking is oriented toward deriving the single best (or correct) answer to a given question. It emphasizes accuracy, correctness, and the like, and it focuses on *recognizing* the familiar, *reapplying* set techniques, and *preserving* the already known. It is based on familiarity with what is already known (i.e., conventional knowledge) and is not aimed at production of novelty, although it may sometimes have this result. It is most effective in situations where the answer already exists and needs simply to be recalled from stored information or where the answer can be worked out from what is already known by conventional and logical search, recognition, and decision-making strategies. IQ scores mainly reflect skill in convergent thinking.

Divergent thinking, by contrast, involves producing multiple answers through processes like *shifting perspective* on existing information (seeing it in a new way) or *transforming* it (e.g., through unexpected combinations of elements usually not regarded as belonging together). The answers arrived at via divergent thinking may never have existed before. Sometimes this notion is true merely in the experience of the particular person or the particular setting, but it may involve what Boden (1995) called *radical originality*. The characteristics of the two kinds of thinking are summarized in Table 3.1.

Both convergent and divergent thinking produce ideas. However, there is a qualitative difference: Convergent thinking generates orthodox singularity (single, "best" ideas that are more or less inevitable because they would occur to anybody who possessed enough information and processed it in a logical way), whereas divergent thinking generates *variability* (ideas that depart from the usual). Boden (1994a, 1994b) made this distinction between the ideas that result from the two kinds of thinking in a dramatic way. Allowing ourselves the freedom of adapting her terminology for our purposes, she concluded that divergent thinking

Table 3.1
Characteristics of Convergent and Divergent Thinking

	Convergent	Divergent
Typical Processes	— being logical — recognizing the familiar — combining what "belongs together" — homing in on the single best answer — reapplying set techniques — preserving the already known — being accurate and correct	— being unconventional — seeing the known in a new light — combining the disparate — producing multiple answers — shifting perspective — transforming the known — seeing new possibilities
Typical Results	— greater familiarity with what already exists — better grasp of the facts — a quick, "correct" answer — improvement of existing skills — closure on an issue	— alternative or multiple solutions — deviation from the usual — surprising answer — new lines of attack or ways of doing things — opening up of exciting or risky possibilities

produces ideas that could not have been produced without a leap in thinking. Examples of processes that produce such leaps are:

- retrieving a broader than usual range of facts from existing knowledge,

- building unusual chains of associations,

- synthesizing apparently unrelated elements of information,

- transforming information in unlikely ways,

- shifting perspective so as to see ideas in a new light, and

- constructing unexpected analogies.

The opposite processes, such as recognizing the familiar, retaining what already exists, or reapplying the tried and trusted, do not generate variability, but rather orthodoxy. It is important to emphasize that there is nothing wrong with orthodoxy, especially in situations where production of variability would be dangerous or where untested variability could have catastrophic consequences. However, a one-sided emphasis on generating orthodoxy—as valuable as this idea is—is fatal for creativity.

> The first crucial property of creativity-facilitating thinking is *generation* of variability/novelty via divergent thinking.

Other Concepts of Novelty-Generating Thinking

In addition to the distinction between convergent and divergent thinking described earlier, other authors have also emphasized the idea of a special kind of thinking that leads to production of novelty, often contrasting it with its mirror image in much the same way as divergent versus convergent thinking. Examples include open versus closed thinking, primary process (not bound by strict adherence to reality) versus secondary process (conscious, rational, logical, and oriented to reality) thinking, or reproductive versus productive thinking. According to psychoanalytic theory, creativity involves biphasic thinking: an initial phase, in which unfettered associations are made in the unconscious via primary process thinking (i.e., novelty is generated), followed by a phase in which these associations are admitted into consciousness in the "realistic" form of secondary process thinking (i.e., they are explored). Thus, creativity involves "tertiary process" thinking, in which primary and secondary process thinking are combined to yield effective novelty.

Rothenberg (1988) introduced the idea of *janusian* thinking, naming it after the Roman God, Janus, who had two faces and thus could look in two directions at the same time (so that he had the ability to deal simultaneously with pieces of information that would not normally be processed together). Rothenburg also introduced the term *homospatial* thinking, the ability to unite apparently conflicting or mutually exclusive ideas by bringing them into the same cognitive space, thus producing novelty. Presumably, homospatial thinking is the opposite of *heterospatial* thinking, which keeps ideas locked away from each other in separate spaces (although we are not aware of Rothenburg using this term).

Although his work is essentially of a popular nature, de Bono (1993) made an interesting and widely reported contribution to the discussion of creative thinking. Initially he emphasized lateral thinking. Unlike conventional thinking, which is strictly sequential in nature and follows a set of logical steps, lateral thinking involves detours or sidesteps. Marginal characteristics of a concept or an object that are not central to its usual definition are emphasized and brought into juxtaposition with similar characteristics of other concepts and objects to yield unexpected associations. To take an example, the fact that a paperclip consists of metal could be emphasized to "see" it as a device for conducting an electric current. A matchbox can be regarded as a nonconductor with movable parts. Seeing these two objects in this way would make it possible to utilize them in an emergency situation as the basic materials for the construction of an electric switch.

De Bono extended his model to distinguish between "rock logic" and "water logic." Application of the first leads to thinking step by step in a straight line according to conventional logic. Decisions on what the next step should be are based on correctness, and this process is decided in terms of absolute norms such as truth, justice, or beauty, which change only slowly. Water logic, by contrast, allows ideas to flow together from many directions according to the natural pathways in the material in question, just as water flows along cracks and depressions in the ground where there is no resistance and forms pools and eventually rivers (creative ideas). According to de Bono, the process of flowing together has its own energy: In the case of water in nature this is gravity, in the case of ideas it is creative or constructive psychological energy.

Table 3.2 lists examples of contrasting kinds of thinking favorable, on the one hand, for production of variability and, on the other hand, of orthodoxy. Variability-producing thinking is characterized as thinking that breaks the rules—of logic. simplicity or symmetry, and social conventions—by bringing together ideas that are usually kept separate.

Self-assessment: Can you think in ways that produce variability?

Table 3.2
Examples of Thinking Leading to Production of Variability/Orthodoxy

Thinking That Produces Variability	Thinking That Produces Orthodoxy
Divergent thinking	Convergent thinking
Open thinking	Closed thinking
Homospatial thinking	Heterospatial thinking
Primary process thinking	Secondary process thinking
Productive thinking	Reproductive thinking
Lateral thinking	Sequential thinking
Thinking based on "water logic"	Thinking based on "rock logic"

THINKING TACTICS THAT GENERATE VARIABILITY

Particular ways of going about these processes are especially favorable for the generation of variability (thinking tactics). Several of these are discussed in following sections.

Constructing Remote Associates

The idea that cognition largely involves seeing connections between bits of information has already been mentioned (e.g., recognizing patterns, synthesizing, uniting, relating, and combining). This process involves making associations. Mednick (1962) argued that what is necessary for producing novelty is that such associations go beyond the traditional, conventional, or orthodox and are remote. He described the formation of remote associates and their connection to novelty production in the following way: In the course of experience, people learn a number of possible responses to any given stimulus. Those responses most frequently linked with a particular stimulus whenever it was encountered in the past have a high probability of being selected as appropriate when the stimulus is encountered once again (i.e., they are common). Responses seldom paired with the stimulus in the past have a low probability of being chosen (i.e., they are uncommon or remote). When the stimulus recurs in a new situation, most people select a common response (they have often made it to this stimulus in the past), which means that people's reactions to familiar stimuli have the advantage of being consistent, but are repetitious. They interpret stimuli in the same way over and over again. In other words, they do not create novelty.

Chicken is a common associate to the stimulus word *egg*, because these two ideas often occur together. Similarly, common associates to egg are *sandwich* or *salad.* An uncommon associate (except perhaps to readers of Dr. Seuss) would be *green,* as in green eggs and ham. A similarly remote associate to *egg* would be *steel.* A person with a high preference for common associates might associate *green* with *grass,* whereas another who preferred remote associates might create novelty by associating *green* with *steel* via their common (remote) link to eggs.

In engineering, we see both the benefits and penalties of different kinds of associations when we examine the functions of common objects. For example, a paper clip's conventional association is with the function "clip paper." The name of the object reinforces this orthodox associate. If engineers are asked to devise alternative uses for a paper clip, they must first overcome their "functional fixedness." These traditional associations do, however, have certain advantages to engineers. Standardized electronic components (e.g., resistors and capacitors with known values), are extremely useful in speeding up design and manufacturing processes. The penalty is that orthodox associates can become so ingrained that it is difficult to make the transition to remote associates in situations where novelty is required. One way that engineers can do this is by thinking of the function of an object as a verb–noun pair. When this is pointed out to engineers, the authors' experience is that they are quick to move from orthodox to remote associates. In response to a request to devise alternative uses for a paper clip, engineers typically initially focus on traditional associations that are anchored to the common function of "clip paper." Such responses will initially be little more than substitutions of other objects in place of the paper. When encouraged to make remote associates and freed from functional fixedness by abstracting the function of the paper clip to a verb–noun pair, engineers quickly generate far greater variability. For example, a paper clip can be used (verb–noun) to conduct electricity, to pierce an ear, to clean teeth, and so on. The question of the merit or effectiveness of the remote associate is left to a later stage of the creativity process.

Remote associates help to generate novelty by connecting apparently unconnected pieces of information.

CASE STUDY: A Remote Associate

In 1865, Friedrich Kekulé discovered the ring or closed-chain structure of the benzene molecule while dozing in front of the fire! With his head full of the problem of the structure of the molecule, about which he had been thinking deeply for a long time, he visualized his tangled thoughts as snakes whirling about in his mind and suddenly "saw" one of them with its own tail in its mouth. He realized at once that this was the structure of benzene. Snakes and molecules belong to areas of knowledge not normally combined, so that the association between them was remote, but extremely fruitful for generating variability that led to effective novelty.

Building Unusual Categories

Bruner's (1964) approach goes further. On the basis of experience, events that repeatedly occur together are recognized as belonging to the same category. Properties that are common to a number of individual exemplars of a category are seen as typical for members of that category. All members of the category of *weapon* are useful for fighting, those of *food* for eating. (It is interesting to note that, in young children, belonging to the same category is understood on the basis of simple temporal or spatial proximity or concrete resemblances such as similar color or shape. In the course of cognitive development, however, people come to understand that events have generalized abstract properties, and that these are the basis of belonging together.)

The process of assigning events to yield categories is referred to as *coding*. A new event is seen to have distinctive and characteristic properties. When these are judged to match the definitive properties of a particular category (i.e., pattern recognition occurs), the new event is encoded into that category. The new event is then treated as if it has all characteristics of the category, even characteristics that have not been directly observed.[1] Thus, coding is a special form of "going beyond the information given" (Bruner, 1964). Furthermore, once an object has been coded into a category, it is difficult to see it as anything other than a member of this category. A simple example is the difficulty people have in seeing a hammer as anything other than a device for driving in nails. It could also be a weight, a hook, or a can opener, but encoding it as tool shuts out most other interpretations. A further example is the difficulty experienced in eating kangaroo meat by many Australians, despite the fact that kangaroo is a plentiful, tasty, healthy, and cheap source of protein. This animal is coded as "lovable and cuddly" or a "symbol of our country," categories that are incompatible with eating them. Eating kangaroo meat is something like eating one's national pride or dignity, an obvious impossibility. Sheep, in contrast, have the misfortune to be coded into the category *food* and are therefore readily eaten, even though they are woolly and much more cuddly, and also contribute far more to Australia's economic well-being than kangaroos.

Coding is useful in everyday life. Without coding, every situation would have to be dealt with anew as if the person concerned had had no prior experience with the external world. It makes it possible to deal with the familiar swiftly and efficiently by activating the category to which a well-known stimulus belongs and thus knowing what it is and what to do about it. It also makes it possible to deal with the unfamiliar. Once something new has been assigned

---

[1]Readers familiar with object-oriented methods in computing will immediately recognize a similarity with concepts such as inheritance, abstraction, and the like.

to a familiar category on the basis of whatever information is available, it has a meaning and the person knows how to deal with it. This meaning gives life consistency and predictability and engenders a high level of confidence in one's own behavior. Consistency and predictability are, however, characteristics of orthodoxy, not variability. When new stimuli are coded into existing categories and the categories remain intact in their existing form, no novelty is generated: Under these circumstances, going beyond the information given simply protects the status quo.

To produce novelty, coding needs to go beyond the obvious and dominant properties of a stimulus so that its membership of categories other than the most obvious can be recognized. Coding also needs to be flexible so that a stimulus can be seen to be capable of belonging to more than one category or of being recoded as the situation demands. How a stimulus is coded depends not only on the properties of the stimulus, but is strongly affected by contextual factors. For instance, in a library rectangular paper objects are likely to be coded as *books*, whereas a hungry person is likely to code a spherical object about the size of a tennis ball, yellowish red in color, and with indentations like those on a golf ball on its surface as an *orange*. Contextual factors act like a key that increases a category's accessibility by unlocking and leaving the door to it ajar. Codings usually reflect past experience in a particular context and are thus usually commonplace and lacking in novelty. They may, of course, be sensible and socially acceptable as well as being readily available, so that coding into these categories trades off production of novelty for ease of processing and avoidance of "cognitive strain" (Bruner, 1964).

As just described, the context predisposes people to code new events into certain categories, which induces a set (i.e., a tendency to see the world in fixed ways). The conventional coding of a wristwatch would be to class it as a device for telling the time. However, it is possible to break sets and code stimuli into unexpected categories, such as coding the watch as an object with weight instead of as a timepiece. This recoding of the watch draws attention to previously ignored properties that it possesses, and the person is then in a position to use the watch to solve problems where a weight is required but time of day is irrelevant (e.g., by using it as a sinker on a fishing rod).

> Unusual categories emphasize what is common to concepts that are not usually linked.

CASE STUDY: Unusual Coding of a Familiar Object

In 1905, in a physics exam at the University of Copenhagen, Niels Bohr was required to answer a question on how to use a barometer to measure the height of a building. Because the customary coding of barometer is *instrument for measuring air pressure*, the expected answer was to use the barometer to measure the air pressure at ground level and at the top of the building, calculating the height of the building from the difference between the two.

Bohr suggested tying a piece of string to the barometer and lowering it until it just touched the ground, adding the lengths of the string and the barometer together to obtain the height of the building.

He was failed, but appealed on the ground that his method would work—in the terminology of this book, it was effective, but it was also surprising. A referee ruled that Bohr was correct, but that his answer showed insufficient knowledge of physics. He was then given a few minutes to answer the question in a way demonstrating such knowledge. He responded by suggesting:

- throw the barometer off the roof and count the seconds until it hits the ground. Calculate the height of the building with the formula $s = \frac{1}{2} at^2$.

- Measure the length of the barometer and of its shadow and calculate the ratio of the two. Measure the length of the building's shadow and multiply it by the same ratio.

- Tie a piece of string to the barometer and set it swinging as a pendulum. Time the period of the pendulum at ground level and at the top of the building. Use Huygens' formula ($T = 2\pi\sqrt{L/g}$) to calculate the difference in g at ground level and at the top of the building and then calculate the height of the building from this difference.

- Use the barometer to calculate the difference in air pressure at ground level and at the top of the building, calculating the height of the building from this difference.

Finally he had given the conventional answer!

However, the irrepressible Bohr apparently could not stop himself. He went on to suggest climbing up the fire escape and marking off the height of the building in barometer lengths with a piece of chalk and then adding up the number of barometer lengths. Finally, he suggested using some social creativity and offering the janitor the barometer as a bribe to reveal the height of the building. What grade Bohr received is not known to us, but he received the Nobel Prize in 1922!

Building Broad Networks

In an analysis of the creative thinking of Poincaré and Einstein, Miller (1992) concluded that the essence of novelty generation is "network thinking." Building broad networks involves combining apparently disparate concepts. Miller defined the mechanism of combination as "proper choice of mental image or metaphor." In terms of concepts outlined above, the building of networks is an extension of the process of coding. Different categories may share properties. For instance, weight, balance, a convenient length, rigidity, and portability are all properties of weapons, but also of bats and racquets used in sports such as baseball, cricket, hockey, or tennis, as well as of walking aids such as a walking stick or a crutch. The three categories overlap and can thus be combined to form a system or network (for a relevant discussion of networks in thinking, see Anderson, 1976). Broad networks linking categories that are usually kept apart would make it possible to break the boundaries of a particular category—in the present example, by combining the categories of *sporting equipment* and *walking aid* and using a baseball bat as a walking stick, thus producing effective novelty.

The concept of networks of interlocking categories was stated somewhat differently by Köstler (1964), who saw knowledge as existing in matrices. Information processing usually involves linking elements from within the same matrix and thus produces no novelty. By contrast, when two matrices are linked via bisociation or three are trisociated, variability is produced. In the extreme form, it would be possible to speak of omnisociation where in principle all matrices could be linked to one another. The potential for production of novelty would then be high. Broad networks, novel configurations, remote associates, and the like do not come from nowhere. Certain strategies in thinking favor their production. Some of these are outlined below.

Broad networks place markedly different ideas into a single context.

Accommodating Rather Than Assimilating

Martinson (1995) identified two strategic dispositions in thinking: Some people consistently seek to deal with the new by reapplying existing knowledge and tried and trusted solution strategies, whereas others try to construct new approaches when dealing with new situations. Thus, there are two contrasting ways of reacting to novelty, uncertainty or ambiguity: The one seeks to absorb the novel into what is already known (i.e., to make it familiar and preserve what already exists), whereas the other seeks to alter the already known (i.e., to produce novelty). This disposition can be characterized by borrowing from Piaget and emphasizing assimilating and accommodating. In the present context, assimilating involves fitting new information in with existing mental structures and thus preserving the status quo, whereas accommodating is based on recognizing that current structures are not adequate and revising them. Intuitively, assimilating (making the new fit the known) is related to the production of orthodoxy, accommodating (changing the known as a result of contact with the new) to the production of novelty.

However, Piaget pointed out that it is the interaction between assimilating and accommodating that produces a creative product. The external world must first be assimilated (e.g., by recognizing that familiar things may appear in a number of diverse situations), or take diverse forms in the different situations. This notion involves recognizing the familiar, seeing connections, and so on, and it requires knowledge of the field (i.e., in Piaget's terms, *assimilated experience*). The second step is accommodation: adapting the already known to solve a new problem.

Self-diagnosis: Are you an assimilator or accommodator?

Assimilation = taking in new information and relating it to what you already know (seeing links, making associations, etc.).

Accommodation = changing existing ideas and concepts on the basis of the assimilation.

Using Creativity-Facilitating Cognitive Styles

Cognitive styles are consistent and stable differences between people in the way they obtain information from the world around them, sort, organize and recall information, and cope with demanding situations. Cognitive styles are often stated in the form of bipolar dimensions, such as leveling versus sharpening, focusing versus scanning, field dependence versus field independence, preference for wide versus narrow categories, or seeking cognitive complexity versus seeking simplicity. Some of these styles (e.g., field dependence, wide categories, or preference for complexity) are favorable to the production of novelty. Some well-known bipolar styles are summarized in Table 3.3. It is important to notice that no particular style of thinking is universally favorable for the production of effective novelty. A style may be favorable in some respects, but unfavorable in others. Thus, to take a single example, field dependence favors broad coding (good for production of effective novelty), but makes it difficult to see things separately from their context, and thus encourages stereotyped perception (bad for production of effective novelty).

Table 3.3

Examples of Bipolar Cognitive Styles

	Cognitive Style	Result
Leveling versus sharpening	Paying little attention to subtle or minor differences among the elements of a configuration	Perceiving globally. Focusing on similarities. Homospatial thinking.
	Exaggerating minor differences and overlooking anything the elements may have in common	Getting bogged down in details. Difficulty in seeing "the big picture." Heterospatial thinking.
Scanning versus focusing	Looking at the entire situation; seeing the forest but hardly noticing the trees	Broad grasp of the big picture. Broad, ill-defined categories. Associating elements with only low similarity. Homospatial thinking.
	Homing in on precise details; seeing the individual trees, not the forest	Precise knowledge of details. Ignoring similarities. Heterospatial thinking.
Field dependence versus field independence	Interpreting stimuli in terms of the context in which they occur	Omnisociation. Homospatial thinking. Broad coding, but discourages seeing things in a new way. Difficulty in breaking out of the corset (if the cat has kittens in the oven, they must be cookies!).
	Interpreting stimuli in terms of their individual properties, regardless of the context; failing to take account of the context	Awareness of contrasting, less obvious, or unexpected properties of stimuli. Heterospatial thinking.
Simplicity seeking versus complexity seeking	Reducing a complex situation to simple, harmonious, closed terms	Undifferentiated understanding of the "big picture." A harmonious (even if simplified) view of the way things are. Ignoring fine differences. Broad categories. Low tolerance for uncertainty.
	Tolerance, even preference, for "messy" situations	Attention to fine detail. Sharp differentiation of stimuli. High tolerance for uncertainty.

Self-diagnosis: What is your preferred cognitive style? What advantages and disadvantages does this have for your creativity?

SELF-DIRECTION IN THINKING—META-COGNITION

Although some contemporary authors have gone so far as to argue that creativity results from random processes, we take the view that information processing leading to effective novelty cannot proceed by "brute force" (Simon, 1989) in a process of perceiving, blindly associating, and occasionally recognizing, perhaps by good fortune, that a new combination happens to offer the required solution. This process would lead to a combinatorial explosion involving huge numbers of empty trials and causing cognitive strain. Thus, thinking processes must be guided by knowledge about how to acquire, organize, or apply knowledge: heuristics, strategies, hunches or "rules of thumb" (Rickards, 1999), or what is sometimes called "meta-cognition" (e.g., Flavell, 1976).

For instance, quickly discerning promising lines of attack would be greatly facilitated by possession of rules or guidelines for recognizing blind alleys from the start and ruling them out, or the opposite, homing in on particularly promising lines of attack. Evaluation skills that made it possible to see that a line of attack was proving inadequate or to recognize that a solution was at hand (e.g., mental blueprints or patterns of what an effectively novel solution might look like and techniques for matching the present state with this blueprint) would be of great help here.

Meta-cognition involves the executive processes in thinking that allow people to organize and keep track of their own cognitions. In the case of creativity, these include:

- redefining plans where necessary,

- monitoring one's own progress,

- changing existing line of attack if necessary,

- being aware of alternative routes,

- recognizing conditions that make a change of approach necessary,

- possessing insight into the costs and benefits associated with the various possible changes, and

- recognizing opportunities.

People's ability to articulate their own meta-cognitions (i.e., to state in words the results of the processes in the following box) is also of considerable importance. Articulation permits conscious self-reflection, identification of pre-cise differences between approaches, discussion of progress with other people, and the like.

> Self-assessment: Can you:
>   review your existing knowledge?
>   direct your own attention?
>   assess and marshal your resources?
>   define problems in your own terms?
>   select an appropriate set of processes for solving a problem?
>   combine the above into a workable strategy?
>   monitor and evaluate your own progress?
>   sense one or more promising alternatives?
>   effectively change course should the evaluation make this necessary?

A striking description of the way in which creative thinking is systematically guided is to be found in the writings of Poincaré (2003[1908]). He regarded production of novelty as a process of selection in which knowledge elements from widely separated domains are combined. Poincaré possessed vast knowl-edge of mathematics and could in principle have produced an endless string of combinations, but somehow homed in on the effective ones. Apparently, nearly all of the theoretically possible combinations are filtered out, leaving only the ones that meta-cognition suggests offer prospects of a solution.

Avoiding the Wrong Approach Barrier

Olken (1964) argued strongly that creativity is partly a trial-and-error process, thus apparently adopting a blind variation position. According to him, initially possible solutions are imagined as mental images and are matched with the desired end result. If this matching process shows that the solution envisaged in the mental image does not match the desired result, it is abandoned. (Of course, if trial solution and desired end result match, the trial solution is retained.) More complex problems are broken down into small steps or subproblems, and these problems are solved one at a time using the trial-and-error method mentioned in the previous sentence. However, Olken emphasized that the mental images are not produced randomly, as would happen in a blind combination approach, but are selected from among the large number of possible images on the basis of "hunches," or, as Olken points out, what are now called *heuristics* (meta-cognitions). The process is iterative: Solving one subproblem provides a new jumping off point for the next, and the process restarts.

Olken extended his discussion by focusing attention on the problem of avoiding dead ends. In an examination of the development of innovations such as the triode vacuum tube, the Astron machine (a reactor for producing power by controlled nuclear fusion), or a device for the simultaneous production of multiple photocopies, he identified the "wrong approach barrier." He pointed out how dangerous it is to start along a wrong approach because the difficulty of getting out of the *cul de sac* increases as the researcher invests more and more resources (money, time, ego-commitment, difficulty of disengaging without loss of face, etc.) in the dead end. In effect, a barrier builds up that blocks finding a productive approach.[2] Thus, the first step in generating effective novelty is to produce variability, to be sure, but to avoid becoming trapped in dead ends. Olken identified three ways of breaking the barrier: a lucky break (see above), letting the work lie fallow (incubating), or continuing along the fruitless line of attack, but gradually veering around to find a new direction (what Sternberg called *redirection*). To this list we would add finding the courage and openness of mind to recognize when one has entered a *cul de sac*.

The wrong-approach barrier:

Investment of time and money, staking of personal status and credibility, and narrowing of attention all raise a barrier against abandoning unsuccessful solutions even when everyone else can see that they are leading nowhere: The greater the investment, the harder it is to climb over the wrong-approach barrier.

STOCKTAKING

Summary Table 3 is more differentiated than the first two. It lists aspects of the dimension **Product**, as these were outlined in chapter 2, but adds **Process**, as discussed in this chapter. In later chapters, the summary is built up to incorporate **Person** and **Press**, and to map **Product**, **Process**, **Person**, and **Press** onto **Phase**, thus developing the differentiated model of creativity which is the goal of the theoretical part of this book.

PRACTICAL GUIDELINES

As in chapter 1, Box 3 summarizes implications for practice of the material presented in this chapter in the form of hints or guidelines for innovation-friendly behavior for students, staff, educators, and managers. Statements in Boxes 1 and 2 are supplemented, not replaced, by the contents of Box 3.

---

[2]This problem is probably most acute for experts, who may have invested a lifetime into a particular approach, so that recognizing this as a dead end means acknowledging that a lifetime's work has all been in vain. Senior professors and managers are probably most at risk of becoming unable to recognize the wrong-way barriers in their own work.

Summary Table 3

Relationship Between **P**hases and **P**rocesses and Sub-**P**roducts

Phase	Process	Subproduct	Criterion of Creativity				
			Relevance	Effectiveness	Novelty	Elegance	Generalizability
Preparation	— "Uncensored" intake of information — Acquisition of broad general knowledge — Acquisition of specific knowledge	— Identification of problem — Establishment of goals	+	+			
Activation	— Problem recognition — Problem construction	— Understanding of the dimensions of the problem — Establishment of broad solution criteria	+	+			
Generation	— Boundary breaking — Making remote associations — Restructuring ideas — Producing configurations	— Many candidate solutions	+	+	+		

Stage	Sub-processes	Outcome				
Illumination	— Recognizing appropriate configurations — Building new categories	— Apparently appropriate configurations		+	+	+
Verification	— Exploration of own ideas — Elaborating and extending ideas — Recognition of a solution	— Privately explored novelty — A single optimal solution		+	+	+
Communication	— Making the novelty available to other people	— A working prototype		+	+	+
Validation	— External exploration of ideas — Seeing wider implications	— Publicly explored novelty: a "truly" creative product	+	+	+	+

Box 3. Practical Advice Based on Chapter 3

Who?	When?	What?
Teachers and managers (Thought leaders)	Attitudes to students and colleagues	Respect students and colleagues who produce novelty ("way out" questions or suggestions), providing they have a recognizable link to reality
		Respect students and colleagues who question or criticize (provided that criticism is informed)
		Regard students and colleagues as a valuable source of ideas, especially when they challenge your own ideas
	Instructional and leadership strategies	Encourage students and colleagues to work in unfamiliar settings, in unusual ways, or with unfamiliar materials
		Encourage trying the already known in new settings
		Invite multiple answers
		Watch for the wrong-approach barrier in your own work
	Assessing other people's work	Be open for novel solutions (even if you can see that they are wrong)
		Look for and respect unexpected combinations of ideas
		Respect the "inspired" error, and check possible latent creativity
		Provide feedback on novelty production, idea combinations, etc., not just accuracy and correctness
Who?	When?	What?
Students and colleagues (Coal-face creatives)	Self-image	Be interested in your own unusual ideas
		Do not be afraid of your own impulses. Regard them as a valuable source of ideas
		Be aware of your preferred cognitive style and ascertain whether it facilitates or blocks generation of novelty
	Learning and work strategies	Let your imagination go
		Seek wide experience (marginally related classes, practical, assignments, etc.)
		Look for links among pieces of information, especially unexpected links
		Look for relevant but remote associates
		Be willing to cross boundaries
		Try to build networks of related knowledge

Who?	When?	What?
Students and colleagues (Coal-face creatives)	Assignments and work tasks	Transfer ideas from outside settings (including previous jobs) to new tasks
		Seek to go beyond the information given
		Avoid treating a new task as simply another example of the familiar (i.e., assimilating)
		Try to look at the new or unexpected elements of the task that make it different (accommodate)
		Try to find multiple answers
		Look for the unexpected *but supportable* answers
		Ask yourself if you have generated *effective* surprise
		Be ready to defend your own ideas, even if they are unconventional

Conventional Thinking and Creativity

Creative thinking involves more than simply generating variability. Evaluation of the novelty is also necessary. Novelty that is accepted blindly can cause a variety of problems in practical situations, including reckless change. In the evaluating phase, which we refer to as *exploration*, knowledge is of particular importance: It is a source of ideas, suggests pathways to solutions, and provides criteria of effectiveness and novelty. The way in which novelty generation and evaluation work together can be understood in terms of thinking styles or phases in the generation of creative products. The extended-phase model is particularly useful here. The extended-phase model also makes it possible to link thinking with the process of emergence of a creative product in a more differentiated way.

EFFORTFUL CREATIVITY: THE PREPARED MIND

Henri Poincaré, the French mathematician, is now remembered as one of the most creative mathematicians of all time. In 1881, as he was about to enter a coach for a sightseeing trip during a conference, he was not thinking about mathematics at all (see O'Conner & Robertson, 2003). Suddenly, the Fuchsian functions (nowadays known as *automorphic functions*) came unexpectedly into his head. Refinements of the equations came later in a second burst while he was having a relaxing walk by the sea. Anecdotes such as this reinforce the idea already introduced in chapter 3—that creativity can come in a sudden burst, more or less as a gift from heaven. Learning of facts, application of strict logic, accuracy, and the like (convergent thinking) were even presented by some writers as conflicting with or blocking creativity (e.g., Getzels & Jackson, 1962) and were sometimes seen as bad, or at best a necessary evil that is greatly exaggerated in education and business (e.g., Cropley, 1967a).

Nonetheless, despite evidence such as the Poincaré anecdote, in this book, we reserve the term *creativity* for goal-oriented, intentional activities carried out by human beings, although it is apparent that, historically speaking, chance sometimes does play a role, as in the Goodyear and Post-It anecdotes in chapter 3.

It seems unreasonable to us to speak of creativity to describe the result if, let us say, a group of monkeys escaped from a university's psychology department, broke into the registrar's office, and, while playing on the computers there, happened to redesign and improve the university's record-keeping system.

> Creativity involves systematic and purposeful thinking, not blind generation of novelty.

Intuition and Convergent Thinking

Despite what has just been said, it is not immediately apparent that Poincaré's idea did not come from nowhere. How could this happen apart from the muse of mathematics whispering into Poincaré's ear or some similar mechanism? One of the processes that seems feasible as a source of effortless creativity is intuition. However, contrary to what is sometimes argued, intuitions do not come from nowhere: They derive from knowledge acquired via implicit learning (for a fuller account of what is meant by implicit learning, see Seger, 1994). In the course of everyday life, people acquire knowledge without becoming aware they possess it. As a result, although they have not consciously prepared themselves to solve a problem, sometimes they already have in their head a rough outline of the solution they are seeking, despite not necessarily being aware of it. This rough outline is referred to as *tacit* knowledge. Under these circumstances, the task involved in solving the problem is that of defining and refining this rough idea, not producing something from nowhere.

CASE STUDY: Incidental Learning

During the course of riding to school every day in a bus and sitting just behind the driver, a child might learn a great deal about how buses work without realizing it and without ever having thought of the ride as a learning experience. The child acquires tacit knowledge about the design and function of buses without being aware of this knowledge. As a result, on being given the task in adult life of designing a new bus, this person would already have many ideas about bus design and possess a preliminary framework that could suggest where the required answer might be found or approximately what the eventual solution might look like. The apparent bolt from the blue would really involve logical extension of what the person in question already knew.

In other words, the basis of intuition—which appears at first glance to be the epitome of creativity coming from nowhere—is knowledge. In fact, in recent years, there has been increasing recognition that actual creative production does not derive from divergent thinking alone, but also requires convergent thinking (e.g., Brophy, 1998; Cropley, 2006; Rickards, 1993). The joint contribution of the two kinds of thinking—working together to generate effectively novel products—is the subject of this chapter.

> Even intuitions are based on knowledge, although this may not be apparent to the person in question.

The Prepared Mind

To return to the example of the discovery of vulcanization given in chapter 3, it can be added that James Goodyear spent many years of his life in apparently fruitless toil and impoverished himself in working his way to the moment when he dropped the rubber and sulfur onto the hot stove. Thus, he did not simply take any two substances at random and throw them on the stove, and the fact that he was heating the rubber (instead of, let us say, cooling it) was the result of his earlier findings. Similarly, the 3M staff was thoroughly familiar with adhesives and paper when they accidentally invented Post-Its. Poincaré was not some mathematically naive person who happened to stumble onto a good thing, but was a codiscoverer with Albert Einstein of the special theory of relativity. He was the most broadly knowledgeable mathematician of his age and had been working on the problem of automorphic functions for many years at the moment when they seemed to him to pop into his head from nowhere.

Thus, none of these was a genuine example of accidental or effortless creativity. As Louis Pasteur, the celebrated father of vaccination, put it in a frequently cited aphorism he uttered in a lecture in 1854 (Peterson, 1954): "Chance favors only *the prepared mind*" (page 493; italics added). Creativity does not usually come from nowhere, but (a) rests on a foundation of knowledge, and (b) requires work. Our advice is not to sit and wait for the lucky breakthrough to come of its own accord!

> The properties of the prepared mind include:
> - relevant special and general knowledge,
> - appropriate skills,
> - curiosity,
> - willingness to take a risk,
> - self-confidence, and
> - competence.

CASE STUDY: The Prepared Mind

In 1896, the French physicist, Antoine Henri Becquerel, while studying properties of minerals that had been exposed to the newly discovered x-rays, happened to leave a photographic plate and a container with uranium compounds in it in a drawer of his desk (Nobel Foundation, 1967). On opening the drawer some time later, he noticed to his surprise that the photographic plate had fogged. This unexpected event piqued his curiosity. Instead of throwing the "ruined" plate away, he began to study it intensively. He eventually concluded that the uranium compounds had emitted some kind of "rays" similar to x-rays, apparently without any source of energy, and that these unknown rays were responsible for the fogging. He was able to confirm that the mystery rays emanated from the uranium compounds and differed qualitatively from x-rays. After initially being called *Becquerel rays,* the newly discovered radiation subsequently became known as *radioactivity.*

Was the discovery of radioactivity an example of creativity? It would be hard to answer, "No." After all, Becquerel shared the 1903 Nobel Prize for physics with Marie and Pierre Curie. Did the creativity, then, come from nowhere, through blind good fortune, intuitive inspiration based on nothing, or in a burst of pure divergent thinking (which, if it did not produce a winner, would be regarded as wild speculation)? Does creativity perhaps involve nothing more than being open for ideas and being able to recognize that a particular idea is a solution to something or other, thus seizing the opportunity when it occurs? Ghiselin (1955) seemed to support this view by arguing that recognizing a solution when one occurs is the key to creativity.

What is easy to overlook is what it was that made it possible for Becquerel to capitalize on the opportunity chance presented. He could not have done this had he not possessed, among other things:

- the general knowledge that permitted him to realize that the fogging was unusual and important,

- the specific knowledge that told him that some kind of radiation had caused the phenomenon, and

- the research skills that enabled him to clarify the whole situation.

Indeed, had Becquerel not already been engaged in relevant research, the uranium compounds and photographic plate would not have been in the drawer together in the first place. Thus, he not only profited from chance (because of, among other things, his knowledge and skills), but he created his own lucky chance. His discovery was not an example of effortless creativity, but required the prepared mind referred to earlier. Furthermore, the properties of Becquerel's prepared mind were largely convergent in nature, involving especially knowledge and specialized technical skills.

> Creativity often arises out of a long history of hard work in an area. Creative people often cause their own lucky break.

The Unprepared Mind

Unfortunately, even diligent and effective workers do not always make use of chances apparently offered by blind good luck. Eugen Semmer (see case study) accidentally cured two dying horses in a novel way, but did not recognize their return to good health as an important discovery at all. To him, the cure was a problem that made it impossible to investigate the cause of the horses' deaths.

CASE STUDY: The Unprepared Mind

In 1870, Eugen Semmer, a pathologist working in the Institute of Veterinary Science in Riga, published a paper in the widely read German-language scientific journal, *Virchows Archiv* (which still exists), reporting on the strange return to health of two horses that had been admitted to the clinic suffering from what we would now call infections (Semmer, 1870). He carefully examined the now-recovered horses (whose corpses he had expected to be examining) and discovered that while at the institute they had by chance been exposed to spores of the fungus *penicillium notatum*. He correctly concluded that the mold had been responsible for the horses inconveniently getting better, and he explained how he had carefully cleaned out his laboratory and succeeded in eliminating the troublesome *p. notatum*, which had been growing in dark nooks and crannies. No further sick horses would be recovering by accident in his clinic!

Apparently, both Semmer and the distinguished readers of the journal failed to recognize that he had discovered a novel (and, as we now know, extremely effective) curative agent (i.e., antibiotics), and medicine had to wait another 70 years for Fleming to discover penicillin. In a sense, Semmer's mind was unprepared not because he possessed insufficient knowledge, because he could hardly be expected to have known about bacteria (whose existence had not yet been discovered), but the wrong kind of knowledge. He was thorough and skillful enough to discover the presence of fungus spores and to see that they had saved the horses, and he was thus well on his way to discovering penicillin. However, unlike Becquerel or Fleming, Semmer failed to appreciate the significance of his observations. He did not realize that he had a solution because he was thinking about a different problem: life-taking rather than life-saving. Had he been a clinician, he might have immediately seen the possibilities of his accidental discovery. This scenario raises the question of what role knowledge plays in creativity and, because knowledge is the principal product of successful convergent thinking, once again of the role of convergent thinking.

> Despite the importance for creativity of experience and activity in an area, it is possible to fail to notice a solution even when it is right in front of your eyes. Noncognitive and social factors play an important role here (see chaps. 5–7).

KNOWLEDGE AND CREATIVITY

Although some writers (e.g., Hausman, 1984) have argued that true creativity is always so novel that it is unprecedented, and thus has no connection to anything that went before, others, such as Bailin (1988), have concluded that creative products are always conceived by both the creative person and external observers in terms of existing knowledge. Indeed, it is clear that many novel ideas are based on what already exists, even if existing knowledge is transferred to a field quite different from the one in which it is already known.

> **CASE STUDY: Transferring Knowledge From One Field to Another**
>
> In the early 1700s, the French entomologist, René de Réaumur, noticed that certain wasps, nowadays known as the "paper" wasp, chewed up wood, digested it, regurgitated it, and used the resulting material to build their nests. The material dried out to form a paper-like substance. Réaumur realized that chemical processes in the wasps' stomachs were making paper out of raw wood. It had been known for several thousand years that plant fibers would form a kind of interlocking mat when separated and suspended in water (i.e., paper). Before Réaumur, old rags were used in France as the source of fiber—an expensive and scarce source because the raw materials had already been subjected to substantial refining and manufacturing. Papermakers applied physical processes to material that had already been subjected to considerable value-adding and were thus expensive. Réaumur proposed transferring the wasps' chemical approach to human papermaking, and thus invented modern techniques (although it must be admitted that he never succeeded in getting the process to work properly).

In about 1840, Charles Babbage transferred the punched card system for controlling the work of the Jacquard loom from the French fabric-making industry (where it was already well known) to guiding the operations of a mechanical calculating machine, thus making it possible for the machine to remember the information stored in the pattern of holes in the cards. By this transfer he created the idea of the analytic engine, a calculator with a memory, or what we now call a *computer*.

At a systems level, in the years around 1900, Fredrick Winslow Taylor applied the principles of systematic observation, measurement, and objective analysis that are well known in scientific research, which he had learned at engineering school, to a field where they had not previously been implemented (organizing work and production in a steel mill). By making this transfer, he devised procedures for isolating and analyzing the various factors operating in any manufacturing, administrative or sales process, and in effect invented time and motion studies. He transferred knowledge that already existed to settings where it was previously unknown.

Although they merely transferred what already existed to a new context, all three of the people just mentioned made breakthroughs that were the basis of revolutions in their fields. Babbage is remembered as one of the fathers of the digital computer, the production of cheap paper was an important part of the industrial revolution, the explosion of mass literacy, and the widespread distribution of knowledge (despite the dawning of the electronic age, the paperless office or school is yet to become reality). Taylor's introduction of scientific methods into organizing work in a steel mill not only improved productivity in the mill in question, but also changed the way work was conceptualized. It ceased to be seen as involving repetition of fixed, traditional procedures originally learned at the master's side and subsequently reapplied without change by the former apprentice, and instead came to be seen as carrying out, with a high degree of precision, specified, highly standardized operating procedures that had been worked out exactly for a particular production step to optimize production. This discovery led to analysis of work requirements and selection of workers on the basis of their ability to be trained in, and to carry out, specific procedures, as against, for instance, inheriting the traditional family job.

In fact, even many of the innovations introduced by America's most distinguished inventor, Thomas Alva Edison, were improvements on existing technology or ideas. Edison worked with a large staff of engineers and technicians who constantly improved their own existing ideas. For instance, over the course of time, they took out more than 100 patents for the electric light bulb alone. Indeed, the Canadian Intellectual Property Office reported (www.strategis.gc.ca/sc_mrksv/cipo/patents/pat_gd_protect-e.html#sec2) that 90% of new patents are improvements of existing patents. In an aphorism that was printed in *Harper's Monthly* in 1932 (Josephson, 1959), Edison concluded that "genius is 1% inspiration, 99% perspiration" (p. 97), thus coming down squarely on the side of convergent thinking.

A further example from a more artistic field is also useful here. Much of Coleridge's imagery in *The Rime of the Ancient Mariner* (1912) is taken from ideas he found in the course of his wide and eclectic reading. He did not invent the ideas, so to speak, from nowhere, but adapted existing images to suit his new purpose, the writing of the poem. Weisberg (2004) showed that even an extraordinarily radical product such as Picasso's *Les demoiselles d'Avignon* arose out of what Picasso had experienced up until the time he painted it. Thus, there is a link between novelty and the already known even in artistic/aesthetic fields.

Lubart (2000–2001) expressed the link between knowledge and creativity in a homely, but convincing, way. He suggested that there may well be no difference between the processes of divergent and convergent thinking, but that differences in outcome may depend instead on "...the quality of the material (e.g., knowledge)." Lubart extended this thought with the concrete metaphor: "The engine is the same, but some people use better grade fuel" (p. 301). Those who have only limited or narrow knowledge (the poorer grade of fuel) would not be able to combine ideas, make unexpected associations between pieces of knowledge, or synthesize apparently unrelated facts, because they would not possess the ideas, knowledge, or facts on which to operate.

Scott (1999) listed a number of creativity researchers who all give a prominent place to knowledge in creativity (e.g., Albert, Amabile, Campbell, Chi, Gardner, Gruber, Mednick, Simonton, Wallas, and Weisberg). Ericsson and Lehmann (1999) summarized the link between knowledge and creativity by concluding that:

> ...the empirical evidence on creative achievement shows that individuals have not been able to make generally recognized creative contributions to a domain unless they had mastered the relevant knowledge and skills in the course of a long preparatory period. (p. 706)

They repeated the idea, usually attributed to Gardner (1993), that there is a "10-year rule": An apprenticeship of at least 10 years is necessary for acquiring the fund of knowledge and skills necessary for creativity. What then, broadly speaking, is the role of knowledge in creativity?

Knowledge is at the heart of creativity.

Knowledge Provides a Well From Which Ideas Are Drawn

In what way is knowledge linked to the generation of effective novelty? Already, before the beginning of the modern era, the idea that creativity draws from the wellspring of conventional knowledge was well established. Rossman's (1931, p. 132) study of inventors, for instance, concluded that they "manipulate the symbols of . . . *past experience.*" He also showed that they combined "*known* movements." Feldhusen (1995) and other writers have made an important point by emphasizing the "knowledge base" of creativity. As Bailin (1988) put it, novelty "always arises out of what already exists" (p. 5). The position of knowledge as the basis of creativity has been put in more formal terms by Boden (1994a), using the language of artificial intelligence. What we call *knowledge,* she called *cognitive maps* of a *conceptual space.* The more structural features of a conceptual space such as music are represented in a person's mind (the more the person knows about music), the more creative the person can be. Boden gave the example of Mozart and concluded that his creativity arose from his vast musical knowledge. Of course, emphasis on the importance of knowledge raises the specter of the wrong knowledge (see the Semmer example above) or too much knowledge (see the discussion of the disadvantages of expertise).

Knowledge Defines What Is Creative

As Sternberg and Lubart (1999) put it, a creative product must be adapted to "task constraints." Boden (1994a) made this point strongly by arguing that it is dealing with the task constraints that makes a product or idea creative, instead of merely original (occurring for the first time). Without task constraints, ideas could not cause surprise because there would be no expectations from which they would deviate. Thus, paradoxically, novelty is determined by existing knowledge, and not just by the product itself. Csikszentmihalyi (1999) extended the idea of existing knowledge as defining creativity when he described creativity as a novel variation in a domain of practice that experts in the domain recognize as novel and effective and regard as worth incorporating into it. The experts judge according to their knowledge of their domain, which they have acquired through convergent thinking.

Although it goes beyond the limits of this chapter, it is interesting to note that, because knowledge in a domain changes with the passage of time (usually by increasing), whether novelty is judged to be effective—and thus creative—may change with time. Indeed, once incorporated into existing knowledge, novelty of necessity ceases to be novel, thus creating a further paradox: Novelty (a) derives from what is already known; (b) is judged effective (or not) in terms of the already known (i.e., orthodoxy determines the novelty of novelty; (c) passes into the body of knowledge if it is judged to be effective, and thereupon becomes orthodoxy; and (d) having lost its own status as effective novelty now influences the assessment of later novelty.

Referring to the way novelty—more or less inevitability—destroys itself, Cropley, Kaufman, and Cropley (2008) spoke of the "decay" of novelty and pointed out that this decay begins from the moment the novelty is first introduced. Thus, to some extent, novelty is a race against time. One era's innovation is the next one's orthodoxy. However, novelty sometimes has the opposite effect. New knowledge can reveal the effectiveness of earlier novelty that was initially regarded as ineffective (or possibly not even novel). Although this phenomenon can result from factors such as changes in conventions, social values, or taste (such as in aesthetic creativity), it can also result simply from increased factual knowledge, which starts as effective novelty, becomes orthodoxy, and then reveals the effective novelty of older knowledge that already existed, but had not previously been recognized for what it was. The anecdote about the mathematician, Evariste Galois, in chapter 2 is an example of how later advances may reveal the creativity of earlier work, creativity thus working backward in time. His divergent thinking could not gain recognition until convergent thinking had advanced sufficiently to make the effective novelty of his ideas apparent.

Creativity is intimately connected with time:

(a) With the passage of time, novelty ceases to be novel; and

(b) Later novelty can work backward in time to reveal the effective novelty of earlier ideas not previously judged to be creative.

Knowledge Guides and Shapes Creativity

Existing knowledge indicates which kind of attack on a problem is likely to be fruitful (or is already known to be fruitless); defines the pathways, methods, and tools through which progress can be made; and specifies the nature of acceptable solutions. To take an absurdly simple example, in a society with no knowledge of the existence of electricity, engineers would not spend much time thinking about radio or the telephone as communication devices because such devices would be unimaginable. Communications engineers would be forced to think along different lines, such as improved megaphones. Alternatively, if they did fantasize about a totally unknown form of energy (electricity), this would be at best quasicreativity, and they would risk being regarded as engaging in wild speculation that ran counter to received wisdom, possibly suffering the same fate as people like Ignaz Semmelweiss or Galileo Galilei, who introduced what we now know was effective novelty, but suffered personal rejection in their own time.

Engineers working in the product development department of a large automobile manufacturer would be unlikely to stake their careers on a nuclear-powered electronic matter transmitter as a means of personal transport. On the one hand, they would have a vested interest in limiting creativity to polishing what already exists, and, on the other hand, their familiarity with automobiles would almost predestine them to think of private transportation as based on the motor vehicle. They would also know that the public expects personal transport machines to take a certain form (the automobile) and that many people are afraid of nuclear power. Such constraints deriving from their knowledge would severely limit their attack on the problem of developing better forms of transport.

> Existing knowledge often influences the emergence of new knowledge by making some avenues of innovation more obvious, safer, more acceptable, or even more profitable.

Even aesthetic creativity in fields such as poetry or music rests on a foundation of skills, expectations, conventions, and the like. Poets or musicians have to know and stick to the rules in order for the novelty they produce to be judged effective. To take a simple example, sonnets always have 14 lines (otherwise they are not sonnets), and there are rules about the rhyme schemes, or even the contents that are permissible: For instance, sonnets are often divided into an eight-line section in which a general theme is introduced, followed by a more specific six-line section offering some conclusions, consolations, or the like. In "On his Blindness," John Milton lamented in the first eight lines that his blindness was hindering him in serving God, but then in the closing six lines consoled himself with the thought that God can get along perfectly well without the humble work of a mere mortal. Sawyer (1999) showed that even jazz improvisation, which may look to the uninitiated like pure divergence, is governed by rules and involves organized reuse of the already known.

CASE STUDY: The Role of Knowledge and Routine in a Highly Creative Activity

The 1940s' jazz saxophonist, Charlie Parker, is recognized as one of the most creative of all jazz musicians. He is especially known for his novel improvisations using the higher intervals of a chord as a melody line and backing these chords with appropriate improvisations. However, these were not invented anew every time he played: He developed a repertoire of about 100 "motifs" or "licks," each between 4 and 10 notes in length. When improvising new music, he combined and recombined these already existing licks to generate effectively novel performances.

> Even in artistic areas, creativity often involves recombining elements of
> existing knowledge to form something new.

Converting Existing Knowledge Into New Ideas

Sternberg (1999) turned to the question of the processes through which existing knowledge is used to produce creativity. He introduced the useful idea of
creativity as "propelling a field" and suggested a number of ways in which this
can occur:

1. *Conceptual replication* (the known is transferred to a new setting);

2. *Redefinition* (the known is seen in a new way);

3. *Forward incrementation* (the known is extended in an existing direction);

4. *Advance forward incrementation* (the known is extended in an existing
   direction, but goes beyond what is currently tolerable);

5. *Redirection* (the known is extended in a new direction);

6. *Reconstruction and redirection* (new life is breathed into an approach previously abandoned); and

7. *Reinitiation* (thinking begins at a radically different point from the current one and takes off in a new direction).

Of these, only the last involves something quite new. All the others are based
on modifying what already exists.

Savransky (2000) also discussed the processes through which existing knowledge is used to develop effective novelty. He argued that inventive solutions to
problems always involve a change in what already exists. He discerned six ways in
which this process can occur. Slightly modified for present purposes, generating
effective novelty involves, according to Savransky, one or more of the following:

1. *Improvement* (improvement or perfection of both quality and quantity
   of what already exists);

2. *Diagnostics* (search for and elimination of shortcomings in what already
   exists);

3. *Trimming* (reduction of costs associated with existing solutions);

4. *Analogy* (new use of known processes and systems);

5. *Synthesis* (generation of new mixtures of existing elements); and

6. *Genesis* (generation of fundamentally new solutions).

As was the case with Sternberg's list, only the last of these involves something fundamentally new.

The Russian researcher, Altshuller (1988), also emphasized the role of the already known in his procedure for finding creative solutions to problems—known as TRIZ (a transliteration of the Russian acronym for "Theory of Inventive Problem Solving"). This procedure is based on an analysis of thousands of successful patent applications (i.e., on effective novelty that is already known). It argues that all engineering systems display the same systematic patterns of change. Creativity is the result of the development of what exists according to these trends. TRIZ identifies these systematic processes of novelty generation so that people working with a new problem can apply them to derive their own novel solutions. This procedure is discussed in greater detail in chapter 9.

> Reuse of what already exists is of particular importance in technical settings and existing functioning systems.

We have already distinguished between generation of novelty, exploration of it to identify effective aspects, and exploitation of this effective novelty. Some writers (e.g., March, 1991) regard exploration and exploitation as conflicting or competing ways of reacting to existing knowledge—existing knowledge can be exploited (i.e., applied immediately in its existing form to do something useful) or it can be explored (i.e., used as the jumping-off point for developing further new knowledge). In the present book, we use the term *exploitation* to refer to the third step in the process of generation, evaluation, and utilization of effective novelty, the step of inserting effective novelty into a functioning system. Exploitation in March's sense refers more to what we call "loops," in which the process of production of an effectively novel product is restarted after a subproduct has been developed.

THE INTERACTION OF DIVERGENT AND CONVERGENT THINKING

What, then, is the joint role of convergent and divergent thinking in generating effective novelty? How do the two combine to produce it?

Generating and Exploring Variability

Finke, Ward, and Smith (1992) distinguished between two broad processes in the production of effective novelty: on the one hand, generating novelty; and, on the other hand, exploring this novelty once it has been generated. The first kind of process produces novelty, to be sure, but on its own can easily lead not to creativity, but to quasicreativity or pseudocreativity (unless there is a blind hit). Suppose that a civil engineer noticed that both steel reinforcing rods and spaghetti are long, tubular, and, under certain circumstances, flexible, and thus saw that spaghetti has some similarities to steel rods. This revelation would involve a changed perception of spaghetti (generation of novelty). There are similarities between reinforcing rods and spaghetti, and it is imaginable that settings exist where this variation from the usual perception of steel and spaghetti really could lead to effective novelty (even if this idea requires a considerable stretch of the imagination). However, most civil engineers would probably reject out of hand the actual use of spaghetti instead of steel and would predict a catastrophe if spaghetti were used as reinforcing rods (i.e., they would explore the novelty and decide against it). This rejection of the novelty would be based on the engineers' knowledge of basic principles of civil engineering, such as strength of materials. Thus, converting mere novelty into effective novelty (i.e., creativity) requires both generation (via divergent thinking) and exploration (via convergent thinking).

Lonergan, Scott, and Mumford (2004) summarized recent thinking in this area and concluded that the idea of a two-step process of production of effective novelty is now widely accepted. In our terms, this would involve novelty generation followed (or accompanied) by exploration of the novelty from the point of view of workability, acceptability, or similar criteria to determine whether it is effective. Only then would we speak of creativity. It is tempting to think of exploration as essentially a process of evaluation, and Runco (2003) supported this view. He argued that creativity requires a combination of divergent and convergent thinking and, further, that convergent thinking involves "critical processes," critical meaning not merely that the processes are necessary for creativity, but also that they involve criticism of the results of the divergent thinking (i.e., what we have called *evaluation*).

Continuing with the (admittedly whimsical) example of making a link between spaghetti and reinforcing rods via divergent thinking, Table 4.1 gives examples of processes of divergent and convergent thinking in both generating and evaluating phases of idea production. The table suggests what the results might be if divergent thinking were not tempered by convergent thinking.

We do not intend to deny the importance of divergent thinking in the production of effective novelty. However, although necessary, it is not sufficient on its own, except perhaps for occasional flukes when blind luck leads to effective novelty. Convergent thinking is necessary, too, because it makes it possible to explore, evaluate, or criticize variability and identify its effective aspects. In the enthusiasm for divergent thinking, it is thus important not to forget the contribution of convergent thinking, although it is also important not to overemphasize it, as may sometimes be done in schools and universities, as well

Table 4.1
Processes of Divergent and Convergent Thinking in Generating Novelty

| Phase | Generation of Variability | | Generation of Orthodoxy | |
	Examples of Processes of Divergent Thinking	Result	Examples of Processes of Convergent Thinking	Result
Generating	Linking Transforming Reinterpreting Branching out	Engineer sees similarity between steel rods and spaghetti	Recognizing the familiar Reapplying the known Sticking to the rules	Engineer does not see a similarity between steel and spaghetti
Exploring	Shifting contexts Exceeding limits Crossing boundaries Creating surprise	Engineer concludes that steel rods can be replaced with spaghetti. Novelty to be sure—but in this case, a disaster!	Avoiding risk Being certain Staying within limits Seeking simplicity Assessing technical and financial feasibility	Engineer sticks to steel rods to reinforce concrete. No innovation but building does not fall down!

as in management settings of various kinds. Table 4.2 gives examples of vital *con*vergent thinking processes in both the generating and exploring phases of generation of variability.

Convergent thinking makes an indispensable contribution to the generation of effective novelty, which is largely connected with relevance and effectiveness of novel products.

The Need for Exploration as Well as Generation

There are considerable risks if novelty is introduced into a functioning system without appropriate exploration (i.e., if novelty generation is not accompanied

Table 4.2
Examples of the Contribution of Convergent Thinking to Creativity

Phase	Contribution of Convergent Thinking (Necessary but not sufficient prerequisites for generation of effective variability)
Generating variability	Accumulating factual knowledge Observing closely Remembering accurately Drawing "correct" conclusions Thinking logically Processing information rapidly
Exploring variability	Recognizing promising lines of attack Zeroing in on potential solutions Seeing limits Being aware of weaknesses Weighing up feasibility Recognizing a solution

by exploration/evaluation). Figure 4.1 considers a number of possibilities. If no variability is generated (no divergent thinking), nothing changes and orthodoxy rules, bringing, however, the risk of stagnation and similar problems. This situation is depicted in the first row of the figure. Of course, it is the safest pathway in settings where errors are punished but doing nothing is tolerated without sanctions, but absence of creativity is of no interest to us here.

A new set of possibilities opens up when variability is actually generated. It is possible for this to be accepted without exploration (i.e., divergent thinking without convergent thinking). If such novelty proves to be ineffective, we can speak of "recklessness," which raises the danger of disastrous change. If, despite the lack of exploration, the novelty proves to be effective, it is more a matter of luck than judgment, and we can speak of "blind creativity," with the danger of overconfidence in the future. Thus, not only does lack of knowledge reduce the possibility of generation of variability in the first place, but even where variability is generated, lack of exploration (convergent thinking) raises the possibility of reckless variability and exposes the system in question to the risk of disastrous change or over confidence.

Figure 4.1 also depicts the various possibilities if exploration does take place (i.e., divergent thinking accompanied by convergent thinking). Where convergent thinking following on divergent thinking leads to a correct decision—in the case

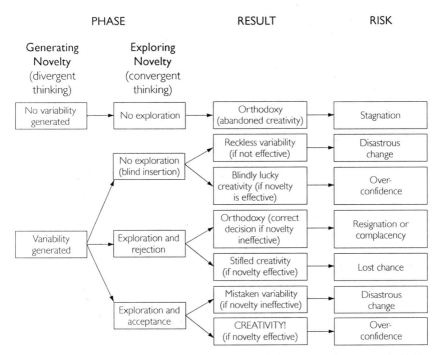

FIG. 4.1. Consequences of differing combinations of divergent and convergent thinking.

of convergent thinking, we can speak of correct and incorrect—creativity occurs, which is the ideal result. Where convergent thinking correctly leads to rejection of the variability generated through divergent thinking, the possibility of disastrous change is avoided, but at the risk of resignation or complacency. Of course the convergent thinking is not always correct: In the Computer Users' Committee at the University of Hamburg in the early 1980s, Cropley Sr. fought against the introduction of remote computer terminals on the grounds that desk-top computing would never catch on. Errors of exploration (mistakes in convergent thinking) can lead to "stifled" creativity (false negatives) or "mistaken" variability (false positives) and raise the danger of a lost chance or, again, of disastrous change.

Despite the danger of stagnation, if novelty is not generated and inserted into functioning systems, insertion of unexplored novelty opens the system to other dangers, which may be catastrophic. Thus, exploration of novelty through convergent thinking is of great importance.

HOW DO DIVERGENT AND CONVERGENT THINKING WORK TOGETHER?

We have argued that insertion of unexplored novelty brings risks such as disastrous change or overconfidence. Thus, both novelty generation through divergent thinking and exploration through convergent thinking are necessary for successful innovation. How do the two work together?

Prerequisite Models

The simplest explanation of the joint roles of divergent and convergent thinking in production of effective novelty is based on the idea that convergent thinking is a prerequisite for effective divergent thinking. An example is to be seen in Vincent Van Gogh (see Case Study).

CASE STUDY: Raw Talent Is Not Enough

Van Gogh's early work was driven by humane impulses (personal disappointment in love and a desire to bring other people beauty and consolation), which he initially tried to express by becoming a missionary, before turning to painting. However, his paintings lacked formal, technical skill (convergent knowledge), and he had to return at the age of 32 to the Academy of Art in Antwerp, where training in painting techniques allowed his flair for color and light to come to fruition. No one had to teach van Gogh how to produce novelty, but it was only after he had mastered basic technique through hours of repetitious, convergent work that his paintings satisfied the prevailing norms for effective novelty.

The simplest prerequisite approach is the summation model: Divergent and convergent thinking seem to add something to each other or even to compensate for defects in each other. More dynamic is the threshold model: Below some threshold level of convergent thinking, effective divergent thinking is thought to be impossible. However, as the level of convergent thinking approaches the threshold from below, the possibility of divergent thinking rises (i.e., divergent and convergent thinking are positively correlated to this point). Once the threshold has been passed, convergent thinking has no further effect on divergent thinking (e.g., van Gogh did not continuously become more and more creative as his technical skills increased). Once these had become adequate as a vehicle for expressing his divergent thinking, creativity was inhibited or facilitated by factors other than convergent thinking.

A further elaboration of this approach is the channel model, according to which convergent thinking provides the channel or pathway through which information reaches the systems responsible for divergent thinking, and thus determines how much and what kind of information is processed. A variant of this is the capacity model, which argues that convergent thinking determines the amount of information that reaches cognitive systems, divergent thinking then being applied to whatever information becomes available. As in the sense of Lubart, convergent thinking would thus influence the level of performance by providing high- or low-octane fuel (channel model) or sufficient or insufficient fuel (capacity model), but divergent thinking (or absence thereof) would influence the kind of performance.

> Divergent and convergent thinking are often conceptualized as supplementing each other, each adding something to the other.

The Superordinate Ability Approach

Ward, Saunders, and Dodds (1999) identified two approaches to conceptualizing the relationship between intelligence and creativity that differ somewhat from the supplementation models just outlined. According to Renzulli's (1986) three-ring approach, creativity and intelligence—together with motivation—are separate subcomponents of a superordinate ability we usually call *giftedness*. According to the overlapping skills model, cognitive skills such as problem definition, selective encoding, shifting context, or transcending limitations are common to both intelligence and creativity (Finke, Ward, & Smith, 1992; Sternberg & Lubart, 1995). Hassenstein (1988) went so far as to argue that a new term is needed to refer to the superordinate intellectual ability that combines both divergent and convergent thinking—he suggested *Klugheit* (cleverness).

Style Models

An alternative way of conceptualizing the interaction between production of variability and production of singularity is the style approach. According to this, convergent and divergent thinking act jointly on the product, but do not directly influence each other. Both involve application of a superordinate ability to acquire, process, and store information, form abstract, general networks, develop knowledge matrices, form systems, and the like. Whether convergent or divergent products result depends on the style in which this thinking power is applied. A convergent style of application would use ability to generate orthodoxy (more of the same), whereas a divergent style would use it to generate novelty. An early example of this approach is seen in the work of Hudson (1968). Cropley

(1999) discussed the interaction of creativity and intelligence in some detail, especially from the point of view of using ability to generate orthodoxy versus using it to generate novelty.

This conceptualization of the interaction regards differences between convergent and divergent thinking as qualitative rather than quantitative. Regardless of level, mental ability can be applied in a convergent or divergent style. Hudson (1968) raised the possibility of people who are good at both and can switch from one style to another—in the sport of cricket, they are referred to as "all-rounders," whereas in baseball, a similar metaphor used to be "switch-hitter." Facaoaru (1985) showed that creative engineers could move freely between divergent and convergent thinking.

A Phase Approach

Even before the modern creativity era, some writers had already reported that the emergence of a creative product seemed to involve a succession of steps. For instance, Prindle (1906) studied inventors and concluded that each invention is the result of a series of small steps, each advancing the development of an invention by a small amount. The gain achieved with one step creates a new jumping off point for the next step, and so on. The classical phase model, first introduced into creativity research about 80 years ago by Wallas (1926), is more general than a small-step model, in that it sees the steps as involving different kinds of operations, rather than simply small gains in content. According to Wallas there are four phases of production of effective novelty (see Fig. 4.2). In the *Preparation phase*, a person becomes thoroughly familiar with a content area. In the *Incubation* phase, the person "churns through" or "stews over" the information obtained in the previous phase. In the *Illumination* phase, a solution emerges, not infrequently seeming to the person involved to come like a bolt from the blue. Finally, in the *Verification* phase, the person tests the solution thrown up in the *Incubation* and *Illumination* phases. The solution may emerge into consciousness all at once, thus seeming to have appeared from nowhere and creating the subjective feeling of effortless creativity. This result would explain why some creative people overlook information and incubation in describing their own creativity.

Empirical studies of the process of creation in people actually engaged in producing something new (see Glover, Ronning, & Reynolds, 1989), as well as retrospective studies in which acknowledged creators described how they obtained new ideas, have cast doubt on the validity of the phase model as an exact literal description of the production of an effectively novel product in real-life settings. Nonetheless, it offers a helpful way of looking at the production of effective novelty as a process, rather than an event, and, as we argue later, of describing the contributions of divergent and convergent thinking to this process.

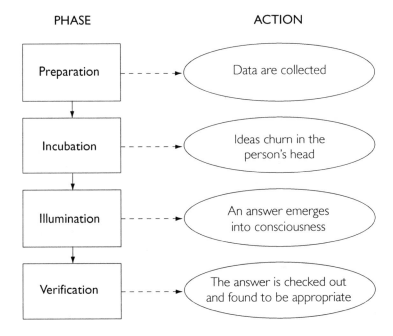

FIG. 4.2. The phases of creative thinking, according to Wallas (1926).

INNOVATION: THE EXTENDED-PHASE MODEL

In the Wallas model, the *Preparation*, *Incubation*, and *Illumination* phases correspond quite well to generation of variability, and the *Verification* phase is similar
to exploration. However, innovation involves more than merely generating and
exploring variability. Effective novelty yielded in the process must be inserted
into a functioning system before we can speak of innovation. Emphasis in this
book on existing knowledge, as well as on the social setting (see particularly
chaps. 6 and 7), suggest that Wallas' four stages need to be extended by adding
further stages. As we discussed in some detail earlier, novelty is not normally
generated in a vacuum, but in the context of what is already known. Thus,
the phase model needs to take account of an initial stage that comes between
Wallas's phases of *Preparation* and *Incubation*. In this phase, the person becomes
aware that there is a problem (in university classrooms, perhaps because the
instructor draws attention to it; and in practical settings too possibly because
of management pressure, but also because of personal expertise, social need, or
commercial imperative; see chap. 6). This is the *Activation* phase.

After *Incubation* and *Verification,* we see a need for two additional phases that we call *Communication* and *Validation.* Although he was not discussing the phases of creativity at all, Dasgupta (2004) summarized the need for *Communication* very aptly: To be judged creative, a product must reach a sufficient state of maturity or completeness to be "manifested publicly" (i.e., it must be communicated to other people). He also gave helpful concrete examples of what the public manifestation looks like. In the case of a scientist, it might well be a series of papers in which experiments are written up, in technology it might be a drawing or artifact, and in literature a novel or poem. We call the public manifestation of a *mature* product *communication.* This idea is by no means new. At the beginning of the modern era, Torrance (1966) defined *creativity* as including ". . . *communicating* the results" (p. 6; italics added)." Finally, as Csikszentmihalyi (1999) stated strongly, a product only achieves the status of creativity when it is judged by external critics to make a significant contribution to a field (i.e., not only is communication necessary, but approval too). We call this *Validation.* These considerations yield an extended model of innovation involving seven phases (see Fig. 4.3) in which we prefer the term *Generation* to *Incubation.*

Information may be vital in the whole process as, for instance, our earlier discussion of Einstein's problem awareness (where others saw none) suggests. Without problem awareness, there is no pressure for divergent thinking. Furthermore, the way the problem is defined, the pathways to a solution that are considered appropriate, and the kinds of solution regarded as feasible may all be determined in the *Preparation* phase via convergent thinking. It may well have been his information that undid Semmer, the nondiscoverer of penicillin. Thus, this phase may be both decisive and yet potentially problematic, as we discuss later, for instance, because it involves placing limits on divergent thinking quite possibly without any intention of doing so. Normally, those who know the most are the best prepared, so that problems of information may apply particularly to experts.

What is striking about the phase model, for present purposes, is that in some phases divergent thinking is needed, in others convergent thinking, and in still others both are necessary. The crucial idea here is that, although both are needed for production of effective novelty, this is not necessarily at the same moment in the process; the creative person may alternate from one kind of thinking to the other, according to the demands of the particular phase of the process of production of effective novelty.

> The phase approach sees divergent and convergent thinking as not directly affecting each other, but as alternating in different phases of the production of effective novelty.

A Precautionary Note—The Problem of Too Much Knowledge

We do not want to imply that convergent thinking is always beneficial for creativity. It is true that lack of knowledge, incorrect information, misunderstanding

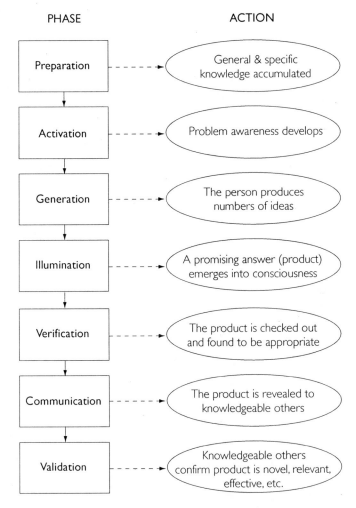

PHASE | ACTION

Preparation – – – – – → General & specific knowledge accumulated

Activation – – – – – → Problem awareness develops

Generation – – – – – → The person produces numbers of ideas

Illumination – – – – – → A promising answer (product) emerges into consciousness

Verification – – – – – → The product is checked out and found to be appropriate

Communication – – – – – → The product is revealed to knowledgeable others

Validation – – – – – → Knowledgeable others confirm product is novel, relevant, effective, etc.

FIG. 4.3. The extended-phase model of creativity.

of ideas or principles, and the like can lead to various forms of bad creativity, such as disastrous change. However, a high level of knowledge can also lead to problems in generating, exploring, and introducing novelty. Thus, from the point of view of creativity, convergent thinking can be both a good and a bad thing. For instance, working successfully in an area over a long period of time (i.e., obtaining a great deal of information and enjoying an extremely thorough preparation, even becoming an expert) can provide a substantial knowledge base that can be manipulated to yield effective novelty (i.e., it can benefit divergent thinking). However, as Gardner (1993) pointed out, there may be "tension between creativity and expertise": The preexisting knowledge of an expert can also act as a corset that blocks novel ideas, so that thinking leads only to production of tried and trusted, "correct" answers.

In addition to making it difficult to recognize effective novelty when it occurs, as in the example of Eugen Semmer (1870), extensive knowledge can thus channel information processing into a narrow range of approaches—possibly without the person concerned being aware of this—and thus limit the variability of what is produced (via divergent thinking) or even block generation of novelty altogether. Research (e.g., Ericsson & Smith, 1991, Root-Bernstein, Bernstein, & Garnier, 1993) has looked at this interesting problem: Although working successfully in an area over a long period of time (i.e., becoming an expert) can provide a knowledge base of both the subject matter and the organization, it can also produce a kind of tunnel vision that narrows thinking and restricts it to the conventional. Thus, despite possessing precisely what seems to be required for generating effective novelty, knowledgeable people can inhibit creativity. To be creativity-fostering, they must not only know the facts, but also be capable of seeing them in a fresh light. Root-Bernstein (1989) spoke of the "novice effect" in this regard. In contrast to the expert, the novice is not inhibited by the negative effects of prior knowledge.

Although the processes that can lead to a negative correlation between creativity and expertise are sometimes cognitive in nature (e.g., sets, functional fixity, and confirmation bias), they can also be noncognitive. For instance, the well-prepared expert can develop a vested interest in maintaining the status quo. Radical new solutions to old, apparently already solved problems may threaten the self-image of experts who labored long on a particular way of looking at a problem. By exposing the inadequacy of their line of attack, a new way of doing things may render an expert's lifetime of work irrelevant and make the person look outdated and incompetent, with dramatic effects on social status. The result may be that experts actively resist introduction of novelty. Thus, for an experienced manager or a professor to return to novice status or even admit to lack of expertise in a team setting requires a high level of self-confidence.

Nonetheless, there are examples of well-established experts who did not lose the novice touch. Cropley Sr. once attended a lecture by the then 58-year-old Hans Selye, the discoverer among other things of the stress syndrome and nominated no fewer than 10 times for the Nobel Prize. He apologized for being in plaster from his toes to his hip—a few days before he had fallen out of a tree after he saw something that seemed odd and interesting in its branches and climbed it to have a better look. A less creative senior researcher would have been too busy with current research problems to bother with something in a tree or would have sent a junior staff member to investigate.

In an empirical study of almost 1,000 employees and managers, van der Heijden (2000) showed that expertise has five dimensions, including special knowledge and specific skills as would be expected after reading this chapter, but also two further important dimensions: meta-cognitive knowledge and growth and flexibility. The former involves self-insights, the latter the combining of fields (referred to in chap. 3 as forming associates or coding). The fields combined may be adjacent, with the result that combining them involves forming commonplace associates or narrow coding (orthodoxy) or, more interesting for present purposes, the fields may be remote, in which case combining them involves forming remote associates or coding broadly, which leads to generation of novelty. In other words, deep knowledge is only favorable for creativity when it is accompanied by insight, flexibility, and similar characteristics. For a more detailed discussion of the role of personal characteristics in production of effective novelty, see chapter 5.

> Introducing effective novelty requires knowledge, skills, and understanding of "the system," which is usually acquired via experience. However, experience with a certain way of doing things can hinder generation of novelty or acceptance of it when others generate it. What is vital is that the knowledge gained by experience be accompanied by openness, flexibility, willingness to start afresh, and so on. What is needed is enough convergent thinking, but not too much.

STOCKTAKING

In this chapter, we have expanded the conceptualization of Process (in the sense of cognitive processes) by emphasizing that not only thinking that generates variability (broadly stated, divergent thinking), but also thinking that generates orthodoxy (broadly speaking, convergent thinking) is required for production of effectively novel products. We have also expanded Process in a second way, by focusing on the sequential steps or Phases in the emergence of a product and developing the extended phase model (see Fig. 4.3). It is now possible to map Process (in the sense of thinking) onto the Phases (see Summary Table 4). Furthermore, this table introduces the idea of intermediate results of thinking in each phase, thus expanding the idea of Product to include subproducts—the result of a phase, but not the whole sequence of events.

In each phase (see left-hand column, in Summary Table 4), psychological processes (second column) produce a subproduct (resembling what Simonton, [1988a] referred to as a *configuration*) shown in the right-hand column that forms the material for the next phase. The third column in Summary Table 4 identifies the broad area of thinking to which the processes belong. The table depicts a process culminating in a socioculturally validated product. Naturally, the product can also fail to achieve validation (i.e., be judged by observers not to be effectively novel). The process can also be broken off before being communicated (e.g., when executive or meta-cognitive processes indicate that the current configuration is doomed to failure). The creative process can also start

Summary Table 4
Creative Processes and Subproducts in the Phases of Creativity

Phase	Process (Cognitive Aspects)	Classification of Process	Subproduct
Preparation	Perceiving Learning Remembering	Convergent thinking	General knowledge Special knowledge
Activation	Identifying problem Setting goals	Convergent and divergent thinking	Problem awareness
Generation	Making associations Bisociating Building networks	Divergent thinking	Many candidate solutions
Illumination	Recognizing promising new configurations	(Mainly) convergent thinking	Novel configurations
Verification	Checking relevance and effectiveness of the novel configurations	Convergent thinking	A relevant and effective prototype *solution*
Communication	Gaining feedback Achieving closure	(Mainly) convergent thinking	Effective presentation of the prototype to others
Validation	Confirmation of relevance and and effectiveness	Convergent thinking	Acclaim of the creative product by relevant judge(s)

partway through, such as when a person who has in the meantime learned more returns to a configuration previously abandoned, thus restarting the *Generation* phase without first passing through *Preparation* and *Activation*.

PRACTICAL GUIDELINES

Once again, the guidelines for practice in Box 4 do not replace or compete with those in earlier boxes, but supplement them. Box 4 adds practical advice for educators and managers based on the concepts presented in chapter 4.

Box 4. Practical Advice Based on Chapter 4

Who?	When?	What?
Teachers and managers (Thought leaders)	Attitudes to students and colleagues	Do not assume that students and colleagues who place great weight on facts are incapable of being creative
		Value the contribution of facts-oriented students and colleagues
	Instructional and leadership strategies	Emphasize the importance of knowledge as the basis of novelty production
		Give examples of novelty being generated from the already known (e.g., case studies)
		Emphasize the uncertainty and complexity of what already exists
		Be on guard against quasi- or pseudocreativity
		Emphasize phases in novelty generation
	Assessment strategies	Reward not just generation but also exploration of novelty
		Provide feedback on rationality, workability, feasibility, and so on, not just novelty
		Reward risk taking, curiosity, and problem finding as much as knowledge (but do not create the impression that facts do not matter)
Who?	When?	What?
Students and colleagues (Coal-face creatives)	Self-image	Do not be afraid of uncertainty or complexity in what already exists
		Be open to the unexpected implications of what is already known
	Learning and work strategies	Seek complexity. Look at things in ways you think might be different from the others
		Look for gaps in material presented. Speculate about why they exist or how they could be filled
		Do not be satisfied with the status quo. Ask how things could be otherwise
		Follow up your own curiosity. Pursue topics that you find fascinating
	Learning and work assignments	Explore novelty you generate
		Try to see the novel in what already exists
		Ascertain what phase of the process of novelty generation you are currently in

5

Intrapersonal Factors in Creativity

Is it simply thinking (see chaps. 3 and 4) that enables people to generate effective novelty or are other aspects of the person also involved—such as personality? Although it is not clear that there is a standard set of personal characteristics that are always found in all creative people, but not in less creative people, there is still a high level of agreement among researchers that certain personality traits help people to become creative and that particular motivational states are also helpful. Creativity is also typically linked with certain emotions and feelings. The link between personal characteristics and creativity is paradoxical: Creativity seems to require simultaneous possession of apparently contradictory traits (e.g., openness for fantasy associated with a strong sense of reality). The phase model of creativity offers a way of understanding this paradox. Different traits are important at different stages in the process. This finding emphasizes the importance in attempts to foster creativity of defining what aspect of the process of novelty production is to be fostered by a particular measure or activity.

THE SEARCH FOR THE CREATIVE PERSONALITY

We have already described Evariste Galois as one of the most creative mathematicians who ever lived. His prodigious mathematical talent was already visible at school, to be sure, but there was what would now be called a downside: He refused to study anything except mathematics! His teachers described him as "original," but they also judged him to be "singular," "withdrawn," "bizarre," and, especially interesting for this chapter, "closed." Is it, perhaps, customary for creative people to display atypical patterns of personality traits?

The first step we take in examining the question of creativity and personality is to ask whether there is a creative personality at all. The idea of a unique personality type that can be labeled *creative* has been questioned strongly by some psychological researchers. Helson (1996) concluded that there is no single, unitary, differentiated personality profile that is typical of all highly creative people and also distinguishes them as a group from the less creative. However, this does not negate the idea that certain traits are related to production of effective novelty, either in a positive way (i.e., they facilitate its appearance) or a negative way (i.e., they inhibit it). The point here is not to discover a personality constellation that makes people creative (indeed we have just suggested that this may not exist), but to look at aspects of personality that make it easy (or difficult) for people to become creative.

> There may well be no such thing as the creative personality: Many kinds of people can be creative. However, some personality traits may make it easier to become creative, whereas others may inhibit it.

Creativity and Mental Illness

One common opinion is that creativity is facilitated by mental illness. Indeed, this topic is one of the oldest issues in psychology and was already a subject of empirical investigation more than 100 years ago. For instance, the idea of the mad artist is central to the romantic view of creativity. It is even conceivable that in the 18th and 19th centuries, some poets, artists, or composers deliberately tried to create the impression of being mad because of the widespread romantic admiration of the mad artist at that time. The French writer, Gérard de Nerval (1805–1895), for instance, kept a lobster as a pet and used to take it for walks on a lead made from a blue ribbon. He said that he liked it because it did not bark and knew the secrets of the sea. The theme has continued to be the subject of psychological investigation right up to the present day. Kaufman and Baer (2002) summarized much of the more recent research in their study of mental illness and female poets. Weeks and Ward (1988) demonstrated the relevance of the discussion not just to literary/artistic domains, but also to practical fields such as engineering innovation. They showed that many people regarded as eccentric hold patents, some of them holding several.

Contemporary research has adopted two approaches to investigating the question of creativity and madness, either studying acknowledged creative people to see whether they are more frequently mentally disturbed than chance would predict, or focusing on people already regarded as mentally ill or at least eccentric, to see whether they show more creativity than the general population. The research has shown that there are some similarities between schizophrenic (schizotype) and creative thinking. For instance, schizophrenics make more remote associations and think more divergently than uncreative people without schizophrenia (for a recent summary, see Schuldberg, 2000–2001). A particularly interesting finding is that Nobel Prize winners, schizophrenic patients, and creative college students all show patterns of schizotype thinking that differ from those of less creative students (Rothenberg, 1983).

However, although creative people resemble schizophrenic patients in some ways, they also differ sharply from them in others. In a study comparing architects and members of other creative professions with schizophrenic patients, Cropley and Sikand (1973) showed that both groups displayed schizotype thinking (remote associations, unexpected combinations of ideas, etc.) by comparison with members of a control group. However, this divergent thinking did not favor production of effective novelty in the schizophrenic patients because they were frightened by their own unusual ideas. The creative people, in contrast, were inspired by them. This theory suggests that, although atypical cognitions may be part of creative thinking, on its own, cognitive disturbance does not produce creativity. Earlier findings supported this view. Barron (1969), for instance, showed that creative writers and architects scored in the upper 15% on all psychopathology scales of the Minnesota Multiphase Personality Inventory (MMPI), a psychological test assessing clinical conditions, but that their high ego-strength made it possible for them to make use of the unusual associations and elevated mood to generate and explore variability. What would be pathological in conjunction with low ego-strength enriched the thinking of people with high ego-strength and led to production of novelty.

Thus, there does not seem to be a straightforward cause–effect relationship between cognitive disturbance and creativity. Indeed, in a recent empirical study, Kinney, Richards, Lowing, LeBlanc, Zimbalist, and Harlan (2000–2001) concluded that the relationship has an inverted-U form: Narrow categorizing, exclusive (as against inclusive) thinking, absence of unusual associations, and similar deviations from the average in information processing, as well as broad categorizing, extreme overinclusive thinking, and excessively unusual associations (i.e., the opposite pattern of deviation) are associated with low levels of creativity. In our terms, the one generates no novelty, whereas the other large amounts of novelty, but with the possibility of problems in the area of effectiveness. A moderate amount of deviant thinking, however, allows production of novelty without abandoning effectiveness.

> Thinking in ways that deviate moderately from the usual is good for creativity, but large deviation is not!

Apart from the question of a connection between cognitive disturbances (e.g., schizophrenia) and novelty production, it has also been shown that mood disturbances such as depression are much more common among acknowledged creative people than in the general public (Andreasen, 1987). Jamison (1993) reported the results of a study carried out with famous British artists and authors, in which she found that manic–depressive disturbances (mood fluctuations ranging from depression to heightened excitement) were six times more common in this group than in the general public. This link appears to be unequivocally established. Indeed, Jamison concluded that mental states such as elation are vital for creativity.

The question that now arises is whether mood disturbance makes people creative or is even necessary for creativity—for instance, by driving them to a state of despair, where they see the world differently from other people, or encouraging them to retreat from their pain into fantasies, or by elation that leads them to regress to infantile kinds of thinking that are free from the rigid rules of everyday adult thinking. It is also imaginable that creativity is related to emotional lability and greater sensitivity to external stimuli or internal mood fluctuations. The mood swings associated with emotional disturbance may provide a rich source of feelings, motives, and unusual ideas for those who are also creative, but only pain to others. It is also possible that the apparent link is an artifact. For instance, mood states such as manic disorders could reduce creative people's fear of embarrassing themselves or promote self-confidence. Reduced fear or increased self-confidence may then encourage people to behave in atypical ways (generate surprise), thus creating an erroneous impression that the manic disorder causes the creativity.

Generally, the position of clinically oriented researchers on creativity is that it requires a high level of mental health (Maslow, 1973; May, 1976; Rogers, 1961). Helson (1999) demonstrated empirically that sound mental health was necessary for the realization of creative potential. Women who as students had shown creative potential, but had problems in areas such as sense of identity, did not fullfil in their adult lives the promise they had shown 30 years earlier. It can even be argued (e.g., Cropley, 1990) that creativity promotes mental health. Studies of highly creative people indicate that creativity is connected with psychological properties such as flexibility, openness, autonomy, humor, willingness to try things, or realistic self-assessment. These characteristics are prerequisites for the emergence of creativity. However, research on normal personality development also emphasizes similar properties as core elements of the healthy personality. Adopting a psychoanalytic position, Anthony (1987) argued that creativity is related to ego-autonomy and ego-autonomy to mental health, with the consequence that creativity promotes mental health. Krystal (1988) showed that uncreative people had difficulty in self-caring and lacked self-coherence. Fostering creativity in such people assists them in these areas and would thus promote self-realization.

This line of argument is easily compatible with Schuldberg's (2000–2001) conclusion that creativity is linked with six subclinical patterns of personal adjustment (i.e., patterns of characteristics that in pronounced degrees are pathological, but at modest levels are not). Three of these charateristics are positively related to creativity:

1. positive schizotype cognitive symptoms (rather like what was called *divergent thinking* in chap. 3),

2. hypomania (elevated mood, as already discussed above), and

3. impulsivity.

The first is associated with the thinking aspects of creativity, the latter two with properties such as courage (even if it is false courage), risk-taking, self-confidence, lack of concern about social norms, and the like. The other three inhibit creativity: negative schizotype cognitive symptoms (i.e., very rigid thinking), negative schizotype affective symptoms (flat affect), and depression. This approach accords well with earlier remarks about the beneficial effects of properties associated with cognitive disturbance (broad categorizing, wide associating, etc.) combined with others related to mood disturbance (reduced inhibitions, positive mood, etc.) within nonclinical limits.

> Heightened sensitivity to stimulation, mood swings, elation, and the like may lead to seeing things differently, daring to break rules, and so on (i.e., to generation of novelty), and thus produce an apparent link between creativity and pathology.

Ludwig's (1998) division of creative fields into four groups (impersonal vs. emotive, objective vs. subjective, structured vs. unstructured, and formal vs. informal) makes it possible to analyze the possible link between psychopathology and kind of creativity. The more impersonal, objective, structured, and formal a field, the lower the incidence of psychopathology in practitioners in the field. This result may have two causes. On the one hand, those who show the emotivity, lack of structure, subjectivity, and informality associated with psychopathology will have difficulty making creative achievements in these fields, so that successfully creative individuals in these fields will show low levels of cognitive and mood disturbance. On the other hand, in some fields, creativity is aided by subjectivity, emotion, informality, and lack of structure, all of which are encouraged by cognitive and affective disturbance, so that psychopathology will encourage creativity in such areas. A second possibility is that subjective, unstructured, emotive, informal fields are attractive to people who have difficulty with structure, formality, impersonality, and objectivity, thus causing a higher incidence of people displaying psychopathology in such areas. This notion does not mean that everybody in these fields is mentally ill or that mental illness is a necessary prerequisite for success in the fields.

> Personality characteristics that are at the limit of what is accepted as normal in a society may be helpful for creativity in certain fields. Alternatively, certain fields may be more tolerant of marginal personalities. In either case, these fields may attract borderline pathological personalities.

STUDYING PERSONALITY AND CREATIVITY: METHODS

The logical way to investigate relationships between creativity and personality is to focus on people who have already produced highly acclaimed products (i.e., to concentrate on those who have successfully introduced effective novelty). As Runco and Charles (1997) pointed out, focusing on real-life examples of functional creativity is safer because it is certain the people involved really are producers of effective novelty (after all, their products have been acclaimed). Although a focus on acclaimed creativity has the advantage of concentrating on people whose generation of effective novelty is self-evident, this approach has the disadvantage that it risks setting the bar too high. It creates the impression that this book is concerned with sublime creativity and that our goal is either to applaud the creativity of geniuses after the fact or to drive on ordinary students in the expectation that they can all be turned into Thomas Alva Edisons, Pablo Picassos, or Ernest Hemingways. This is not the case. Our goal is to encourage generation and exploration of variability in all kinds of settings and to encourage all students to be innovative. Nonetheless, it is interesting to look briefly at people who have achieved universal acclaim.

Case Studies

Case studies are an excellent device for obtaining information about, for instance, distinguished creators. A common approach is the intrinsic case study, which focuses on a single person because of the overpowering interest of the case in question. Gardner (1993) carried out case studies of Freud, Einstein, Picasso, Stravinsky, Eliot, Graham, and Gandhi. Such people offer examples of overpowering cases. The data obtained from a case study may be in the form of a narrative provided by the person in question (e.g., an interview) or notes, audiotapes, videos, and the like yielded by observation of the case. In some studies, the data have been second-hand in the form of diaries and letters, autobiographies or biographies, or similar documents.

The data can also be works of the person being studied (e.g., the paintings of Picasso), which could be analyzed for the presence of certain themes such as violence, joy, despair, and the like, or for other kinds of content such as original scientific ideas or prophetic statements (e.g., the writings and technical drawings left by Leonardo da Vinci). An example can be seen in a case study at the University of Hamburg of the German poet, Friedrich Leopold von Hardenburg, known as "Novalis," whose work greatly influenced 19th century romanticism. He wrote many short poems whose contents were analyzed to identify themes related to death. Because the dates when the poems were written is known, it was possible to relate the appearance of the death theme in the poems to real events in Novalis' life, such as the early deaths of both his brother and fiancée, Sophie von Kühn, and to show that his creativity was shaped by things that happened in his immediate, everyday life.

The case study approach is beset by a number of problems. The data may be highly idiosyncratic (i.e., specific or peculiar to a single respondent or even to the interaction between a particular respondent and a particular researcher). A case study of the development of Picasso's creativity would obviously require only a single case (Picasso) and would obviously be extremely interesting and informative. However, such a study demonstrates two problems centering on the representativeness of case studies: idiosyncrasy and generalizability. Nonetheless, case studies provide a rich source of hypotheses about creativity and the person. It is well known, for instance, that women experienced severe difficulties in intense relationships with Picasso, who seems to have been uncaring, selfish, cruel, and exploitative of them, raising questions about whether these are typical characteristics of men hailed as creative geniuses. More generally, without prejudging the nature of the relationships, it could be asked whether there is a systematic connection between interpersonal relations and creativity.

> Case studies offer insights into the creativity of acknowledged creative people, but they are beset by problems, including distortions or even misinformation, as well as doubt about whether they can be transferred to people who have not become famous for creativity.

Occupational Creativity

One way of doing this is to focus on people who pursue occupations regarded as inherently creative such as writer, musician, or actor, treating them as creative simply by virtue of the area in which they work regardless of level of achievement (occupational creativity). Examples are the works of Barron (1972), Cattell and Drevdahl (1955), Drevdahl and Cattell (1958), Eiduson (1958), Götz and Götz (1979), or MacKinnon (1983). One finding is that such people possess special personality characteristics that set them apart from people in less creative occupations (i.e., highly creative vs. less creative people). Early research on the psychology of patent holders, such as that of Prindle (1906) and Rossman (1931), also indicated that there is a link between personality and creativity.

A variant of this approach is to study people in occupations not regarded as inherently creative, but offering opportunities for creativity (e.g., architecture, research science) or even occupations thought (rightly or wrongly) to offer few opportunities for creativity, such as business, the armed forces, or engineering. Creative members of these professions are then compared with less creative colleagues. Participants are often identified as creative by means of ratings of their creativity in their job by colleagues or other qualified persons. MacKinnon (1983) showed that there were personality differences between creative and less creative architects, whereas Helson (1983) reported similar differences for creative mathematicians, and Barron (1969) studied, among others, Air Force officers. Facaoaru (1985) investigated engineering students and engineers, contrasting those rated creative with others rated less creative, and showed that there were differences in thinking, personality, and motivation.

Some researchers (e.g., Cattell & Butcher, 1968; Roe, 1953) looked at possible differences in personality between people who had achieved creative eminence in different fields (e.g., creative chemists vs. creative psychologists, creative social scientists vs. creative physical scientists, creative scientists vs. creative artists). This research involves comparing creative people with other equally creative individuals, the difference being the field of eminence. Certain traits seem to differentiate between people who are creative in aesthetic fields, such as art or literature, and those who are creative in science. Examples include radicalism and rejection of external constraints. Art and literature people tend to be radical and to reject social constraints, whereas engineers (even those who generate variability) tend to be conformist and restricted by external factors. This finding emphasizes once again the difference between functional and aesthetic creativity.

Unacclaimed Behavior

Without losing sight of the importance of actual functional creativity, however defined, the criterion of creativity can be set even lower by concentrating on humble activities that nonetheless produce effective novelty (i.e., everyday creativity; Cropley, 1990). We are referring here to the paradox of creativity in people who will never produce anything novel, effective, and ethical (Nichols, 1972). Finally, it is possible to study people—especially children—who have not yet displayed creative behavior, but seem likely, on the basis of test scores (especially tests of creative thinking; chap. 8), to become creative if they receive appropriate encouragement (i.e., potential or latent creativity). We are mainly interested here in ordinary or everyday creativity. Everybody is capable of this.

STUDYING CREATIVITY AND PERSONALITY: RESULTS

Although there is debate about whether a unitary creative personality exists, the possibility remains that certain personal characteristics in some way help people to generate effective novelty or learn to generate it. Several comprehensive reviews of research on creativity and personality traits have appeared over the years. These summaries confirm that a fairly stable set of findings has emerged, although different authors name traits somewhat differently or give differing weight to particular traits according to their own areas of interest.

Personality-Facilitating Traits

Several comprehensive reviews of research on creativity and personality traits have appeared over the years, including Dellas and Gaier (1970), Farisha (1978), Barron and Harrington (1981), Motamedi (1982), Treffinger, Isaksen, and Firestien (1983), Dacey (1989), Albert and Runco (1989), and Eysenck (1997). A relatively stable set of personal characteristics seems to be particularly helpful for creativity. By and large, the positive traits are:

- nonconformity (both in attitudes as well as in social behavior),

- autonomy/inner directedness,

- intuitiveness,

- ego strength,

- tolerance of ambiguity/preference for complexity,

- flexibility,

- openness to stimulation/breadth of interests,

- risk-taking,

- androgyny (possession of both male and female characteristics),

- acceptance of being different (i.e., self-acceptance), and

- positive attitude to work.[1]

However, some creative traits are less positive (e.g., lack of concern for social norms, and antisocial attitudes).

---

[1]Although such considerations may seem to be of purely academic interest, looking at creativity from the point of view of **P**erson offers interesting perspectives on practical issues. For instance, in this book we analyze gender differences in creativity in terms of personality. A possible and thought-provoking further practical application of these traits would involve mapping them onto known characteristics of the behavior of terrorists, which we have argued elsewhere (Cropley, Kaufman, and Cropley, 2008) displays many characteristics of creativity. At the theoretical level, this would aid understanding of differences between socially desirable and undesirable creativity. In practical settings, it might aid understanding how and why people become terrorists, how to provide them with remedial treatment, or how to deter them.

More specific studies have given particular weight to a smaller number of traits that are thought to be of central importance. Barron and Harrington (1981) listed:

- preference for complexity,

- autonomy,

- self-confidence,

- the ability to tolerate contradictory aspects of one self, and

- high evaluation of aesthetic qualities.

Parloff, Datta, Kleman, and Handlon (1968) emphasized autonomy and complexity, whereas Albert and Runco (1989) focused on independence. Barron (1969) showed the importance of ego-strength, including acceptance of conflicting aspects of oneself.

Interestingly, Dellas and Gaier (1970) concluded that the personalities of young creative people are similar to those of creative adults, and this notion is supported by studies focusing on children. Heinelt (1974) studied schoolchildren identified on the basis of test scores as highly creative and concluded that they were significantly more introverted, more self-willed, intellectually more active, more flexible, and possessed greater wit and a stronger sense of humor than less creative youngsters. According to Neff (1975), they are flexible, tolerant, and responsible, as well as being sociable and success-oriented. They are also characterized by being less satisfied and less controlled than children who display lower levels of creativity. In social situations, they are less willing to conform and less interested in making a good impression.

Some personality traits make it easier to become creative. These traits include autonomy, flexibility, preference for complexity, self-confidence, and ego-strength. Taken together, such characteristics define a special pattern of personality that we call *openness*.

The Importance of Openness

A telling aphorism, whose origins we do not know, is the following: "The human mind functions in the same way as the immune system. When it encounters something unfamiliar it rejects it!" This problem of resistance to novelty is the subject of the present section. Basadur and Hausdorf (1996) drew attention to the fundamental importance for creativity of placing a high value on new ideas, which is true for both individuals and societies, although we concentrate here on individual people (for a discussion of society and creativity, see chaps. 5 and 6). One of the basic personal characteristics associated with creativity thus seems to be a general willingness to work with or an ability to tolerate novelty—openness. Cropley (1992a), for instance, particularly emphasized "openness to the spark of inspiration." *Openness* was defined by McCrae (1987) as interest in novelty for its own sake: The open person likes to go beyond the conventional and enjoys the unexpected, even without any observable payoff. Linked with openness are traits like tolerance for ambiguity and self-confidence.

Gough (1979) described the opposite personality configuration from the one just described, calling it *cautious*. In fact, openness versus caution seems to be a fundamental dimension of personality. Our observation is that differences from person to person in openness are already visible in early childhood. Many people, even as children, reject out of hand anything that departs from the familiar by more than a small amount, preferring novelty to arise, if at all, out of small, barely perceptible changes to the status quo (cautious personality). Others welcome variability or even seek to generate it (open personality). The size of the maximum tolerable change in the status quo may correlate with creativity. In view of the well-known importance of collative variables in the environment (such as incongruity, unexpectedness, and unpredictability) for maintenance of optimal cognitive and emotional functioning (Berlyne, 1962), and the negative effects of monotony, as seen in for instance the hospitalization syndrome in small children, the drive in many people for maximum sameness and stability is unhealthy. In studying the effects of stimulus deprivation on mental and emotional functioning, Heron (1957) described the "pathology of boredom," whereas Burkhardt (1985) referred to society's *Gleichheitswahn* (sameness psychosis).

> Many people cannot tolerate discrepancies, weaknesses, gaps in knowledge, and the like: They are closed. Open people, by contrast, seek novelty.

Play and Humor

Linked with openness are play and humor. Early studies (e.g., Getzels & Jackson, 1962) emphasized these traits as personality characteristics associated with creativity. More recently, Graham, Sawyers, and DeBord (1989) demonstrated the relationship between playfulness and creativity in schoolchildren. Isen, Daubman, and Nowicki (1987) showed that children did better on creativity tests after they had seen a comedy film. According to Bruner (1975), a playful approach fosters creativity because play is not chained to the strict rules of reality and is freed from social pressures. Play is also less risky than real life because situations imagined in play can be cancelled out if they prove too problematic, and everything returned to what it was before. Hence, in play, novel situations can be tried out without risk. Picasso's well-known observation that he played with ideas is often cited as support for the importance of play even for acknowledged creators. Torrance and Safter (1999) saw play as a central element in what they called "making the creative leap."

> In play, it is possible to take risks without sanctions and to correct mistakes if necessary.

DYNAMICS OF PERSONALITY AND CREATIVITY

An interesting question is how personal factors affect production of effective novelty. Is one the cause and the other an effect? It is usually assumed by researchers that personality influences creativity, although it is theoretically conceivable that the reverse is true (i.e., that creativity influences personality). For instance, the experience of producing novelty and having this accepted by other people seems likely to increase self-confidence, willingness to deviate from the commonplace, openness for new ideas, and similar traits. However, in the first comprehensive review of research on personality and creativity in the modern era, Dellas and Gaier (1970) concluded that personality traits affect creative behavior, rather than the reverse. In any case, the question of the effects of personality on the production of effective novelty is of central interest in this chapter, because this book is concerned with fostering functional creativity, not promoting favorable development of personality.

The Dynamics of a Cause–Effect Relationship

A putative causal relationship between personality and creativity can be looked at in two ways. The first posits a threshold effect, the second a linear relationship. According to the threshold model, possession of certain decisive personality traits beyond some minimum level (the threshold) is necessary for creativity to occur (a qualitative approach: If you have the personality you are creative, if you do not you are not). According to the second model, certain special characteristics would increase the likelihood of creativity, the more strongly a person possessed them (a quantitative approach): As the strength of the necessary traits increases, the probability of creativity would also rise. The quantitative approach is more optimistic, because strengthening existing traits (or weakening negative ones) seems intuitively easier than inculcating what is not there.

Does personality push people to generate variability, allow them to do it, or increase the likelihood that they will do it? Five possibilities will be looked at in this section:

1. direct causal relationship (certain personality traits actively trigger generation of variability, etc., almost perforce),

2. threshold relationship (certain traits are necessary for generation of variability, exploration, etc.),

3. facilitatory relationship (certain traits make generation of variability and the like easier),

4. common source relationship (personality and novelty production both derive from the same fundamental roots), and

5. interaction relationship (personality and novelty production mutually affect each other).

Personality as a Compelling Cause

It is conceivable, at least as a theoretical possibility, that certain personality characteristics may directly trigger generation of variability and the like. In fact there are writers, especially psychoanalytically oriented authors—including Freud—who emphasize a link of this kind. The most obvious examples of such characteristics would be negative properties like lack of impulse control or rejection of social norms. These traits would lead more or less inevitably to surprising behavior as antisocial impulses were expressed (i.e., they would cause generation of variability). Not only negative traits, but also positive characteristics, could also force people to generate variability. For instance, a strong sense of justice could impel a person to turn to literature, the theatre, or medical research in the hope that these careers would provide a pathway to righting what the person regarded as social wrongs. To take one example, Emile Zola was moved to write *Germinal* by the outrage he felt at the injustice experienced by French coalminers. Other admirable traits, such as determination and strength of character, could energize a person who had experienced misfortune and hardship to turn to literature or art to communicate to others the sorrow and disappointment these experiences had caused, or they could cause a person who had been refused a research grant to work hard to achieve a major scientific breakthrough against all the odds.

Creativity need not always be a reaction to negative factors either in the individual's personality or the environment, as might seem to be the case from the examples just given. Positive personality characteristics, such as the drive for self-realization or generative motives (the desire to build something up), may lead to the production of effectively novel products even without deprivation, injustice, or the like. Indeed, some acknowledged creators are born into environments of wealth and privilege, or at least of acclaim and success, and seem to become creative either because the production of effective novelty is simply a natural part of the ethos of their environment or because their social privileges give them the time and facilities to pursue their interests.

CASE STUDIES: Creativity as an Environmental Norm

The three generations of Becquerels—Antoine César, Alexandre Edmond, and Antoine Henri (Nobel Prize in 1903)—successively held the chair in physics at the Museum of Natural History in Paris between 1837 and 1895, each becoming one of the creators of modern knowledge in his particular field: electrochemistry, the nature of light, and radioactivity, respectively. After studying medicine in London and then attending Cambridge University without graduating, Sir Francis Galton traveled widely before accompanying his cousin, Charles Darwin, on the voyage of the Beagle, apparently motivated by nothing more than curiosity and spare time. Darwin subsequently published the theory of evolution, while Galton published books on geography and meteorology and went on to lay part of the foundations of modern statistics, which he invented because he needed it to pursue his interest in quantitative analysis of the inheritance of ability (which he called *genius*, although he later retracted the term).

It is important to notice, however, that effective novelty can only occur if the cognitive elements such as knowledge, skills, and divergent thinking are also present. These elements determine what level of effectiveness the novelty achieves even if noncognitive factors are decisive for its emergence or nonemergence. Emile Zola displayed extraordinary imagination and poetic fantasy in his work, it is true, but without his mastery of the French language, painstaking research, and detailed drafting of plot, his manuscripts would still have been surprising, even shocking, but would have lacked effectiveness and may well have produced no more than quasicreativity (surprisingness unaccompanied by effectiveness).

Even in people who seem to be driven to be creative by their personal properties, this quality is not sufficient on its own for production of effective novelty.

Personality as a Facilitator/Blocker

Personality may function not so much as a sufficient cause—a press or goad that almost drives a person to production of novelty in the way just outlined—but rather as an assister. This theory would mean that certain personality characteristics might be necessary or at least helpful for creativity but not actually cause it. (In the case of some negative traits, it could be their absence that is necessary or helpful.) This approach involves the idea of personality as a necessary, but not sufficient, cause. Relevant personality characteristics may include courage, interest in the novel, self-confidence, a generative or growth orientation, and similar factors. These traits are looked at more closely in later sections of this chapter.

This way of conceptualizing the relationship between personality and creativity can be grasped easily by examining negative personality characteristics that seem to inhibit production of effective novelty. For instance, a person could conceivably be cognitively equipped to produce effective novelty and even highly motivated to do this, but be inhibited by personality characteristics such as fear of looking foolish, excessive need for certainty, or exaggerated social conformity. In this case, the personality characteristics in question can be thought of as blocks to creativity. Not encouragement, but weakening of such characteristics would facilitate realization of creative potential.

> Some personality traits make it easier to generate novelty, whereas others make it more difficult.

The Common-Cause Explanation

Although she was studying the possible relationship between creativity and psychosis, Jamison's (1993) conclusion that mental states such as elation are vital for creativity—but do not cause it—is of considerable interest here. Traits such as excitability, nonconformity, or risk-taking may well be an expression of more fundamental characteristics, such as emotional lability, greater attentiveness to internal mood fluctuations, or greater sensitivity to small changes in external stimuli. These characteristics also underlie production of novelty, resulting is an apparent direct relationship among excitability, nonconformity, and risk-taking and creativity. To give a more concrete example, elevated mood could lead to flamboyant (nonconforming) behavior in people by reducing fear of embarrassing themselves (i.e., it could remove a blocker). Simultaneously, it could promote making remote associates and thus lead to production of novelty. It could then seem logical to conclude that the nonconformity had led to the production of novelty, whereas in reality both might be the result of euphoric mood.

Although he was referring specifically to creativity and psychopathology, Schuldberg (2000–2001) also emphasized that an apparent link between personality and creativity could result not from a direct cause–effect relationship, but from a diathesis factor: an earlier risk factor that leads to later behaviors, of which some are viewed as pathological symptoms and others as creativity. This kind of approach introduces the interesting idea that some later deviations from the norm resulting from a single risk factor may be labeled pathological by observers, but other deviations creative. In other words, what is creative may be decided by the surrounding society (see chaps. 6 and 7 for a more detailed discussion). This model makes the phenomenon of pseudocreativity easier to conceptualize. A fundamental state—let us say, impulsivity—might lead some people to behave in ways that the majority regards as rude, wild, or antisocial. At the same time, it might promote generation of variability. If the antisocial behavior were repeatedly seen paired with generation of variability, it might come to be regarded as essential for creativity or even be regarded as a cause of it. Ultimately, it might even be mistaken for creativity, thus reducing creativity to nonconformity (pseudocreativity). Pseudocreativity is attractive to some people because it eliminates the need for effective novelty and the hard work this often entails.

> The apparent link between creativity and personality is sometimes an artifact.

MOTIVATION AND CREATIVITY

Studies of famous creative people from the past have confirmed that motivation plays an important role in their achievements. For instance, Cox (1926) showed that geniuses such as Newton, Copernicus, Galileo, Keppler, and Darwin were marked by tenacity and perseverance, in addition to high intelligence. Goertzel, Goertzel, and Goertzel (1978) also showed the importance of motivation in their case studies of historical figures, while Hassenstein (1988) too commented on the obsessive nature of the work of gifted individuals. Biermann (1985) concluded that fascination with the subject matter, and consequent extreme motivation, was one of the most important characteristics of creative mathematicians of the 17th to 19th centuries. Facaoaru (1985) showed that creative engineers were characterized not only by special intellectual characteristics, but also by motivational factors such as determination. Among more recent acknowledged creative people, Sir Harold Kroto, winner of the Nobel Prize for Chemistry in 1996 for the discovery of fullerenes ("Bucky Balls"; stable carbon spheres consisting of as many as 60 individual atoms), greatly emphasized intrinsic motivation in discussing his own work, while William Phillips, winner of the 1997 Nobel Prize for Physics for the development of techniques for cooling and trapping atoms with laser light, was repeatedly described as possessing "insatiable curiosity." Both Kroto and Phillips were characterized by a high level of ability to work in teams, and both emphasized how important this trait was to their innovative work. Picasso was innovative and original, even before he became famous, and he was marked by a strong experimental urge.

According to Perkins (1981), creativity is the result of six elements, of which four are closely related to motivation:

- drive to create order out of chaos,

- willingness to take risks,

- willingness to ask unexpected questions, and

- feeling of being challenged by an area.

Henle (1974) gave a Gestalt psychology perspective to the drive to create order out of chaos by emphasizing that perception of dynamic gaps (inadequacies and inconsistencies) in existing knowledge leads in creative people to a drive to build a good gestalt by reorganizing knowledge. Einstein's (Miller, 1992) description of how his recognition that existing theories of thermodynamics were inadequate motivated him to develop the special theory of relativity, and then the general theory is an example of this phenomenon. Einstein continued to be dissatisfied with his own theory and worked on it for much of the rest of his life. Mumford and Moertl (2003) described two case studies of innovation in social systems (management practice and student selection for admission to university) and concluded that both innovations were driven by "intense dissatisfaction" with the status quo.

> Dissatisfaction with the status quo and willingness to take a risk seem to be important aspects of creative motivation.

Linked with dissatisfaction with the status quo as motivation to produce something new and better is belief in one's own ability to do better: People who are dissatisfied with gaps in what exists, but do not believe that they can do anything about it, are hardly likely to be motivated to generate effective novelty, especially if this requires long years of toil or even hardship, as is sometimes the case. Thus, self-confidence, or what Ajzen (1991) called *creative self-efficacy*, is necessary. For our purposes, this idea involves people's personal perception of a task as lying within their ability to solve—in the present context, their image of themselves as capable of generating the necessary effective novelty. Creative self-efficacy intuitively seems to be related to openness, tolerance for ambiguity, risk-taking, and the like. It is one of the important personal properties that managers and teachers can foster.

Park and Jang (2005) investigated motivation for scientific creativity by interviewing both theoretical and applied physicists. They concluded that, in addition to more affective motives such as interest or curiosity (states more related to affective conditions within the mind of the person in question), these scientists were also affected by what they called *cognitive motives*—essentially deriving from their knowledge about phenomena in the external world. In particular, they identified (a) recognition of gaps in existing knowledge (incompleteness), (b) a

drive to round out recently emerging novelty (development), and (c) identification of contradictions in accepted knowledge (conflict/discrepancy) as cognitive
motives for creativity. They gave examples from statements by Albert Einstein that
indicate he experienced all three of these motivating forces at various times. It
is apparent that the cognitive motives identified by Park and Jang have a great
deal to do with discovering problems.

CASE STUDY: Problem Discovery and Creativity

In 1890, Max Planck and his wife received a social visit from a colleague,
Heinrich Rubens. Rubens mentioned that his latest, still unpublished research
had demonstrated the inadequacy of Planck's attempt to use classical physics
to explain why Wien's law was only valid at high frequencies (this law was
accepted at that time as the explanation of radiation of energy from black
bodies). Planck saw at once that a radically novel approach was necessary.
This dissatisfaction with existing theory motivated Planck to think more
about the nature of energy. In the course of that evening, he worked out
the answer—quantum theory—and mailed it to Rubens on a postcard.
There was, at the time, no empirical evidence to suggest quantum theory,
but Planck's dissatisfaction with existing approaches drove him to seek a
radically new solution because he could not tolerate the inadequacy of
existing knowledge. He described his discovery (Planck, 1901) as "an act
of despair." He received the Nobel Prize for Physics in 1918.

Intrinsic Motivation

The factors such as personal dissatisfaction with the status quo or intolerance of
incompleteness and the like that are discussed above suggest that the motivation
for creativity may arise within the individual, rather than in the external world. A
widely accepted position is that creativity is based on intrinsic motivation (Amabile,
1996): the wish to carry out an activity for the sake of the activity, regardless of
external reward. This position can be contrasted with working for external rewards
such as praise, awards, pay raises, promotion, and even avoidance of punishment
(extrinsic motivation). In the case of extrinsic reward, it is argued that people
become active only to gain the reward and shape their behavior to conform to
whatever is necessary to receive that reward, usually generation of orthodoxy.
Even where variability is generated, it is said to be done only in accordance
with external directives—generation of variability as a form of conformity. The
importance of intrinsic motivation was strongly supported by Sir Harold Kroto,
whose Nobel Prize in 1996 was already mentioned.

This issue is vital in discussions of fostering creativity: Can it be encouraged
by teachers through a system of external rewards? If external encouragement

actually blocks creativity, there does not seem to be any chance of actively fostering it, especially in individuals who do not produce novelty more or less spontaneously. The only possibility of fostering creativity would then seem to be avoiding blocking it. More recently, however, the possibility of fostering creativity by the application of external rewards has been demonstrated by Eisenberger and Armeli (1997). These authors showed that extrinsic reward led to enduring improvements even in a creative area such as music, provided that: (a) teachers knew precisely what they wanted to foster; (b) students knew what was required of them; (c) students were rewarded for specified creative behaviors, such as incorporating unexpected elements into a problem solution or producing alternative possibilities; and (d) students were not rewarded for uncreative behaviors.

However, research has yielded contradictory reports on the effects of external rewards; some studies indicate that they can increase creativity, whereas others indicate that they block it. This contrast is attributable to the fact that external supervision of activities supposed to generate variability can take two forms: It can focus on (a) controlling behavior, or (b) providing information. In the latter case, feedback, rewards, and the like do not inhibit production of variability and are perceived by the people receiving them as facilitating. This finding provides an important hint on how teachers, supervisors, and similar people should go about facilitating creativity. It also reinforces the importance of a clearly defined concept of creativity that specifies: (a) what behaviors are necessary in order to be creative; (b) where and how each individual's behavior needs to be changed, and (c) what aspects of personality, attitudes, and motivation are facilitating as well as blocking of such behaviors.

Cropley and Cropley (2000) demonstrated that engineering students who received a concrete definition of what was meant by *creativity* in a particular class, and were also counseled individually on the basis of a personal profile of their own specific strengths and weaknesses, were more original on creativity tests and built more creative models in a laboratory exercise, even though they were working for grades (extrinsic motivation). This study is discussed in greater detail in chapter 10.

> Extrinsic motivators such as grades or other feedback from an instructor or rewards, promotions, and so on from supervisors do not necessarily lead to conformist behavior. They can promote creativity. Important, however, is that the extrinsic motivators are used as a source of information, not as sanctions.

From the point of view of motivation, creative people are the ones who recognize and explicitly identify the defects in what exists and are driven to try to do something about them. Why do they do this? There are many possibilities: to gain fame, to get paid (extrinsic motivation), because they just assume that it is their job, because they are annoyed, because they are curious, and so on (intrinsic motivation). To turn problem recognition into creative action, problem finders must, among other things:

1. experience dissatisfaction with defects,

2. be motivated to eliminate them,

3. have confidence in their own judgment and be willing to act on it,

4. possess the courage and other personal properties needed to act,

5. be capable of generating variability (knowledge and skill plus risk taking and the like),

6. be capable of exploring the variability (knowledge and skill plus self-evaluation, strong reality orientation, etc),

7. be able to communicate the new solution and to interact with other people (both supporters and detractors), and

8. be able to deal with negative as well as positive feedback.

Recognition of defects and an urge to correct them is a powerful motivator for creativity. However, it is not sufficient on its own.

Preference for Complexity

Early research in aesthetics (e.g., Eysenck, 1940) showed that two fundamental dimensions of visual preference are involved in judging the pleasingness of works of art: on the one hand, good taste; on the other hand, preference for simplicity versus complexity. The latter is of particular interest here. Research (e.g., Götz, 1985) has shown that this dimension is stable and can be measured reliably. Gestalt psychologists also emphasized preference for complexity and developed instruments for measuring it (e.g., Welsh, 1975). Shaughnessy and Manz (1991) reported a substantial number of studies that showed that preference for high complexity and asymmetry is an indicator of creativity. In creative people, complexity and asymmetry energize behavior aimed at creating good gestalts that nonetheless contain original and unexpected combinations. Nardi and Martindale (1981) showed that the preference for asymmetry goes beyond visual perception. They found that creative people preferred dissonant tones when passages of music were played to them.

The material just reviewed demonstrates the existence of two fundamental dimensions of individual difference in motivation that are central to the present discussion: openness versus closedness, on the one hand (i.e., willingness to accept the different); and preference for complexity versus for simplicity, on the other hand. Taken together, these dimensions seem to define two basic approaches to life. The one involves welcoming the new and different and being positively motivated by incompleteness, disharmony, and uncertainty, and the other involves rejecting novelty and having a drive to maintain neatness, harmony, and closure. The first combination is favorable for production of novelty, the second favors orthodoxy. It is not being suggested here that this distinction provides an exhaustive definition of the motivational aspects of creativity, but it appears to be well-founded both in terms of research and also of practical observation of youngsters and adults confronted with novelty.

Figure 5.1 shows how people could be rated on a grid defined by closedness-openness on one axis and level of tolerance for complexity on the other. Person 1 represents an idealized combination of high tolerance for complexity paired with great openness, a state of affairs highly favorable for creativity. Person

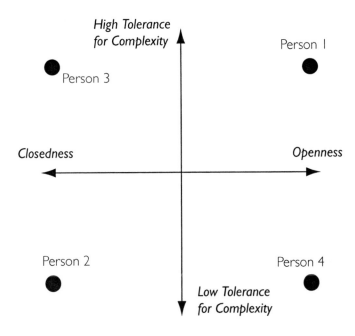

FIG. 5.1. The openness–complexity grid.

2 represents the negative stereotype of a person who cannot tolerate complexity and is closed. All other combinations are theoretically possible, but only some seem likely in practice. For instance, Person 3 (high tolerance for complexity paired with extreme closedness) and Person 4 (low tolerance for complexity paired with high openness) seem intuitively to be unlikely.

> Self-assessment: Where do you stand on the openness–complexity grid? What remedial measures do you need?

Feelings and Emotions in Creativity

Shaw (1989) expressed concern that creativity research has not paid sufficient attention to a further noncognitive aspect of novelty production: the feelings and emotions people experience when they generate effective novelty. Basadur and Hausdorf (1996) emphasized a related aspect of the personal correlates of creativity: attitudes favorable to creativity (e.g., placing a high value on new ideas, believing that generating variability is an appropriate thing to do, and admiring creative people in one's immediate environment and not just in the abstract). In a study of acknowledged creative engineers, Shaw showed that, at various points of the process of production and insertion of effective novelty, they experienced feelings such as fascination, self-confidence or self-doubt, frustration, relief, excitement, and satisfaction. These various feelings can be regarded as part of the joy of creating. Shaw's respondents seldom mentioned negative feelings and emotions, such as aggressiveness or triumph at having beaten someone else, perhaps because they knew that these are socially undesirable, but perhaps because it really is more a matter of joy in creating.

> Creativity also involves feelings and emotions such as hope, joy, or despair.

The Paradoxical Personality

Quite early in the modern era, McMullan (1978) concluded that, despite the high level of interest in the issue, there is no simply definable creative personality. On the contrary, the evidence shows that creative people are characterized by seven polarities:

1. openness combined with drive to close incomplete gestalts,

2. acceptance of fantasy combined with maintenance of a strong sense of reality,

3. critical and destructive attitudes together with constructive problem solving,

4. cool neutrality combined with passionate engagement,

5. self-centeredness coexisting with altruism,

6. self-criticism and self-doubt together with self-confidence, and

7. tension and concentration side by side with relaxedness.

These polarities appear to be mutually incompatible, but seem to occur together in creative people. Hence, such people are marked by what MacMullan called a *paradoxical* personality. More recently, Csikszentmihalyi (1996) made a similar point when he emphasized the importance in creativity of a complex personality, combining among others sensitivity with toughness or high intelligence with naiveté.

> The paradox of creativity: The personality and motivational characteristics connected with creativity often contradict each other.

The phase model introduced in earlier chapters is helpful in making sense out of the paradoxes of creativity. When the cognitive processes of novelty production outlined in chapters 3 and 4, and the personal characteristics and motives associated with the processes described here, are related to the expanded-phase model, specific processes, motives, personal traits, and feelings can be associated with specific phases, whereas different, apparently contradictory ones are necessary in other phases, thus creating an apparent paradox. For instance, in the *Preparation* stage, convergent thinking, naiveté, and extrinsic motivation might be of paramount importance, whereas in the *Illumination* stage, divergent thinking, general knowledge, and openness might predominate. In the *Verification* stage, by contrast, specific knowledge, convergent thinking, and intrinsic motivation might be vital. In the *Validation* phase, however, toughness, courage, and extrinsic motivation are important. The extended-phase model also offers insights into fostering creativity. For instance, it is necessary to specify which phase of the production of novelty is to be fostered by a particular activity: To take one example, promoting *Activation* might require different activities from those needed to foster successful behavior in the *Verification* stage.

> A phase model is capable of resolving some of the paradoxes of creativity. It also helps to integrate discussions of creative products, creative processes, favorable personality traits, and favorable motivation.

A DYNAMIC SYSTEM

It is not being suggested here that the stages are followed in a lock-step and linear fashion; innovative thinking always beginning with preparation and proceeding in order through the other phases. It is obvious that the process could be broken off before it was completed or could start at a later phase than *Preparation*, for instance, because the person had already carried out extensive preparation earlier. A situation is easily conceivable where, let us say, attempts at verification indicated that more information was needed, returning the process to an earlier phase (e.g., *Activation*) and triggering off renewed *Generation*. Shaw (1989) extended this approach by considering not only the interaction of cognitive and noncognitive factors, but also incorporating consideration of the product. He called the interactions *loops*: (e.g., acquisition of information interacts with stewing over a problem in what he called the "Arieti loop," thinking about a problem interacts with the "Aha" experience of unexpectedly seeing a solution [the "Vinacke loop"], seeing a solution with verifying its apparent effectiveness [the "Lalas loop"], verification with communication of the product to other people [the "communication loop"], and communication with validating the product in public ([the "Rossman loop"]).

With the exception of the communication loop, these are named after creativity researchers. Rossman, for instance, has already been mentioned several times in this book because of his research with people holding successful patents. The appropriateness of his name for the phase of communicating and validating a product is obvious. Shaw concluded that there must also be more complex loops involving three or more aspects. The complexity of the interactions among the elements of creativity is emphasized by the fact that the information obtained during *Communication* could affect the gestation process of *Generation*, thus providing the possibility of a new "Aha" experience (Vinacke loop), and so on.

In his typology of creative giftedness, Necka (1986) took the idea of a dynamic relationship among the steps in generating effective novelty further. He emphasized that it requires a combination of ability, personality, and motivation. He saw these as defining an individual profile for each person. More important for the present purposes, he argued that this profile is dynamic in nature—it changes as the person acquires new knowledge or as different motives become more important. Gruber and Davis (1988) went into greater detail about these dynamics: They regarded the achievement of an effectively novel product not as an isolated event that stands alone, but as the result of a long developmental process that can last for years before coming to fruition. In the course of this process, knowledge, opinions, and attitudes are not only acquired, but constantly subject to reorganization. They called this the *evolving systems* model. Three systems are involved: knowledge and abilities, motives and feelings, and goals. All three change continuously as a result of interactions between them and the external environment (e.g., new knowledge is acquired, emotions and attitudes change, and new goals emerge), as well as among themselves.

An understanding of the dynamic relationship between production of novelty and personality and motivation is of great importance in the deliberate fostering of novelty production. As Eisenberger and Armeli (1997) showed, even young children can be taught to generate variability through the application of external rewards. Crucial, however, is that teachers (or, in our case, professors, supervisors, managers, etc.), know precisely what it is they wish to promote, and that students (or, in our case, colleagues, team members, assistants, etc.) know what it is that they are supposed to do differently and how they are to do it. A global, undifferentiated model of novelty production would be restricted to general statements such as "Be daring in your thinking!" and would not be able to reconcile apparently contradictory principles of novelty production. For this reason, we regard a phase approach such as the one outlined earlier as central to an understanding of how effective novelty comes into existence and how to foster its production.

> The relationship between production of novelty and personality and motivation is dynamic: It changes according to the phase in the process of production under consideration.

STOCKTAKING

The findings of this chapter are summarized in Summary Table 5, which extends the maps in earlier chapters by mapping aspects of the Person onto the Phases, Processes, and Products. These personal characteristics are divided into motivation, personality, and feelings. Summary Table 4 already showed that in the *Activation* stage the main processes in generating effective novelty involve identifying the problem and setting goals and that these lead to the subproduct of increased knowledge. Summary Table 5 extends this by showing that the processes are facilitated by a critical attitude to what already exists and trust in one's own ability to find something better (optimism), a feeling of dissatisfaction, and problem-solving drive, possibly linked with the hope of gain. Subsequent phases are analyzed in a similar way. This summary makes it possible to identify a phase in the process of generation of effective novelty and specify what needs to be fostered within individual people.

PRACTICAL GUIDELINES

Once again, the guidelines for practice in Box 5 do not replace or compete with those in earlier boxes, but supplement them by drawing on the specific concepts addressed in this chapter.

Summary Table 5

Creative **P**rocess, **P**erson, and **P**roduct in the Phases of Creativity

Phase	**P**rocess	**P**erson			Sub-**P**roduct
		Motivation	Personality	Feelings	
Preparation	• perceiving • learning • remembering	• hope of gain • willingness to work hard	• optimism • self-discipline • openness	• interest • curiosity	• general knowledge • special knowledge
Activation	• identifying problem • setting goals	• preference for complexity • problem-solving drive (intrinsic) • dissatisfaction with the status quo	• critical attitude • willingness to judge and select • self-confidence	• dissatisfaction • excitement • hopefulness	• problem awareness
Generation	• making associations • bisociating • building networks	• freedom from constraints • tolerance for ambiguity • willingness to take risks	• relaxedness • acceptance of fantasy • nonconformity • adventurousness	• determination • fascination	• many candidate solutions
Illumination	• recognizing promising new configurations	• trust in intuitions • willingness to explore ideas • resistance to premature closure	• sensitivity • openness • flexibility	• excitement	• novel configurations

Verification	• checking relevance and effectiveness of novel configuration	• desire for closure • desire to achieve quality	• hardnosed sense of reality • self-criticism	• satisfaction • pride in oneself	• a relevant and effective prototype solution
Communication	• achieving closure • gaining feedback	• desire for recognition (intrinsic) • desire for acclaim or reward (extrinsic)	• self-confidence • autonomy • courage of one's convictions	• anticipation • hope • fear	• effective presentation of the prototype to others
Validation	• confirmation of relevance and effectiveness	• desire for acclaim • mastery drive	• toughness • flexibility	• elation	• acclaim of the creative product by relevant judge(s)

Box 5.   Practical Advice Based on Chapter 5

Who?	When?	What?
Teachers and managers (Thought leaders)	Attitudes to students and colleagues	Do not write off disorganized or erratic students, but do not assume that they are automatically "creative"
		Do not assume that apparently conforming, quiet students and colleagues are incapable of being creative
		Value nonconformity in students and colleagues: Protect the questioning, "unconventional" person
	Instructional and leadership strategies	Build up students' and colleagues' belief in themselves as capable of being creative
		Promote curiosity
		Encourage dissatisfaction and problem *finding*
		Encourage students and colleagues to have the courage to take on difficult tasks
		Expose students and colleagues to uncertainty
		Encourage intense focus on topics of special interest to students and colleagues
	Assessment strategies	Provide feedback on performance in the form of specific and concrete *information* on what you want to foster
		Provide feedback on risk taking, openness, courage, etc. (not just factual correctness)
		Reward risk-taking, curiosity, and problem finding as much as knowledge (but do not create the impression that facts do not matter)
Who?	When?	What?
Students and colleagues (Coal-face creatives)	Self-image	Do not be afraid of uncertainty or complexity
		Be open to the new and unexpected
		Do not be afraid of your own impulses. Regard them as a valuable source of ideas
		Do not be inhibited by contradictory motives such as need for security vs. adventurousness
	Learning and work strategies	Seek complexity. Look at things in ways you think might be different from the others
		Do not be satisfied with the status quo. Ask how things could be otherwise
		Follow up your own curiosity. Pursue topics that you find fascinating
	Learning and work assignments	Avoid conventional answers
		Have the courage to try something new
		Use study and work assignments to explore issues that you are interested in or to expose gaps

6

Creativity and the Social Environment

Creativity is defined by the society in which it occurs and is socially motivated. It is also facilitated (or blocked) by the surrounding social environment. Social settings differ in the degree to which they will allow deviation from the usual, some accepting more variability than others or being more willing to accept change, while the openness of a society for variability also depends on the person generating the variability, the effects of the variability on other people, and the area of the society's way of life into which variability is to be introduced. In addition, the environment is not simply passive, either supporting or blocking whatever innovators choose to offer, but influences the amount and kind of novelty that are generated in the first place.

A SOCIAL APPROACH TO CREATIVITY

Creativity has frequently been treated as a form of self-expression or a way of understanding or coping with life that is intimately connected with personal dignity, expression of one's inner being, self-actualization, and the like (e.g., Maslow, 1973; May, 1976; Rogers, 1961). Moustakis (1977) summarized the individualistic approach to creativity by seeing it as the pathway to living your own life your own way. Barron (1969) even concluded that creativity requires resistance to socialization, and Burkhardt (1985) took the theme of the individual against society further by arguing that the creative individual must fight against society's pathological desire for sameness. Sternberg and Lubart (1995) called this fight "defying the crowd" and labeled the tendency of certain creative individuals to resist society's pressure to conform *contrarianism*. Although it may not have been the intention of the writers just mentioned, or others who took a similar view, creativity theory has thus sometimes involved "the glorification of individuals" (Boden, 1994a, p. 4).

However, there is also well-documented interest—going back to the ancient world—in creativity as a socially useful phenomenon. The Chinese Emperor, Han Wu-di, who reigned until 87 BCE, was intensely interested in finding innovative thinkers and giving them high rank in the civil service, and reformed the method of selection of mandarins to achieve this. Both Francis Bacon (1909[1627]) and René Descartes (1991[1644]), two of the founders of modern science, saw scientific creativity as involving the harnessing of the forces of nature for the betterment of the human condition.[1] Nowadays we would recognize the human capital approach, and this view of creative people has become well known (e.g., Walberg & Stariha, 1992). Indeed, the original modern-day burst of popular interest following the Sputnik shock emphasized the possible consequences for society of lack of creativity.

However, psychologists and educators in the post-Guilford phase of the modern era tended to emphasize themes deriving from the psychology of the individual (see chaps. 3–5), such as cognitive aspects of creativity and personality, and this emphasis encouraged the individualistic approach to creativity. Nonetheless, in recent thinking, creativity is increasingly seen as a force for developing society in desirable ways, as outlined in chapter 1, thus giving greater weight to its social aspects: creativity as the servant of society.

Analysis of the social aspects of creativity may be considered as having three dimensions:

1. Understanding creativity as a social force with social responsibility,

2. Defining what is creative in social rather than individual terms, and

3. Attributing the driving force for creativity (motivation) to social rather than intraindividual factors.

> Although early scholarly emphasis in the modern era was on individual creativity, there has long been interest in creativity and society.

Ethical Aspects of Creativity

Sternberg (2003) argued that creativity (along with intelligence) must be balanced or tempered by wisdom, assuming that creative people's wisdom will ensure that their creativity serves the common good. Several authors have proposed a "moral creativity" (Gruber, 1993; Runco, 1993; Runco & Nemiro, 2003; Schwebel, 1993). However, even well-intentioned creativity does not always produce unmitigated benefits for society.

---

[1] Interestingly, and not insignificantly, this statement is close to modern definitions of the discipline of engineering. For example, the U.S. Accreditation Board for Engineering and Technology (ABET) defines *engineering* as: "…the profession in which a knowledge of the mathematical and natural sciences gained by study, experience, and practice is applied with judgement to develop ways to utilize economically, the materials and forces of nature for the benefit of mankind."

> **CASE STUDY: Negative Consequences of Well-Intentioned Creativity**
>
> In 1935 the cane toad (*bufo marinus*) was introduced into the sugar fields of the Australian state of Queensland as a novel way to combat the grey-backed cane beetle and the frenchie beetle. These were great pests in the sugar farming industry, and the introduction of the cane toad promised an environmentally friendly remedy that avoided, for instance, the use of ultimately harmful pesticides. (Unfortunately, the novelty proved to be ineffective mainly because the cane toad is a ground feeder, whereas the beetles just mentioned live well above the ground on the plant's foliage! This fact, however, is not relevant to the present discussion.) Now, however, the toad has become a major pest in Australia and is threatening to spread throughout the country. Because it is extremely poisonous, it is a serious danger to the survival of native Australian fauna. Introduction of the toad was a novel approach to combating insect pests, to be sure, but it ultimately had negative effects despite the good intentions.

Such unintended negative effects of the introduction of novelty are not uncommon. Even the highly acclaimed discoveries of Edward Jenner and Louis Pasteur about the transmission of disease, to take one example, laid the foundations for germ warfare. Thus, creativity has a "dark side" (McLaren, 1993).

Creativity's dark side includes not only accidental harm, as in the example above, but also creative activities that are carried out to satisfy personal vanity or overweening pride, or that benefit narrow, short-term interests. Even more disturbing, it is also possible for effective novelty to be introduced in the full knowledge that it will damage others. This can occur without the damage being the primary object of the exercise, as for instance in business, when a new product is introduced to make a profit, in the knowledge that it will inevitably harm a rival product. It is also often seen in criminal behavior. Fortunately, as Eisenman (1999) showed, prisoners rated by guards and other inmates as creative typically generated little or no effective novelty, but rather showed lack of inhibitions and low levels of social conformity (i.e., pseudocreativity), which suggests that at least unsuccessful criminals (those who have been imprisoned) are not particularly novel or innovative. As a result, anticrime measures are reasonably successful even without high levels of novelty, elegance, and generalizability.

Unfortunately, it is also possible for the negative consequences of creativity not only to be fully intended by the person or group introducing the effective novelty, but to be their central purpose—harm to others as the main goal of creativity. Obvious examples of such creativity are seen in war. Cropley, Kaufman, and Cropley (2008) have grudgingly conceded that terrorists such as the 9/11 murderers are capable of generating highly effective novelty and successfully inserting it into a functioning system, so that—in a sense—they are creative, and indeed innovative, despite their evil intentions. D. H. Cropley (2005) first used the term *malevolent* as one way to describe such creativity. Such examples confront us with particularly difficult issues. Suppose, for instance, that an employee found effectively novel ways of making a colleague's life miserable through harassment or mockery, not for any personal gain, but simply out of malice, or a hacker applied the principles of code writing in an ingenious, unexpected, novel, and effective way to distribute a virus that caused economic loss to millions of Internet users simply for the thrill of damaging others. Along with particularly murderous weapons of war and effectively novel acts of terrorism, both of the situations just mentioned might well involve generation of novelty that was highly effective in achieving the goals of a particular individual. But are they examples of creativity?

A strictly individualistic approach might indeed conclude that they are. In the same way, effectively novel techniques of a mass murderer might be regarded as in principle having the same virtues as the innovative work of a creative engineer, or the poetic fantasy of a poet, because all reflect the workings of a mental ability, creativity, to generate effective novelty. However, we believe that such a conclusion is unsatisfactory for the overwhelming number of teachers and managers: Few of them are interested in fostering the creativity of, let us say, an ax-murderer.

Nonetheless, it is apparent that the generation of novelty really does require deviating from the usual, so that in a sense it requires social deviation! We thus need an understanding of creativity that goes beyond a purely abilities/personality approach. A social approach can help here. An understanding of the social aspects of creativity also helps to clarify where creativity comes from, what factors facilitate its appearance, how it can be fostered or applied in groups (such as a university classroom or a work setting), and so on. Emphasis on the social aspects of creativity does not deny the importance of the cognitive and personal aspects discussed in chapters 3 to 5, but adds an additional dimension to these.

> Creativity serves social ends, and its effects can be judged in terms of its social consequences. Thus, it is necessary to confront the issue of production of effective novelty for ends that are, at the least, socially questionable and, at worst, overtly malevolent.

THE SOCIAL DIMENSIONS OF CREATIVITY

Social Definition of What Is Creative

As we have argued already, the essence of any kind of creativity is the production of effective novelty. But how are novelty and effectiveness determined? From a psychological point of view, the decisive property of novelty is that it causes "surprise" in beholders (Bruner, 1962), that is, it is people's surprise that defines novelty, not the product. Surprise occurs when something is unexpectedly different from the usual (i.e., it deviates from what things have been like until now). It is the contrast with what already exists that yields the surprise. In other words, production of novelty does not occur in a vacuum, but in a social context. In a certain sense, it is not the product or process that determines novelty, but the particular setting (the contrast of the novelty with the existing state of the art or the constraints of the external world). Without existing external norms, there would be no such thing as novelty, simply variability.

Nonetheless, as emphasized in chapter 2, the term *creativity* is not applied to anything and everything that surprises people: What is crucial in converting novelty into creativity is effectiveness. But this too is determined by the surrounding environment. Indeed, Csikszentmihalyi (1999) described creativity as requiring "acceptance by a particular field of judges" (p. 316), thus arguing that creativity is essentially a positive category of judgment in the minds of observers, a term they use to praise products that they find exceptionally good. When a number of observers agree that a product is creative, then it is. Csikszentmihalyi called this social definition of effectiveness *sociocultural validation*.

Although social recognition or acclaim defines effectiveness, and is thus necessary for creativity, the judges need not be experts. For example, it is not necessary to be a civil engineer to be capable of recognizing the effectiveness of a bridge. In other words, the everyday users of many products may well be in the best position to determine their effectiveness. As Wernher von Braun is reported to have said, "The eye is a fine architect, believe it!" (Rechtin & Maier, 1997). In effect, good products are easily recognizable as good products. In chapter 8, we review research supporting this view. Therefore, sociocultural validation can be carried out by a wide range of "judges."

> Something is only creative when it surprises the social environment in which it occurs and is accepted as effective; creativity is in the eye of the beholder.

The Problem of Changing Standards

A practical problem with sociocultural validation as the criterion of effectiveness is that what is regarded as creative in one era or society can be uncreative in another. Brahms was unable to obtain the post of director of the philharmonic orchestra in his native city of Hamburg because his music was initially judged to be too conservative. He had to go to Vienna to find acclaim, eventually settling there in about 1872, although he never forgave Hamburg. In Georgian England, Shakespeare's plays were regarded as indecent and had to be edited to make them respectable—in 1818, Dr. Thomas Bowdler published the *Family Shakespeare*, in which he removed expressions that could not with propriety be read aloud in the family (he bowdlerized Shakespeare's work, as we now express it).

The problem of changing social standards is possibly most obvious in the area of fine art, where what is regarded as creative may vary from society to society and from epoch to epoch within a society, while the foremost experts may disagree on the creativity of a given work. Nonetheless, similar problems also exist even in areas that are more objective and rely less on taste or judgment, as the example of the French mathematician Evariste Galois shows. Although he is now regarded as an extremely original mathematician, the value of the body of mathematical writings he left was at first underestimated because external judges could not see their effectiveness: His ideas were not sufficiently grounded in the mathematical knowledge of the time. It was only several years later, after conventional mathematics had caught up with his thinking, that their creativity was recognized. Galois is famous today despite the lack of sociocultural validation in his own brief lifetime.

> What a society regards as creative differs from society to society and from epoch to epoch within a society.

Social Definition of Who Is Creative

In addition to deciding what is creative, the social environment also identifies certain people who generate novelty as creative, and others as "strange," mentally ill, or criminal. One mechanism through which the society determines who is creative can be demonstrated by returning to Schuldberg's (2000–2001) discussion of psychopathology and creativity, especially his concept of *diathesis*. Some cause in an individual's development—the precise nature of which is irrelevant for the present discussion—leads to psychological states that encourage behavior that differs from the average or normal, such as linking ideas usually kept separate, coming up with unexpected suggestions, freely expressing excitement and elation, and so on. If society applauds the resulting behavior the person is regarded as creative, whereas if it frowns on the behavior the person is regarded as criminal or crazy. All this despite the fact that the behavior in question is the same. Once again, we have the idea that it is not so much the actual deviation from the usual that determines creativity, but how the environment reacts to the deviation.

In particular, the precise social group in which the person in question displays the deviation may be decisive. For instance, someone who was active in a setting where unbridled expression of impulses and ignoring the conventions were regarded as odd or incompetent (let us say, an engineer) would be treated differently for the same behaviors than someone in a setting where such behavior was admired—in, perhaps, *avant-garde* theatre or dance. The second person might be fortunate enough to have the behavior accepted as not only surprising, but also effective, and thus creative. By contrast, generation of novelty through application of a high level of technical skill might be highly prized among engineers, but regarded as boringly conventional in the dance or theatre groups just mentioned.

> A person is only creative when the social environment agrees that this is the case. People who generate socially disapproved novelty are "odd," "crazy," or "criminal."

Social Determination of Amount and Kind of Creativity

The relationship between the surrounding social environment and creativity may be looked at from both qualitative and quantitative points of view. One possibility is that large departures from the usual are labeled *mental illness* or *criminality*, whereas moderate departures are labeled *creativity* (i.e., that it is the *amount* of deviation that is decisive). This seems to be the case with the diathesis example. It is also possible, however, that it is not so much the amount of departure from the usual, but the *kind* of departure that is decisive in determining whether deviation is condemned or acclaimed. This notion seems to be more obvious in the engineers versus dancers example.

As we show in more detail later, society can tolerate only a certain amount of variability, and this is also true of narrower social settings such as the family, everyday social life with peers, recreational or similar activities, educational institutions, work settings, and so on. Within a setting, there may be considerable differences in the amount and kind of variability that is tolerated or applauded: One family may tolerate wild or undisciplined behavior, whereas another will not. Some circles of friends demand greater conformity from their members than others. Some vocational groups regulate the behavior of their members closely, others far less. The social setting thus determines what kinds of new ideas emerge by setting limits on both the amount and also the kind of divergence that is seen, or by guiding creative thinking into particular channels. One way it can do this is via motivation: There is little incentive to produce novelty or surprise that no one else is willing to support. Nevertheless, exceptional individuals who swim against the current—such as Galileo—are still seen.

> The social environment will only tolerate a certain amount and certain kinds of deviation from the usual, the amount and kind differing from area to area of social life.

The Effect of the Amount *of Creativity*

Apparently, the *amount* of deviation from the customary is decisive for public acceptance of novelty. Large departures from what the group in question is used to may be socially unacceptable and even labeled *cheating, mental illness,* or *criminality.* which means that people who generate novelty need to learn how to link this novelty with what already exists so that the amount of deviation is not too great for other people to tolerate. Otherwise, they risk being labeled *rebellious,* or *weird,* as happened to, for instance, Galois, or *insulting* and *crazy,* as happened to the Austrian doctor Ignaz Semmelweiss.

CASE STUDY: Effective Novelty That Goes too Far

In 1997, after losing a chess match to the computer program "Deep Blue," Garry Kasparov complained in the press that the program had not actually played chess, despite adhering to the formal rules. To Kasparov, Deep Blue's moves, although within the rules of the game, seemed to involve cheating because, although novel and highly effective (after all, Deep Blue won), they lay too far outside the traditional boundaries. In a study with schoolboy soccer players in Hamburg, a student of one of us (Herrmann, 1987) taught his team to make totally unexpected moves, such as passing the ball straight to an opponent with the words, "Here. Have it if you want it!" Although perfectly legal, this caused consternation among opposing players and outbursts of rage among their coaches, who found it so surprising that they denounced it as cheating!

Do not deviate from what is usual in your social environment to an extent that is more than the setting can endure.

The Effect of Kind *of Creativity*

However, the *kind* of deviation may also be important. The socially derived distinction between *kinds* of creativity can be regarded as involving, on the one hand, socially *radical,* and, on the other hand, socially *orthodox* effective novelty. From a social point of view, radical novelty arises out of a willingness to venture into the area of socially frowned-on ideas or actions. Orthodox novelty involves generating effective novelty while remaining within socially prescribed limits. This distinction is similar to the one Millward and Freeman (2002) made between change that stays *within* the existing social system (what we call *orthodox* creativity) and change that *challenges* the system (i.e., *radical* creativity). In a recent paper, Sternberg (2006) also linked his own cognitive approach to creativity with social factors when he divided the processes of his propulsion model into those that accept current paradigms (what we call *orthodox* creativity) and those that reject current paradigms (what we call *radical* creativity). Sternberg also suggested the existence of a third variant—creativity that synthesizes current paradigms—although it seems to us that synthesis could be done in an orthodox or a radical way.

CASE STUDY: Socially Challenging Creativity

In the 1840s, the Austrian obstetrician, Ignaz Semmelweiss, dramatically reduced the incidence of death from puerperal fever in the lying-in hospital in Vienna simply by requiring the obstetricians under his supervision to wash their hands before touching women who had recently given birth. However, this novelty, although highly effective in reducing the death rate, was seen by other doctors as insulting because it implied that they were dirty. Far from showing gratitude, his colleagues labeled him a crackpot who was insulting their honor, and he was rejected and hunted into madness. The death rate returned to its earlier levels! Had Semmelweiss found a socially acceptable way of presenting his effectively novel procedures, the outcome would probably have been quite different.

These considerations suggest a 2 × 2 classification system in which the *x* axis would define *kind of deviation* from the usual (orthodox vs. radical; i.e., a qualitative social dimension), the *y* axis the *amount of deviation* (a quantitative social dimension). An appropriate grid is shown in Fig. 6.1. The upper right-hand quadrant involves above average to high levels of radical creativity, the

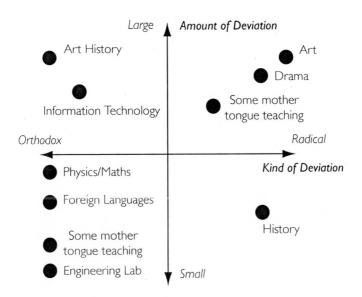

FIG. 6.1. Examples of hypothetical placement of disciplines on the novelty grid.

lower left-hand quadrant its opposite, below average to low levels of orthodox creativity, and so on.

Differences among disciplines, teachers, and students, as well as among managers and organizations, can all be classified using this grid. Some disciplines are frequently open to high levels of radical creativity (e.g., drama or art), whereas others are mainly restricted to low levels of orthodox creativity (perhaps physics, mathematics), some to neither (e.g., foreign languages, as they are often taught), and so on. Thus, placement of the discipline "Engineering Lab" in the lower left-hand corner means that this subject is rated as typically involving low levels of orthodox novelty, and the placement of "Art" in the upper right-hand corner that this discipline is rated as typically involving high levels of radical novelty. It is important to note that where we have placed disciplines in this figure does not reflect objective data: The ratings are offered purely for exemplary purposes and are based on our own subjective assessment of the disciplines in question, as we have experienced them.

Glück, Ernst, and Unger (2002) showed that differences along these lines exist among teachers, too (e.g., art and physics teachers). As a group, the former tolerate or encourage originality, risk-taking, impulsivity, and nonconformity (in our terms, radical creativity), whereas physics teachers as a group prefer problem solving, responsibility, and reliability (orthodox creativity or no creativity at all). In a similar way, some students display radical creativity, some orthodox creativity, and some little of either.

This classification system can be expanded to take account of a further distinction. Research such as that of Simonton (1997) suggests that some societies are product-oriented (they focus on producing novel works such as art, literature, machines, and gadgets, preferably high-tech gadgets, etc.), whereas others are process-oriented (they focus on techniques, production, and management procedures, etc.). Different communities of experts or specialists may also reflect this difference. Engineers, let us say, may place greatest value on product-oriented novelty, philosophers on process-oriented novelty. Much the same may be true of teachers. An example would be the difference between those mother tongue teachers who prefer students to produce imaginative and original text (product orientation) and those who emphasize planning, correct grammar and syntax, checking for accuracy, and the like (process orientation). These considerations suggest an extension of Fig. 6.1 by adding a third dimension: process orientation versus product orientation. In schools, mathematics, for instance, may typically be oriented toward processes showing low levels of orthodox novelty, drama toward products showing high levels of radical novelty, and so on.

We take the view that this classification can also be applied to other kinds of organizations. "Teachers" would have to be replaced by "managers" and "students" by "staff," "colleagues," or "employees." "Disciplines" would then be areas of organizational life such as sales, advertising, operations, staffing, customer relations, and so on. Intuitively, the ideal situation would occur when manager/teacher, individual, and discipline/area of operations were all located in the same quadrant, especially in the case of creative individuals. Indeed, as is discussed further in chapter 9, Harrington (1999) argued that there is no single "best" set of environmental circumstances that is favorable for everybody's creativity, but that the decisive factor is the goodness of fit between the characteristics of the environment and those of the individual. Figure 6.1 can thus be regarded as providing a starting point for developing a schema for diagnosing goodness of fit in terms of demands of the discipline or area of operations, teachers' or managers' orientation to novelty, and students'/workers' production of novelty. Chapter 8 presents some of the formal procedures for carrying out the necessary diagnosis of people and settings.

> Self-assessment: How well does the environment in which you operate fit with the characteristics of creative individuals? How can you change the environment for the better?

Social Influence on the Content of Creative Behavior

The social environment is not simply a passive recipient of whatever novelty people generate, with its function confined to being surprised or not and applying or withholding the seal of approval in the form of the term *creativity*. As well as influencing—at least to some extent—what kind of novelty and how much novelty is produced, the society affects the fields in which people become active, the novelty-generating tactics they employ, and the contents of their creativity. These effects are not only personal—affecting the creativity of a particular individual—but also general: Environmental factors influence the novelty produced by both individuals and society in general. Not uncommonly, several workers in a domain all adopt a similar novel approach or come up with the same novel idea at about the same time. An example would be the simultaneous, but independent, invention of calculus by Newton and Leibnitz. However, the phenomenon is more general than this. Research (e.g., Simonton, 1994) has shown convincingly that in times of economic prosperity or depression; before, after, and during political and social upheavals; or following a successful or an unsuccessful war, differing patterns of creativity are seen. This phenomenon involves not only the number of creators who emerge, but also the domains in which creativity occurs and the kind of novelty that is generated (amending what exists, finding new lines of attack, generating radical and unprecedented novelty, etc.). To take one concrete example, Simonton (1998) showed that "melodic originality" is higher among composers in wartime.

Such phenomena are commonly referred to as reflecting the *zeitgeist*. The internal explanation of the *zeitgeist* is that a domain possesses its own pattern or pathway of growth that is inherent in the domain in question; one thing, so to speak, leads almost perforce to another. Closely related is the idea that each domain has its own system of internal logic and growth in the field must follow this logic. Related to products, this theory would mean that novel products can only occur in a relatively fixed order and at the right time, after earlier events have opened up the field in a new way. For instance, electronic devices could only be invented after the discovery and harnessing of electricity. Of course electricity did not predetermine that, let us say, TV would be invented, but simply opened up the possibility. This statement is a generalization of the argument in chapter 4 that individual novel products are frequently extensions of what already exists, rather than unprecedented breakthroughs.

By contrast, the external model of the appearance of effective novelty in various domains sees the influences on creativity as lying outside the domain in the surrounding environment. Fluctuations in people's production of novelty are obviously linked to broad social conditions such as tolerance of variability by those who wield power over their lives. It is easy to see that the Spanish Inquisition would have discouraged open expression of novel views on religion or the nature of the cosmos, while the Soviet era in Russia severely limited novel interpretations of history by the country's historians or daring forms in its literature (except perhaps for *samizdat* publications). However, the phenomenon goes beyond this. Societies seem to need certain kinds of creativity at certain times in their social, economic, and political development, and to transmit this need to creative people.

An interesting question for educators is how this process occurs. An early answer was the proposal that all societies, as a kind of natural law, oscillate in long waves between a "sensate" and an "ideational" orientation. The sensate orientation is empirical and deterministic, the ideational intuitive and based on feelings. Differences between empirical and intuitive novelty production would hardly be surprising. For our purposes, however, a mechanism requiring decades or centuries to take effect and occurring without human intervention offers limited perspectives for the deliberate encouragement of creativity. We take the view that, at least to some extent, societies directly influence people's creativity through various social mechanisms that influence behavior. These have effects in both the short and long term. They are discussed herein.

The social environment influences what kind of creativity is produced and in what areas.

THE SOCIAL NATURE OF THE CREATIVE IMPULSE

It may be asked why people produce novelty at all. The answer is partly bio-logical. Berlyne (1962) argued that novelty and uncertainty act on the central nervous system to help people maintain an optimal level of neural activity. A certain amount of exposure to novelty production is biologically necessary. Studies of sensory deprivation (e.g., Zuckerman, 1969) and the effects of monotony on children raised in orphanages (Dennis, 1973) have shown the effects of denial of novelty in a dramatic way. The effects include anxiety, hallucinations, bizarre thoughts, depression, and antisocial behavior. In the case of young children denied novelty, effects include apathy, dullness, and stunted emotional and intellectual development. Heron (1957) called this the *pathology of boredom*. Of great interest is that the nature of the novelty is important: Unexpectedness, incongruity, and the like (surprise) are more effective in promoting "normal" development than simple fluctuations in the usual (mere variability)—the novelty must be relevant and effective.

> A certain amount of relevant and effective novelty is necessary for main-tenance of optimal levels of mental functioning. It is a biological necessity, not just a fringe luxury.

Social Motivation of Creativity

However, the impulse to be creative is also (a) economic (to make money); (b) professional (because it is part of the job), (c) personal (e.g., because some-one is curious), or (d) social (e.g., because it brings status and acclaim). Thus, in addition to affecting the kind and amount of novelty produced, as well as determining which novelty is judged to be effective, the social environment also plays a substantial role in determining whether people are inclined to produce novelty at all (i.e., in motivating [or not motivating] production of novelty.) Many creative products are developed "to satisfy the needs of . . . social groups" (Sosa & Gero, 2003, p. 25). The needs may be concrete and down to earth, such as cheaper power or a cure for a particular disease, but they may also be more general, such as better educational methods or more beautiful ways of combining colors on canvas, or more abstract, such as improved ways of expressing feelings through music. Generally, the social groups consist of people who are knowl-edgeable in a domain—specialists or experts—and users of the domain: Someone who does not know that a particular domain even exists cannot experience a need for effective novelty in it. The people who are motivated to solve the problems are most commonly people active in the domain. Those who do not work in an area seldom, although perhaps not never, produce effective novelty in that domain. Interestingly, this view resembles Socrates' line of argument about creativity in Plato's *Ion*.

The idea that creativity is linked with meeting the needs of social groups means that the problems creative people seek to solve are at least partly socially determined. Where there is no social awareness that a problem exists, there may be no drive to produce solutions and no creativity. A simple example is the area of design. A common artifact may be awkward to use, inefficient, and even dangerous. However, it may be so familiar to so many people that they have become accustomed to its disadvantages, and may be able to use it effectively despite the disadvantages and inconvenience. They may even be incapable of imagining that things could be different. In this case, there is no social pressure to introduce effective novelty and, in a sense, no problem, no matter how bad the design may be.

An example is the automobile. The internal combustion engine is inefficient, and cars are dangerous and they pollute the environment. However, novelty in automobile design is limited to tinkering with details, and no genuinely radical originality has been seen since the introduction of the horseless carriage about 100 years ago. In fact, the motor car is only a coach or wagon with a motor replacing the horses! The basic design of a rectangular box, with a wheel at each corner, into which people climb, was well known thousands of years ago. Even the hybrid car is nothing more than a standard automobile with a different fuel system. Problem awareness is limited to the issue of how to polish what already exists.

Radical novelty in this area might include a device that does not have its own power source, but is propelled from outside (e.g., by a spring or by being fired from a canon), one that does not travel longitudinally at all, but holds passengers steady while the earth moves beneath them (such as a rocket fired straight up), or one that does not move the passengers' body at all, such as a matter projector. (We are not seriously proposing these designs, but trying to show that radical approaches are imaginable, although they are probably laughed out of existence if anyone mentions them.)

Problem awareness in the individual, as against the social group, has already been discussed (see chap. 3). There may even be tension between the society's problem awareness and that of individuals. The problem may be apparent only to well-informed workers in an area, or perhaps only to one such person, and may not provoke a publicly perceived need for novelty—only the insiders or even a single insider are dissatisfied and experience the urge to produce relevant effective novelty (see e.g., the case of Einstein's dissatisfaction with existing theories of thermodynamics at a time when others were experiencing no such dissatisfaction). In this case, the society's lack of problem awareness may inhibit motivation to introduce novelty, and thus block creativity. This notion suggests that a culture of problem awareness would foster creativity.

The impetus for creativity often comes from the social environment, especially from society's perception that there is a problem in some domain. Sometimes an individual who perceives a problem may be blocked by lack of social awareness.

SOCIETY'S MECHANISMS OF SUPPRESSION/SUPPORT OF CREATIVITY

Society, the Individual, and Creativity as a System

Fredrick Winslow Taylor, the father of modern studies of work and work training, started his own work career as a machinist on the shop floor of the Midvale Steel Works and advanced through supervisory positions to become a member of senior management. He learned about scientific methods of observation and systematic drawing of conclusions when he studied engineering while an employee, and he later transferred these to analysis of work practices in the steel works—work changed Taylor, and Taylor changed work. Furthermore, his suggestions for scientific management came at a time when the new technology of fast steel cutting made new management practices possible (because of its highly organized and systematic nature, the steel cutting technology permitted the new style of management), while fast steel cutting could not be organized within existing management practices (i.e., because of their highly organized and systematic nature, the new management practices made fast steel cutting possible). Thus, there is a reciprocal relationship between introduction of effective novelty and the environment into which the novelty is introduced. Furthermore, the dynamics of the relationships do not all go in one direction: As has been shown, the environment permits or calls forth and directs or guides creativity, but creativity changes the environment.

Another variant of this interaction is to be seen in the way creativity not only is determined by social criteria, but determines the criteria. Among other things, especially among domain insiders, effective novelty may:

1. push thinking about how to solve certain problems into a particular pathway (which may later become a corset, possibly acting as a source of tension for those active in the area and, paradoxically, blocking the emergence of further effective novelty: earlier creativity blocking later);

2. alter the way other solutions in the area are judged (sometimes causing them to be judged uncreative, the added value of the effective novelty preempting less value-rich novelty);

3. provide new criteria for judging later solutions (with the danger of the corset effect mentioned in 1);

4. expand the way the domain is conceptualized in the society, thus opening up new possibilities for creativity (seminality);

5. suggest new issues not previously noticed (germinality); or

6. suggest new ways of solving problems in the area.

Creative products thus not only reflect social forces, but may alter those forces or even influence the way societies see the world. For instance, Sosa and Gero (2003) argued that the Sydney Opera House not only provided a solution to the problem of an opera house for Sydney (whether effective or not is still debated) and changed architecture and building techniques (there seems to be little doubt about this), but has also become part of the Australian consciousness and, in their view, has become "an emblematic icon" of the Australian identity. The social aspects of creativity thus exert their influence in both directions: The environment influences generation of novelty and judges its effectiveness, and the novelty influences society's willingness to tolerate novelty and how it judges effectiveness.

This interaction is also seen at the individual level. To give some examples, remote associates (see chap. 3) arise out of deep domain-specific knowledge, broad, open perception, and networking in the processing and storing of information. Resistance to group pressure is necessary for nonconformist behavior and autonomy of thinking—at least at certain times and in certain settings (such as the workplace). Readiness to take risks permits remote associates, while playfulness and willingness to experiment go with fluency and flexibility, and tolerance of ambiguity is supported by passion. In fact, the influence pathways run in both directions: As Shaw (1989) put it, there are "loops."

The systemic nature of the interacting factors in the production of effective novelty is shown diagrammatically in Fig. 6.2.

> The interaction between creativity and the social environment is a two-way street.

Society's Ability to Tolerate Novelty

An unusual design for contemporary automobiles—albeit one with only a low level of orthodox creativity compared with radical possibilities—would be to arrange the seats so that all passengers except the driver faced the rear. This design would also be effective in dramatically reducing deaths and injuries among occupants of motor vehicles involved in serious collisions. However, it has

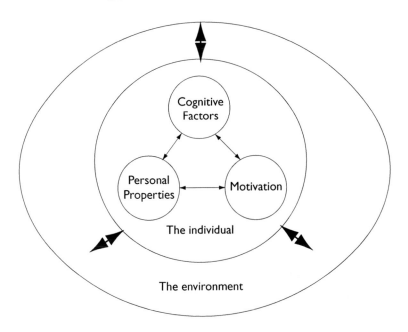

FIG. 6.2. The interaction between properties of the individual and the environment.

never even been tried by auto manufacturers because it is clear that car buyers would not accept it. Despite the value placed on creativity and innovation in contemporary discussions, not all deviations from the commonplace are equally acceptable to a society.

This phenomenon goes beyond acceptance or not of specific pieces of novelty, and extends to generation of novelty. Pseudo- and quasicreativity (see earlier discussions) are often treated as harmless dreaming, letting off steam, and so on even if they are regarded as having no social value. However, some behavior that deviates from the social norms awakens anger, resentment, or rejection. Galois, for instance, was urged to leave his secondary school in France because he was deemed to be wasting his time by focusing to excess on mathematics. Even his mathematics teacher, whom Galois regarded as having opened new worlds for him, found the student's failure to fit into the social framework unacceptable. As already mentioned, Einstein's dissertation was rejected despite (or because of) the originality of his ideas. In fact, only certain deviations will be tolerated by a particular environment. Some people even have a vested interest in maintaining the status quo. For instance, scientists who have invested a lifetime's work in a particular paradigm are understandably likely to resist novelty, even if it is effective.

CASE STUDY: Creativity That Shakes Deeply Held Beliefs

Until the 17th century, cosmology was dominated by the authoritative Aristotelian view that the earth is the center of all things and the sun therefore rotates around the earth. In 1633, although the Church was no longer openly persecuting radical cosmologists, Galileo Galilei was sentenced to permanent house arrest for supporting the now universally accepted Copernican position that, in fact, the earth orbits the sun. The degree of novelty in this idea was simply too much for colleagues, church dignitaries, and the society in general to tolerate, despite the fact that it was correct. In this case, perhaps fortunately for Galileo in that he was not delivered into the hands of the psychiatry of the day, deviation from the usual was treated not as crazy, but as criminal.

Of course many of the behaviors that lie outside a society's norms and are labeled criminal really are unacceptable in anyone's terms. However, other proscribed behaviors are really guilty only of deviating too much from what the society will tolerate at the present time. The society's reaction to levels of novelty that exceed the limits (i.e., that introduce intolerable levels of surprise) are closely connected with the age, occupation, or social role of the person involved. An artist is allowed to be more outrageous than an engineer or a brain surgeon, for instance, while the society is more tolerant of deviation in children than in adults. Indeed, as we argue, there seems to be an inverse relationship between age and tolerance of deviation: The older people are, the less they are expected to generate effective novelty.

The social environment can only tolerate a certain amount of novelty. It reacts negatively when people go too far.

Social Mechanisms That Encourage or Discourage Creativity

In the course of their development, people learn specific behaviors in concrete situations, such as how to obtain food or move about in safety, rules for living with other people, special cultural skills such as a language or how to obtain information, social roles and a self-image, a concept of the good person, and techniques for dealing with stress, anxiety, and the like. These are acquired through interactions with the various instruments of socialization: family, schooling, peers, role models, media, and so on. Furthermore, they are strengthened by having an affective or evaluative component. Thus, children learn not only that *we* do something in a particular way, but that those who do it differently are stupid, ignorant, wilfully wrong, or evil. A child in one social group may be taught to eat with the fork in the left hand and the knife in the right, placing food in the mouth with the fork, but always with the tines curving downward. The child may learn that those who eat differently are ignorant and of lower class. On first encountering the North American way of transferring the fork to the right hand and spooning up food with the fork held upside down, a child from Australia might be amazed at how many ignorant and lower class people there are in North America.

In effect, generating variability involves breaking the social rules. All people are capable of a wide range of responses to life situations, but in the process of growing up, they learn that most ways of behaving are forbidden and usually restrict their responses to a narrow range of socially tolerated behaviors. Anderson and Cropley (1966) studied the reactions of schoolchildren in social situations where a number of alternative courses of action were possible, of which one was highly socially desirable (e.g., "You have promised to visit your grandmother but are tempted to go to the movies instead"). They concluded that the children were guided by "stop rules" that forbade most of the wide range of possible reactions in a particular situation in favor of the socially approved, correct one. As Fromm (1980) put it, societies have "filters" that inhibit divergent behavior or even discourage thinking about different possibilities. There are rules not only about behavior, but also about which opinions are correct, indeed about the right way of thinking and the contents of correct thought. Societies conduct "surveillance" (Amabile, Goldfarb, & Brackfield, 1990) to detect people who deviate.

A simple example of the way society controls what novelty is generated can be seen in the phenomenon that is nowadays referred to as *political correctness*. Ideas that can, possibly by drawing a long bow indeed, be interpreted as criticizing certain groups, showing lack of respect for them, or denying their status as victims are not even discussed. Indeed, in some countries, it is illegal to consider explanations of particular historical events that deviate from the conventional or official version. Only certain causes for problems such as pollution are discussed, and only certain approaches to finding a solution are tolerated. In the 1970s and 1980s, mention of the role of heredity in psychological differences among human beings could lead to a professor's office being trashed, as happened to one of us in Hamburg. Society's openness for novelty is limited. Thus, introducing novelty requires a special form of courage.

However, as already discussed in chapters 2 and 4, not every act of undisciplined, disruptive, or ignorant behavior, or every case of defiance, aggression, or nonconformity should be acclaimed in the name of creativity. Knowledge, accuracy, speed, good memory, and the like are obviously important, most obviously for relevance and effectiveness. The society makes a substantial effort to train its members in its ways because it means that that they can function effectively in a social environment. Indeed, acquisition of the social rules has an important survival value. To take a simple example, if city children do not know how to cross the road safely in high traffic areas, many of them will die. Society has a strong interest in preserving most of the achievements of the past, as well as in limiting the extent to which people's behavior deviates from the well established. Some writers equate introduction of effective novelty exclusively with evolutionary change and imply that it cannot be introduced where the forces of preservation are strong. It is certainly true that most people would probably prefer the engineers who build the jumbo jets in which they fly to stick to the tried and trusted, rather than introducing too much novelty into the situation. Nonetheless, even such areas are not completely static. Caution is not the same as total absence of change.

A high level of conformity to social norms has the advantage that life becomes predictable, because it is more or less known what can be expected in everyday situations. However, the disadvantage is that unusual, unexpected behavior may become rare. In some societies, dislike of deviation may penetrate the public consciousness and become part of everyday, normal attitudes and values to such an extent that generation of novelty is subjected to extremely strong and widespread everyday sanctions. Gribov (1989) reported that the former Soviet Union was marked by a widespread public resentment of and hostility toward individuals who deviated from narrowly prescribed social norms and generated novelty. Burkhardt (1985) went so far as to refer to a societal mass psychosis involving *Gleichheitswahn* (sameness psychosis), an almost pathological drive in societies to resist change.

> Both the society and the individual have an important and legitimate interest in maintenance of the status quo. The problems arise when this goes too far.

There seem, in fact, to be two opposite forces in any society: forces of conservation and forces of renewal. The nature of these forces is summarized in Table 6.1. Because these forces are opposite, they are often treated as opposing, but in fact both are capable of producing change while they can also work together. From a practical point of view, the difference is that the conserving pressures in a society allow only slow, gradual evolutionary change, whereas the reforming pressures encourage more dramatic changes that are larger and occur quickly (i.e., they lead to "revolutionary" change). This kind of change is what people have in mind when they talk of creativity.

Table 6.1
Opposing Forces in a Society

Force	Effect	Change Mode	Benefits
Conserving	Change: • is relatively slow • builds on what already exists • may appear to be blocked	"Evolutionary"	Despite change: • the world remains orderly and understandable • existing knowledge and skills remain useful • people's feeling of security is not threatened • experts' self-image of competence is preserved • power structures and the like remain intact

SLOGAN: "If it ain't broke, don't fix it!"

Force	Effect	Change Mode	Benefits
Renewing	Change: • is rapid (paradigm shift) • sweeps away what already exists	"Revolutionary"	As a result of change: • novelty is obvious • progress is often rapid • problems are often solved quickly • people are encouraged to introduce novelty • existing structures are theatened

SLOGAN: "Altius, citius, fortius!"

Degree of Openness of the Society

Thus, openness to the new (or lack of openness) is a characteristic not only of individual people (see chap. 5), but also of societies. People who produce novelty in societies that are not open for it are likely to suffer various kinds of negative sanctions. The situation of such people is exacerbated by the fact that some traits associated with creativity may lead to disorganized and even chaotic behavior or to behavior that is regarded as antisocial or arrogant (e.g., impulsiveness, lack of concern about social norms, lack of interest in making a good impression, tendency to lose themselves in their work; see chap. 5). Cognitive characteristics such as making remote associations that are too remote for most observers worsen the situation. The result may be that observers concentrate on the deviant or unpleasant, even antisocial behavior of the people concerned, and the link between their behavior and the production of effective novelty may become difficult for others to recognize.

CASE STUDY: Novelty That Others Cannot Understand

The French mathematician, Henri Poincaré, submitted in 1879 a dissertation that was highly original. In it he devised a new way of studying functions defined by differential equations, and he was the first person to study the geometric properties of these functions. He also showed their practical application in studying problems such as the stability of the solar system. However, after the first 30 or so pages, the novelty became increasingly difficult for the examiners to understand (their report is still in the relevant files in Paris), and they criticized it on the grounds that after a good beginning it became progressively more disorganized (difficult for them to understand). Fortunately for Poincaré, the examiners showed a degree of openness. They eventually concluded that the level of mathematical knowledge and original thinking displayed at the beginning was so high that the dissertation could be accepted anyway. Not all highly original thinkers have been so fortunate—to take one famous example, Einstein's dissertation was rejected by the Technische Hochschule in Zurich.

In general, there are rules about breaking the rules. People publicly acclaimed as creative break the rules, but succeed in staying within acceptable limits. If they do not, they are likely to be regarded as eccentric, immoral, mentally disturbed, or criminal, rather than creative, with the possibility of being criticized, shunned, or even locked away. A conversation a number of years ago with the coach of a team in the Canadian Football League demonstrated this point clearly. He was asked why his team had not made use of the, at that time, still legal but never-used drop goal (worth three points) in a game in which they were in possession of the ball at the 30-yard line for the last play of the game and trailed by only two points. Instead of trying for the match-winning three points with a kick that would have been quite easy for a rugby player, they preferred instead a conventional, completely predictable long pass into the end zone. The opposition—because it knew what was coming—had its defense perfectly organized for this play, which was more or less inevitably unsuccessful.

The coach explained this meek acceptance of a loss by insisting that, had he called for an attempted drop goal, he would have been written off as an idiot who had lost it when the pressure went on. Even if the kick had succeeded, far from being celebrated as the innovative genius who had engineered a surprising victory when all had seemed lost, he would have been regarded as some kind of cheat who had somehow succeeded by trickery. An unsuccessful long pass, by contrast, caused great excitement among the spectators and sent them home feeling that their team had fought bravely to the end and only lost through bad luck. Creativity is allowed in sport as in other areas, but only within the limits of what the environment can tolerate.

> Different social environments are more or less open for introduction of novelty. Openness is related to the area of a social environment's life affected by the novelty and differs in different eras.

Socially Assigned Roles and Creativity

One effect of society on creativity can be examined by looking at research on creativity and age. There is a well-documented relationship between the two. Focusing on people who actually became famous for their creative achievements (i.e., producers of acclaimed novelty), the early classic study of Lehman (1953) reported that peak performances occurred most frequently between the ages of 30 and 40. This view is still widely supported (see Simonton [1988b] for a detailed analysis based on case studies of famous people). Lehman's findings indicated that the age at which peak performances occur varies from discipline to discipline, mathematicians tending to become famous particularly early. Nonetheless, there is agreement in the research literature that, allowing for differences in definitions and methodology, somewhere around age 40 is the most productive age. Despite this, it should be borne in mind that many famous creative individuals continued to produce until well into later life: Darwin, Freud, and Einstein became famous in their 20s and remained active into their 70s. Those who start youngest seem to continue longest.

However, a major weakness of many case studies of age and acknowledged creativity is that they often include creative people who died young. Naturally such people made their creative achievements at an early age. The picture becomes somewhat different when people who lived into their 70s and longer are studied separately. Lindauer (1993) showed that the average age of peak performance of long lived artists was not 35, but 50. Focusing on individual people, he reported substantial differences from person to person in patterns of creativity and age. In general, longer lived famous artists maintained a high peak of creativity over a period of three decades—usually in their 30s, 40s, and 50s. Peak creativity was unusual in the 20s (although not nonexistent) and fell off in the 60s and later, although it was more common after 50 than before 30. A high level of creativity even in old age was quite common. Two members of the group of artists studied by Lindauer reached their peak in their 20s, to be sure, but six reached it in their 60s. There were noticeable sex differences: Famous women artists produced more creative work in their 20s, men more in their 60s or even later, although both sexes experienced their peak years between 30 and 50. These results suggest a social effect—in this case, possibly sex-role expectations—on the development of creativity. We return to the issue of roles and creativity, as well as to gender and creativity, in chapter 7.

Turning to scientists, Root-Bernstein, Bernstein, and Garnier (1993) studied the productivity of 40 men who had all made enduring high-impact contributions in physics, chemistry, biochemistry, and biology, including several Nobel Prize winners and a number of men who had been nominated for the Nobel Prize without actually winning it, some of them on more than one occasion. The contributions of these men were studied over a period of 20 years. The authors concluded that a falloff in creativity after early achievements is common, but by no means necessary. Many of the people they studied went on producing into their 50s and 60s. Of particular interest for the present discussion is that those who made a single achievement early and then ceased to be creative tended to have moved into management, whereas those who continued to be creative avoided administrative work. Dudek and Hall (1991) showed that architects who resisted retiring were creatively productive for many years more than those who retired early.

Thus, existence of a negative correlation between creativity and age may be due, at least in part, to social factors, and not to disappearance of the psychological potential for creativity at all. These factors include the social convention of ceasing to work at about 60 to 65; the expectation that older members of a craft, trade, or profession will concentrate on training the next generation and supervising their work; the expectation that such people will focus on exploring novelty generated by younger people; or that they will become guardians of the status quo. These are all examples of the mechanisms through which social factors may lead to reduced creativity at older ages, and the mechanisms are more closely connected with socially defined career patterns and the behavior expected in certain social roles than with ability, personality, or motivation.

> The social roles people are expected to play at different ages may influence their creativity. This may be a particular problem for older people.

STOCKTAKING

Summary Table 6 again extends earlier summaries by mapping aspects of the environment (Press) discussed in this chapter onto Phase, Process, and Product. Press has been looked at in this chapter from the point of view of properties of the individual that are closely related to the external environment, such as the individual's awareness of social norms (the interaction of Press in this sense with Person has already been mentioned). The *Activation* phase has already been analyzed by showing that in this stage the main processes in generating effective novelty involve identifying the problem and setting goals, and that these lead to a rich supply of cognitive elements (see Summary Table 3), as well as that the processes are facilitated by a critical attitude to what already exists, trust in one's own ability to find something better (optimism), a feeling of dissatisfaction, and a problem-solving drive, possibly linked with the hope of gain (see Summary Table 4). This analysis is now extended by showing that awareness of the social consequences of a perceived problem, socially positive values, and willingness to accept an outsider role would facilitate completion of this phase in a way favorable to the generation of effective novelty.

PRACTICAL GUIDELINES

Box 6 makes a number of suggestions, in addition to previous advice, for applying the principles outlined earlier in practical settings, especially higher education and organizations.

Summary Table 6
Creative Process, Product, and Press in the Phases of Creativity

Phase	Process	Sub-Product	Press (individual)
Preparation	• Perceiving • Learning • Remembering	• General knowledge • Special knowledge	• Product orientation • Focus on the socially unexpected
Activation	• Identifying problem • Setting goals	• Problem awareness	• Problem awareness • Awareness of the social consequences of the situation • Socially-positive values • Willingness to accept an outsider role
Generation	• Making associations • Bisociating • Building networks	• Many candidate solutions	• Rule breaking • Interest in revolutionary change • Tolerance for radical novelty
Illumination	• Recognizing promising new configurations	• Novel configurations	• Openness of the individual • Seeing beyond what the society accepts
Verification	• Checking relevance and effectiveness of novel configuration	• A relevant and effective prototype solution	• Resistance to judging according to social norms
Communication	• Achieving closure • Gaining feedback	• Effective presentation of the prototype to others	• Understanding of what the society can tolerate • Willingness to deviate • Awareness of rules about breaking rules
Validation	• Confirmation of relevance and effectiveness	• Acclaim of the creative product by relevant judge(s)	• Understanding of the zeitgeist

Box 6. Practical Advice Based on Chapter 6

Who?	When?	What?
Teachers and managers (Thought leaders)	Attitudes to students and colleagues	Be aware of the social roles you and others are playing, and the effect of these on generation of novelty
		Provide an environment where "deviance" is accepted
		Support those who are "different"
		Regard all existing and accepted ways of doing things as hiding problems
	Instructional and work strategies	Show public respect for those who generate novelty
		Encourage willingness to generate novelty in front of other people
		Discuss the effects of social factors on the creativity of people mentioned in your classes (amount and kind)
		Discuss the social consequences of innovations stemming from your discipline
		Discuss the effect of society on creativity in your discipline
		Discuss the effect of your discipline on how society sees creativity
		Discuss ethical issues in creativity in your discipline
	Assessment strategies	Set problem-finding assignments, not just problem-solving ones
		Encourage breaking the rules, but do not accept or reject ideas simply because they support or oppose the *zeitgeist*
		Encourage students to test the limits of the socially acceptable in their assignments
Who?	When?	What?
Students and colleagues (Coal-face creatives)	Self-image	Do not be afraid to be different or to defy the social framework
		Identify your own stereotypes
		Remember the importance of ethicality
		Remember that there are rules about breaking the rules
		Identify your own stop rules

Who?	When?	What?
Students and colleagues (Coal-face creatives)	Learning and work strategies	Avoid pursuing what is merely trendy or faddish. Do not confuse this with creativity
		Identify sources and kinds of conformity pressure in your surrounding environment
		Look for the problems in all socially accepted solutions
		See yourself as solving problems
	Assignments	Avoid the bandwagon if you can
		Remember there is a limit to how much novelty can be tolerated by those around you

7

The Institutional Environment
and Creativity

The environment in which people learn or work plays a major role in encouraging or discouraging generation of effective novelty. The environment
goes beyond physical structures and equipment and includes the people in
it; their attitudes, values, goals, and the like, and the way these are perceived
(organizational climate or culture). Working with other people in groups
and teams has both favorable and unfavorable effects on production of
effective novelty, largely through roles people play, power, group processes,
the system of rewards, and so on. Thought leaders (professors, managers)
can affect an organization's climate through the role models they offer, the
way they acknowledge performance, and their effects on communication.

ORGANIZATIONS AS THE SITE OF CREATIVITY

There are two broad ways to approach the fostering of creativity: what Sosa
and Gero (2003) called *bottom–up* (focused on dispositional characteristics of
the individual such as intelligence, personality, interests, or motives) or *top–down*
(focused on leadership, roles, group pressure, distribution of power, system of
rewards, etc. in the environment in which novelty is to be generated, explored,
and inserted). As Sosa and Gero pointed out, behaviors that seem to be remark-
able and to require a complex explanation in terms of personal dispositional
factors (i.e., bottom–up) may seem unremarkable when looked at top-down. For
instance, from the top–down, the creativity of three generations of Becquerels
(see chap. 5) can be seen as simply a matter of fulfilling the role expected by
their family tradition, whereas when looked at bottom–up it raises complicated
questions about the development of general and specific ability, genetic factors
in intelligence, the development of personality, and the like.

Earlier chapters have worked bottom–up, whereas the present chapter
examines the effects of the external environment on production, exploration,
and implementation of effective novelty (i.e., top–down). The extent of this

influence is often underestimated, especially in psychological discussions. This fact is probably due, in part, to the so-called *fundamental attribution error* identified by social psychologists (e.g., Ross & Nisbett, 1991). When explaining behavior, observers tend to overestimate the importance of characteristics of the individual and underestimate the effects of the environment. This tendency is known to be particularly marked when attempting to explain unusual behavior. Because creativity is, by definition, surprising (see chap. 5), its study would be particularly susceptible to the fundamental attribution error.

The early approach to creativity in the Guilford era emphasized its psychometric aspects (i.e., it was bottom–up), scarcely surprising in view of Guilford's background and interests. This approach regarded creativity as essentially a mental ability, analogous to intelligence. The urgent need for creativity experienced after the Sputnik shock, and the fact that satisfying this need was regarded as an educational matter, strengthened the psychometric approach. This process involved regarding problems with creativity in much the same way as problems of conventional school learning. The issues were conceptualized in cognitive terms, and dealing with problems was seen as a matter of measuring abilities using appropriate tests. A major result was that creativity was thought of as a set of cognitive processes that take place in people's minds (such as divergent thinking; see chap. 3) or as a cluster of properties of individual people that facilitate such processes (e.g., openness, nonconformity, tolerance for ambiguity; see chap. 5).

However, 25 years after Guilford, more emphasis was being given to creativity as a property of products. A simple example would be the idea that a creative product is one that surprises onlookers. Amabile (1983) was one writer who focused attention on creativity as a property of products: Reduced to its bare essentials, when products are surprising and useful in a particular environment, they are creative. Amabile also made the point that links the product-centered approach to the present chapter: Creativity is a property of products that is readily seen in favorable social settings. We see this point of view as a top-down approach in the sense of Gero and Sosa. This approach implies that the prime focus should be on setting up a creativity-facilitating environment (i.e., top–down). The interesting question would then be not, "How can we make people more creative?", but "How can we make the environment better for the emergence of creativity?"

Emphasis on top-down creativity can be contrasted with chapters 3 to 5, which were concerned with creativity as a psychological complex within the individual (i.e., bottom–up). In this chapter, we do not reject out of hand the analysis of creativity in terms of properties of individuals (cognitive, personal, motivational, and social). However, we emphasize that the appearance of creativity in organizations (such as institutions of higher education, firms, or businesses) depends on an interaction between personal properties and the environment. For the purposes of the present chapter, we are interested above all in the way in which institutional settings enable (or disable) people to become creative. One way of conceptualizing this enabling/disabling function without disregarding personal properties has been suggested by Harrington (1999). He suggests that it is a matter of goodness of fit between the organizational environment and the properties of individuals (see chap. 8).

> Actual creative behavior in institutional settings (e.g., college classrooms, work settings) is not the result of properties of the individual person alone, but is also influenced by the environment, perhaps more strongly than usually thought.

A Broad Understanding of Organization

It might be asked what we mean here by *organization*. In our sense, an organization incorporates:

1. *material institutional structures and facilities* such as work stations, laboratories, information-processing facilities, libraries, classrooms and workshops, and so on. These are found in businesses, factories, and the like, but also in schools and universities;

2. *people*, not only managers or instructors, but also fellow workers or students;

3. *immaterial institutional factors* influencing the interactions between (1) and (2) such as traditions, standards, norms, and customs; and

4. *psychological institutional factors* influencing these interactions, such as roles, relationships, social hierarchies, interaction rules, communication pathways, and the like.

> An organization consists of physical structures and arrangements, people, interactions among the two, and mechanisms and factors that moderate this interaction. For our purposes, the latter are most interesting.

The Congenial Environment

Reference has already been made in chapter 6 to an environment that encourages production of effective novelty—there, however, the emphasis was more on the role of the environment in providing source material that can be manipulated to generate novelty, in deciding what is creative, or in determining effectiveness. In this chapter, a congenial environment can be thought of as providing conditions that permit, release, encourage, or foster the creativity of individual people or groups. These include, broadly understood,

- the amount of divergence or risk-taking that is tolerated/encouraged,

- the kind of variability that is tolerated/encouraged (e.g., routine extensions of the already known vs. radical deviations),

- the resources that are made available (not only material, but also human) to support production of novelty, and

- the rewards (or punishments) that are offered to people who diverge from the usual.

The quality, quantity, and timing of these factors affects the production, exploration, and insertion of novelty by people functioning within the organization. For instance, a combination in an environment of encouragement of risk-taking, tolerance of even "way-out" or radically surprising novelty, provision of ample time and other resources (e.g., funding, lab equipment, access to information, etc.) and high levels of reward for those who depart from the usual (e.g., promotion, bonuses, high grades, etc.) would intuitively be highly congenial and, not surprisingly, would be expected to encourage generation of novelty.

The beneficial effects of such circumstances are not restricted to encouraging divergent thinking (i.e., cognitive aspects of novelty production), but also promote:

- a positive attitude to generation of variability in general;

- positive social status of creative individuals in teams, work, and social groups;

- a positive self-image among divergent thinkers;

- appropriate motivation (e.g., the urge to innovate, willingness to take risks, tolerance of ambiguity); and

- willingness to express personal characteristics such as openness, nonconformity, independence, and flexibility.

> The congenial environment encourages risk-taking, tolerates variability, rewards divergence, and provides resources for generation of novelty. In many organizations, sadly including many universities, most of these conditions are not met.

One of the better known examples of the deliberate creation of an environment that we would call *congenial* in the context of creativity is the Lockheed Martin Skunk Works® concept. Responsible for the company's Advanced Development Programs, the Skunk Works traces its origins to the development of advanced fighter aircraft in World War II. The term has become synonymous with any small and loosely structured team of people engaged in the development of a project where a primary consideration is innovation. Typically, a Skunk Works will operate with a high degree of independence from normal managerial and reporting constraints and will be protected from interference by a champion (in the following section, we refer to such a person as an *assister*). By operating outside the normal rules of product development, physically separate from the main site of its parent company, and with minimal communications overheads and strong autonomy, a Skunk Works seeks to achieve rapid development of novel product concepts that subsequently may be reinserted into a normal product development cycle.

Some of the *rules* of Skunk Works that are relevant to the present discussion are:

- Teams must have a high degree of autonomy,

- Project teams must be kept small (typically only 10%–25% of normal teams),

- Reporting requirements must be kept to a minimum,

- A high degree of cooperation and communication between developer and customer must be maintained, and

- Reward systems must be based on outcomes achieved.

Environments that are simultaneously challenging and supportive have been shown to sustain high levels of creativity in individuals and teams (West & Richards, 1999). According to Mathisen and Einarsen (2004), creativity-fostering organizations are characterized by:

- ambitious goals, which promote dissatisfaction with the status quo;

- freedom and autonomy in choosing tasks and deciding how they are carried out;

- encouragement of ideas;

- time (for creating ideas);

- feedback, recognition, and rewards;

- lack of threat of sanctions when brave attempts go wrong;

- interest in excellence;

- expectation and support of creativity;

- permission to take risks;

- tolerance of errors; and

- loosely specified objectives (or clearly specified objectives plus opportunities to challenge them).

Self-assessment: How congenial is the environment you create?

Assisters and Resisters

However, not just the organization of work and study are important in encouraging creativity. Individual people also play an important role. Diaghilev is remembered as the father of Russian ballet. Stravinsky was one of the most famous composers born and bred in that country, yet both were law students at university in Saint Petersburg around 1900. While still law students, both came under the influence of the revered musician Rimsky-Korsakoff, who advised each of them to give up law and focus on music, although he strongly advised Diaghilev against trying to become a composer as he intended. Diaghilev then focused on ballet. The result of Rimsky-Korsakoff's influence on Stravinsky and Diaghilev was perhaps a loss to the law, but a vast enrichment of world music.

The facilitating effect of people such as Rimsky-Korsakoff is well known: Treffinger (1995) referred to the presence in organizational environments of *resisters* (people or circumstances that inhibit production of novelty) and *assisters* (people or circumstances that facilitate it). Although assisters can be objects such as special tools or specialized literature, physical conditions such as access to an important source, or even abstractions such as lucky timing, we are interested here in human assisters: people, such as teachers or managers, who foster generation and insertion of effective novelty by merely tolerating appropriate behavior, actively encouraging it, or even functioning as models of it.

A comprehensive study of 20th-century British novelists (Crozier, 1999) concluded that differences in their productivity were largely attributable to the influence of social support factors. Csikszentmihalyi (1988) postulated that social support networks are vital determinants of creativity in the lives of individual creators: These include parents, teachers, mentors, colleagues, and managers. In a discussion of the introduction of novelty into an organization, Mumford and Moertl (2003, p. 264) emphasized the importance of, among other things, a "persuasive and effective advocate," in other words, what we would call a powerful human assister. These people are not always single individuals; they may also consist of groups or networks.

Assisters seem to be important among other things for development and maintenance of the intense motivation that is needed to generate, explore, and apply high levels of novelty. Petersen's (1989) study of hobby authors showed that support from other people, whom we call *assisters* in this book, was vital in her participants' ability to avoid writer's block and maintain their motivation to write, thus demonstrating the importance of the social support system not only in acclaimed, but also in everyday, creativity. As Bloom (1985) showed, human creativity assisters need not be powerful figures like Rimsky-Korsakoff at all, but in certain settings can be humble and unsung people such as a grade school teacher or perhaps a manager or colleague. Thus, some assisters energize, activate, or release creativity in others without necessarily producing effective novelty. This role is a major responsibility for instructors and managers—to facilitate the creativity of their students and colleagues.

An important function of such people is to offer creative individuals a safe space where they can break the rules without punishment, thus protecting them from social or other sanctions (such as having research funding cut off, being fired, or, in the case of students, failing a course). Another is to offer them a positive perspective on themselves (e.g., the view that their ideas are not crazy, but creative). This recognition can help foster the courage to deviate from what everyone else is doing, among other things by offering an opportunity to test the limits of the acceptable without risk or feelings of guilt. Human assisters can also help creative people to communicate their ideas to others (e.g., to repeat ourselves, by acting as an advocate).

> Teachers, managers, colleagues, and similar people can function as assisters who foster creativity in others. They do this by protecting novelty-generators from negative sanctions, enhancing their self-image, and facilitating communication of their ideas.

> Self-assessment: To what extent are you an assister? Whom have you assisted lately? How do you assist creative people?

Institutional Climate

In addition to relatively concrete and specific assisters and resisters, however, it is possible to speak of a more general element of an innovation-friendly environment: its climate. Litwin and Stringer (1968) focused on more concrete aspects of *climate* by defining it as "a set of measurable properties of the work environment that are perceived by those working in the environment and influence their motivation and behavior." These include:

- recognition of the value of generation of variability through promotion or raises or, in the case of colleges, praise, high grades, scholarships and assistantships, and the like;

- decision-making processes that do not stifle change by bogging it down in a quagmire of discussions and procedures;

- contact with models of creative behavior;

- provision of appropriate opportunities to generate novelty; and

- presence of people who encourage generation of variability.

As Ekvall (1996, p. 105) explained, an institutional climate is also a percept in the mind of the people working in it: "a conglomerate of attitudes, feelings, and behaviors that characterize life in an organization." These include a feeling that generation of novelty is welcome and that people who generate it are respected. It also involves factors like feelings of tolerance and safety. These also define a congenial environment.

From a psychological point of view, the climate of an institution consists of people's perceptions of what is allowed or encouraged, perceived openness for the novel, feelings of being accepted even if you deviate, a sense of personal security, and personal identification with the goals of the institution.

MANAGEMENT FOR INNOVATION

Although they were discussing innovation in social systems, Mumford and Moertl (2003) listed a number of characteristics of organizations that encourage creativity. We have grouped them into categories (prerequisites, institutional factors, and processes):

- *Prerequisite factors:* intense dissatisfaction with the status quo in some individuals in the organization, availability of relevant expertise within the system, a culture of problem-finding;

- *Institutional support factors:* flexible core concepts in the organization, availability of resources, existence or development of appropriate technologies, congruence of the innovation with existing trends; and

- *Process factors:* build up of a cadre of supporters, bringing important people into the fold, use of protracted tryout periods (delay of critical judgment), meeting the needs of varying constituencies.

In an organization, especially a large one, the presence of many of these factors can be influenced by management processes, especially provision of: (a) elite support (e.g., through a persuasive and effective advocate); (b) visionary and charismatic leadership.

> Leaders in educational and other organizations can provide conditions that foster the generation of novelty by students and colleagues.

Creative Leadership

An important part of the organizational environment is thus the people who are in a position to create the conditions just listed. This concept leads to the consideration of creative leadership and the management of creativity (e.g., Rickards, 1993), not only in education, business, and industry, but also in government, the armed forces, and similar large organizations. This discussion is necessary despite there being something inherently paradoxical about deliberately applying administrative procedures or management techniques to creativity, which involves, after all, novelty, unexpectedness, surprise, and the like. For the purposes of the present book, institutions of higher education, firms and businesses, and other organizations can be regarded as social environments and the members of the organization in leadership positions (including teachers in higher education) as managers of creativity. The question then is, "How can managers, including teachers in universities and colleges, foster (or inhibit) creativity?"

Brophy (1987) concluded that the effects of teachers as leaders occur through (a) modeling, (b) communication of expectations, and (c) direct instruction. The aspects of an organizational setting involved in the production of effective novelty that managers can influence can be stated in a more psychological way as: (a) workplace culture, (b) communication processes, and (c) role expectations.

Workplace Culture. Workplace culture is related to what we called *climate.* However, it refers to more abstract factors such as norms or deep underlying beliefs or philosophies. The workplace culture affects:

- the kinds of behavior that are tolerated or encouraged by leaders,

- the kind of behavior they themselves display (i.e., model),

- the way they provide rewards and sanctions (what is rewarded, what punished, and how),

- the way they assign status and power,

- the attitudes toward deviant behavior that they display and foster in others, and

- the resources they make available for generation of variability (or of orthodoxy).

Organizations frequently claim in mission statements and the like that they want to encourage creativity, but people in leadership positions stamp down hard when subordinates generate even small amounts of novelty, thus negating the official policy. The culture is then anticreative despite lip service to the contrary.

> The task of managers (including university teachers in their function as managers of student learning) is to accept divergent behavior and, better still, to act as a model of it; provide rewards and status to those who diverge; and accept dissatisfaction with the status quo (problematization).

Communications. As the extended-phase model of creativity (see chap. 4) emphasized, creativity requires that novelty is not only generated, but also made available to other people (communicated). Innovation (as against simply dreaming of change) is a three-step process: generation of novelty, exploration of the novelty, and insertion into a functioning system. Although contact with other people may be favorable for the first step, the latter two steps are impossible without communication. If the creative individual fails to communicate ideas effectively to others, the novelty cannot be socially validated. Failure to communicate can result from lack of communication skills, but it can also occur because the creative person makes no attempt to communicate ideas to others (e.g., because of fear of being ridiculed or making other people angry or unhappy). The manager's task is not only to welcome communication of novelty, but also to assist people who generate it to communicate it to others in a way that they too can understand and tolerate.

> Managers (including professors) should encourage people to communicate their novel ideas to others. This role requires both skills and courage and is facilitated by acceptance.

Roles. In explaining behavior, a focus on roles emphasizes not individual characteristics such as abilities, motivation, or personality, but the influence of people's position in groups, most interesting for present purposes the learning or working groups of which they are part. Within these groups, people have roles—expectations that other people and they themselves expect them to fulfill. For instance, professors typically define the subject matter of a course and assign grades, and managers make tactical or, if they are senior enough, strategic decisions—this is their role and they themselves and other people simply expect it.

Sometimes roles in an organization are laid down in formal codes such as a job specification that states who has what authority to do what and must report to whom under what circumstances. Not seldom, however, roles in an organization are implicit or established through time-honored custom and acquired through processes of socialization (e.g., via observation of role models). We have already given the example of the three generations of Becquerels. Using a roles approach, it could be said that they acquired the role of senior scientist by observing people within the family and simply fulfilled this role in their professional lives. As Cropley (2003) pointed out, professors and managers seldom receive specialized training in the leadership aspects of their job. In academia, a PhD degree is frequently assumed to confer not only scientific skill, but also knowledge and techniques for teaching other people. Because they rarely experience formal training in leadership, many professors and managers model themselves on their own teachers. In addition to emphasizing once again the importance of leaders as models, this state of affairs means that those who have been poorly taught pass on the same problems to the next generation of students.

The way people understand their role in a given situation and its interaction with the roles of others helps to determine their behavior in that setting, and changes in roles and role expectations result in changes in behavior. It is thus apparent that roles and the behaviors, attitudes, values, motives, and personal characteristics displayed by role models (such as professors and managers) are an important social factor in encouraging people to generate and insert effective novelty (or to avoid doing so). James, Clark, and Cropanzano (1999) summarized the effects of role models on creativity in organizations. They concluded that, through the way they behave, models such as professors and managers: (a) make people aware of the possibility of generating effective novelty, (b) legitimize creativity as a worthwhile goal, (c) show how to generate novelty, (d) awaken positive emotion about creative activity, and (e) provide rewards for being creative. Points (a) and (b) involve both general and specific effects: Creativity is legitimized as a general goal, while attention is directed toward certain kinds of creativity. The effects of role models seem to follow the well-known tendency for people to be most strongly affected by role models who have power and are like themselves in visible attributes such as gender or ethnic group membership (e.g., Bandura, 1962).

> Managers and teachers can foster generation of effective novelty by the way they themselves behave (i.e., through their function as role models). This may be particularly important in higher education.

CREATIVITY AND GENDER

One of the most interesting social issues in the discussion of institutions and creativity is the question of possible gender differences. Put in a provocative way, "Can women be as creative as men?" It cannot be denied that, historically speaking, far fewer women than men have been acclaimed for what in chapter 5 was called *sublime* creativity. This remains true despite the many contributions in the past of creative women and the fact that women's opportunities for receiving acclaim may have been severely limited by, for instance, a refusal of those (men) who had the power and status to give sociocultural validation to the novelty they generated. How is this to be understood?

Characteristics Needed for Creativity

Cropley (2002) carried out a psychological analysis of this issue based on concepts outlined earlier. He started by listing some of the personal characteristics thought to be linked to creativity (see chaps. 3–5). These are summarized in Table 7.1. These characteristics were then used as the basis for an analysis of the relationship between gender and creativity (see next section).

Table 7.1

Examples of Motivational, Personal, and Social Factors
Associated With Innovation

Psychological Domain		
Motivation	Personality	Social Skills
• goal directedness	• openness to the novel	• team work
• persistence	• flexibility	• willingness to go it
• curiosity	• independence	alone
• risk taking (courage)	• acceptance of things	• willingness to risk
• drive to ask questions	that are "different"	looking foolish
(even "uncomfortable")	• self-image as innovative	• communication skills
• unwillingness simply to	and daring	• confidence in a group
carry out orders	• tolerance for ambiguity	• willingness to admit not
• desire to do things	• sensitivity to problems	having an answer
differently	• mental toughness	• low level of respect for
• drive to reveal one's	• autonomy	"sacred cows"
own unusual ideas to	• self-centeredness	• willingness to be
others	• intuitiveness	disrespectful to authority
• mastery drive	• playfulness	• willingness to risk
• desire for acclaim		hurting people's feelings

Stereotypes of "Male" and "Female"

Without disputing the existence of biological differences between males and females, it can be said that there is a great deal of disagreement about the nature and extent of social and psychological differences between them. It is also obvious that *male* and *female* are not discrete categories: Some biological females display some characteristics traditionally socially labeled *male* and some biological males display socially defined *female* characteristics. In fact, it is unclear to what extent gender is a matter of biological destiny, and to what extent a social construct. Thus, as psychological categories, *male* and *female* are best regarded as stereotypes. Nonetheless, typical differences are widely thought to exist: Of relevance for this discussion is Lipman-Blumen's (1996) distinction between male and female achieving styles (see Table 7.2). The table is based on discussions in Millward and Freeman (2002), Powell (1993), and Schein (1994) and strongly reflects the classic analysis of Maccoby and Jacklin (1974). However, we have mapped them onto the psychological dimensions used to structure the discussion of creativity in this book.

When the requirements for creativity in Table 7.1 are juxtaposed with the stereotypes of male and female in Table 7.2, it quickly becomes apparent that the male stereotype fits the requirements for creativity outlined in chapters 3 to 5 and summarized in Table 7.1 much better than the female stereotype.

We already pointed out that the gender profiles in Table 7.2 are stereotypes. Nonetheless, these stereotypes exert a strong influence on aspects of experience, such as the way boys and girls are educated or treated by their parents. To take a simple example, it is commonplace in Australian TV reports to see the fathers of adult female athletes who have just won a world title or an Olympic gold medal refer to their daughter as "my little girl." Apparently the fathers are astonished that their cuddly little baby in pink ribbons has become a highly focused, competitive, high-achieving adult. By contrast, it is almost unimaginable that the parents of a similar male athlete would talk about their "little boy." Millward and Freeman (2002) linked society's stereotypes of male and female directly to management by drawing attention to evidence indicating that the stereotypes have consequences for the way female managers are regarded by their seniors (and thus for factors like authority and promotion), as well as for females' actual management behavior. In fact, Schein (1994) concluded that the stereotypes dog female managers from the beginning of their careers. An important mechanism through which stereotypes affect the behavior of females and males is role expectations. Scott and Bruce (1994) showed that these expectations have direct effects on innovative behavior. For instance, not only do male managers expect their female colleagues to avoid risks, but the women too are familiar with the stereotype and the associated role expectations and often tend to behave accordingly.

Table 7.2
Stereotypes of Male and Female

| Area | Stereotype | |
	Female	Male
Cognition	—concrete —narrowly focused —convergent —intuitive	—abstract —broadly focused —divergent —logical
Motivation	—gives up quickly —seeks security (avoids risks) —seeks to avoid failure —reactive —pursues long-term goals	—persistent —takes risks —seeks success —proactive —pursues short-term goals
Personality	—cautious —empathic —timid —sensitive —oriented toward feelings —lacking self-confidence —responsible	—daring —egocentric —aggressive —insensitive —oriented toward ideas —self-confident —adventurous
Social Properties	—people-oriented —wants to be liked —communicative —slow to come forward —allows herself to be dominated —gives in to authority —fears criticism	—task-oriented —wants to be respected —taciturn —seeks limelight —tries to dominate others —challenges authority —fights back when criticized

Lipman-Blumen (1996) carried out an extensive analysis of male–female stereotypes and the way males and females are shaped into different achieving styles during the process of psychological development. There are a number of psychological mechanisms that could lead people to acquire existing stereotypes:

- imitation (e.g., Bandura, 1962);
- identification with the same gender parent who conforms to the stereotype (e.g., Hoffman, 1971);

- differential reinforcement by parents, teachers and the like of what are perceived as gender-appropriate behaviors (e.g., Fagot & Leinbach, 1993); or

- the view that acquisition of clear gender roles is vital for healthy psychological development (e.g., Kohlberg, 1966).

Thus, even if they are no more than stereotypes, a society's ideas on gender can affect not only what others regard as normal in men and women, what duties women are assigned, and so on, but also, through internalization of the stereotypes by women, what ambitions they develop, what kind of management behavior they exhibit, and so on. What, then, is the answer to the question about men, women, and creativity?

The Paradoxical Personality

Cropley (1997b) drew attention to the relevance for answering this question of what he called the *paradoxes* of creativity. These are polarities: apparently mutually exclusive or contradictory properties or states that have to be simultaneously present for effective novelty to be generated. To give a few examples, which do not by any means exhaust the list, creativity requires:

- openness for multiple solutions versus drive to find the best possible solution;

- openness to material from the subconscious versus a strong orientation to reality;

- a critical, almost destructive, attitude versus constructive problem-solving;

- openness to a variety of possibilities versus passionate engagement for a particular solution;

- a self-centered attitude versus consideration for others;

- emotional involvement versus cool self-control;

- a "loner" work style versus capacity for team work;

- a high level of expertise versus ability to think like a novice;

- playfulness versus strong sense of responsibility; and

- low level of need for feedback versus high level of willingness to communicate results to others.

What is striking about these paradoxes is that at one pole they involve stereotypical male characteristics (e.g., coolness, independence, secretiveness, preference for logic), and at the other pole stereotypically female properties (e.g., emotional involvement, team attitude, communication skills, intuitiveness). Thus, the answer to the central question is that creativity requires both "typically male" and "typically female" characteristics even if this state of affairs is paradoxical in nature. What is necessary to promote creativity in organizational settings is thus "integration of opposites" based on "the art of balancing" (Urban, 1997, p. 39). This point of view has been extensively elaborated by Lipman–Blumen (1996), who called for a fusion of stereotypically male and female styles to yield connective leadership.

> Creativity simultaneously requires stereotypically male and female characteristics. Thus, it is both men's business and also women's work!

GROUPS AND CREATIVITY

Groups

As Harrington (1999) put it, groups can provide a "responsive" or "nourishing" audience. Paulus (1999) listed a number of beneficial effects of working in a group on creativity: They can: (a) provide broader and more varied information than that possessed by a single person, (b) motivate creative activity, (c) provide models, and (d) give feedback. One of the most frequently cited benefits of working in groups is the positive effect they are thought to have on idea production. VanGundy (1984) pointed out that groups usually:

- possess more knowledge;

- arouse intense interest in group members;

- develop a broader perspective on the problem;

- generate more and higher quality ideas;

- come up with more candidate solutions;

- make riskier decisions;

- explore candidate solutions, to use our terms, more effectively;

- enhance acceptance of novel solutions (in our terms, are more open); and

- lead to greater satisfaction with solutions.

Groups also tend to enhance implementation of solutions, not surprising, because a solution offered by a group will have the support of a greater number of "persuasive advocates" (the members of the group) than a solution worked out by a single person. All in all, VanGundy concluded that groups are most effective for solving problems that can be solved through division of labor either because the problem can be broken into separate areas on which subteams can work simultaneously or because it can be broken into sequential stages that can be worked on and solved sequentially.

However, groups can also inhibit creativity. Larey and Paulus (1999) listed a number of creativity-inhibiting tendencies in groups:

1. free riding (individuals reduce their effort and leave it up to the group),

2. evaluation apprehension (fear of negative reactions from the others),

3. production blocking (one person dominates and blocks others),

4. social comparison (people make sure that their ideas conform to the group tendency),

5. matching down (e.g., out of solidarity, the standard drops to that of the weakest member of the group),

6. focus on shared information (special knowledge of individuals is ignored or kept hidden because of the factors already listed),

7. premature closure (to keep the peace or because of the urge to be democratic or respectful, group members agree too quickly), and

8. fixed roles or fixed power structure (in the group there are leaders and followers or bosses and minions; the former possess authority, whereas others do what they are told).

In numerous studies, group brainstorming has been shown to produce fewer ideas than the same number of individuals brainstorming alone (Paulus, 1999). Apparently some of the group members hold back on ideas possibly because of the factors just listed. This notion is particularly true where the individuals who come together to form the group all possess much the same knowledge base. The group does not broaden knowledge or add new perspectives, but just has more people working on the same knowledge. As Puccio (1999) pointed out, research also shows that the effectiveness of brainstorming groups in generating effective novelty (as against producing a large number of ideas) depends strongly on the number of highly innovative people participating in the brainstorming. Groups without innovators do not generate much effective novelty even if they do brainstorm and produce ideas. Thus, brainstorming makes use of what is available in the group, rather than adding some new element that transcends the individuals in the group. The group is simply the sum of the links in the chain, not a new entity.

> To be effective in generating effective novelty groups should contain highly creative members with widely differing knowledge bases.

Teamwork

Abra (1994) showed that achieving spectacular breakthroughs often requires cooperation with others. Sir Harold Kroto (winner of the 1996 Nobel Prize in Chemistry for the discovery of Fullerenes) and William Phillips (winner of the 1997 Nobel Prize in Physics for the development of methods to cool and trap atoms with laser light) are two examples of contemporary Nobel Prize winners who emphasized teamwork when discussing their own processes of innovation. Kroto (see Frängsmyr, 1997) argued that competition must be avoided at all costs. In the 1997 Nobel Lecture, Phillips emphasized that he always worked in a team. He gave as examples of the team's function "testing out ideas," "getting other people's feedback," "getting their suggestions," "asking questions," and "answering questions."

Despite the benefits listed for working in teams, actions like taking a strong stand in favor of an innovation are risky, and people's willingness to be publicly innovative is thus affected by, among other things, fear of being publicly wrong, exposing themselves to criticism, or looking foolish. Production of novelty also depends on people's dissatisfaction with the status quo, which may require standing against the team or not accepting existing situations that the team sees as perfectly satisfactory. As a result, considerable courage and willingness is required to stand alone in a team. This situation is one in which a human assister can be of great value.

> Teams may block generation of effective novelty by imposing a conventional opinion on all members.

Downstream Consequences

Earlier discussions (see chap. 4) emphasized that the introduction of novelty into a functioning system must build on what already exists. Thus, creative people must operate on the basis of a foundation of knowledge. In an organizational setting, this means that they must not only know about the material the team is working on, but must also be able to take account of factors such as the goals of the organization, and to calculate an innovation's "downstream consequences." This concept is as true of institutions of higher education as of business. For instance, there is no point in teaching students to learn in ways that will cause them to fail in other professor's classes or make them incapable of getting a job after university. Thus, successful innovation also requires knowledge of the organizational status quo and the ability to make accurate decisions based on existing knowledge. This in turn requires familiarity with the facts, good memory, rapid recall, logical reasoning, and the like, aspects of what we have called *convergent* thinking.

STOCKTAKING

Summary Table 7 continues the pattern of earlier summaries. However, in this case, the right-hand column (**Press**) involves aspects of the organization that are favorable for completion of a particular phase, whereas Summary Table 6 involved environmentally affected aspects of the individual. Summary Table 7 shows, for instance, that **P**rocess and **P**roduct in the **P**hase of *Activation* are favorably affected by generation of novelty as a goal of the organization, loosely specified organizational goals, loosely defined roles of the people in it, visionary leaders, and the presence of appropriate role models in the work or study setting. Although social in nature, these are not characteristics of a person, such as awareness of the social consequences of novelty or willingness to resist group pressure to conform (see chap. 6), but of the setting.

PRACTICAL GUIDELINES

The guidelines in Box 7 now supplement those in earlier boxes by focusing on advice stemming from the discussion of the impact of the institutional environment on creativity.

Summary Table 7
Creative Process, Product, and Press in the Phases of Creativity

Phase	Process	Sub-Product	Press (organizational)
Preparation	• Perceiving • Learning • Remembering	• General knowledge • Special knowledge	• Expectation of novelty • Loosely specified goals • Loose roles • Visionary leaders • Presence of models • Open authority structures • Supportive authority figures
Activation	• Identifying problem • Setting goals	• Problem awareness	• Resources for acquiring information • Time to acquire information • Loosely specified solution methods
Generation	• Making associations • Bisociating • Building networks	• Many candidate solutions	• Time to stew things over • Encouragement to explore • No demand for quick results
Illumination	• Recognizing promising new configurations	• Novel configurations	• Openness of the setting for radical novelty • Open/loosely specified goals
Verification	• Checking relevance and effectiveness of novel configuration	• A relevant and effective prototype solution	• Opportunities for testing and checking • Tolerance from leaders and colleagues

Phase	Process	Sub-Product	Press (organizational)
Communication	• Achieving closure • Gaining feedback	• Effective presentation of the prototype to others	• Encouragement to share ideas • Interest in novelty from others • Good relationships with others • "Safety" for "deviants"
Validation	• Confirmation of relevance and effectiveness	• Acclaim of the creative product by relevant judge(s)	• Tolerance for radical novelty • Positive feedback for novelty • Rewards for novelty

Box 7. Practical Advice Based on Chapter 7

Who?	When?	What?
Teachers and managers (Thought leaders)	Attitudes to students and colleagues	Be aware of the social roles you and others are playing, and the effect of these on generation of novelty
		Do not be blinded to promising novelty by your own expertise
		Be aware of your role as a model of appropriate behavior
		Identify your own stereotypes about students and colleagues
		Regard female students and colleagues as capable of generating effective novelty
	Instructional and leadership strategies	Constantly question the organization's goals
		Make yourself a role-model of creativity
		Show respect for those who generate novelty in front of others, especially in classes or meetings
		Discuss both positive and negative effects of groups and teams on creativity
		Build working groups whose members have varied background knowledge
		Encourage communication of ideas to other people
		Discuss the effects of stereotypes, including gender stereotypes, on generation of effective novelty
		See that sufficient resources of all kinds are available to those who produce ideas
		Do not centralize all power in your own hands
		Provide a setting in which it is safe to present ideas
	Assessment strategies	Radiate a concern with achieving excellence
		Provide challenging tasks
		Make sure that people have time to generate varied potential solutions
		Reward generation of novelty with grades, status, promotion, etc.
		As much as possible, allow people to choose their own tasks and decide how to carry them out
		Place emphasis on productivity
		Assign ownership of ideas to those who produce them
		Allow students and colleagues to choose the pathway to a solution themselves

Who?	When?	What?
Colleagues and students (Coal-face creatives)	Self-image	Do not be afraid to defy the social framework
		Strive for excellence
		Remember the importance of ethicality
		Identify your own stop rules
	Learning and work strategies	Constantly question the organization's goals
		Identify assisters and blockers in your learning environment
		Try to build with other students and colleagues learning support networks that foster creativity
		Do not be intimidated into conforming to group pressure
		Identify sources and kinds of conformity pressure in your surrounding environment
		Remember that there are rules about breaking the rules

8

Diagnosing Creativity of
Products and People

The purpose of testing creativity is not labeling or selection of the worthy, but diagnosis leading to focused and differentiated efforts to foster creativity. People in organizations and institutions need to be able to recognize elements of creativity when they see them, in both products and people, which would make it possible to promote it in themselves and others. Instruments for assessing effective novelty in products can be used by different observers with substantial levels of reliability. There are also psychological tests for assessing relevant psychological traits in adults. Psychological potential needs to be supported by an appropriate organizational environment, and this too can be assessed. Thus, a foundation exists for a differential diagnosis of creativity focused on product, person, and setting.

THE NEED TO DIAGNOSE CREATIVITY

We hardly need help in deciding that, let us say, inventing the electric light bulb, writing Macbeth, or painting the *Mona Lisa* involved creativity. However, organizations (including institutions of higher education) do need to be able:

- *in solutions*: to recognize creativity that is not self-evident and say systematically where the creativity lies, as well as where and how it can be improved;

- *in people*: to identify potential for creativity and react appropriately to it; and

- *in organizations*: to detect impediments to creativity and remove them, as well as to identify favorable conditions and strengthen them.

The purpose of this is not retrospective certification of creativity or anointment of the chosen few. The practical purpose is, on the one hand, ascertaining what it is that needs to be developed in oneself and encouraged in others and, on the other hand, recognizing when behaviors, environmental circumstances, and products are at least moving toward generation of effective novelty. It is important, for instance, that personal characteristics known to be associated with creativity are identified and positively valued in a classroom or an organization, and that people displaying such characteristics are respected by others and encouraged to respect themselves.

Goodness of Fit

An important advantage to be gained from identifying creativity in people, solutions, and organizations involves goodness of fit: Harrington (1999) argued that there is no single best set of environmental circumstances that is favorable for everybody's creativity. According to him, the decisive factor is the goodness of fit between the characteristics of the environment and those of the individual. Oldham and Cummings (1996) discussed the interaction among individual factors (thinking, personality, motivation), contextual factors (properties of the environment such as climate, management practices, etc.), and properties of the task. They found—as common sense would suggest—that creative performance was highest when people with high creative ability and creative personality worked under supporting and noncontrolling supervision on complex, challenging tasks.[1] Lipman-Blumen (1991) also argued that an appropriate fit between an individual's style and that of the organization in which the person works is best, and accordingly developed two versions of her *Achieving Style Inventory*, one for individual people and the other for organizations. Scoring of the *Achieving Style Inventories* can then be carried out in such a way as to investigate the goodness of fit between person and organization.

Creativity needs to be identified in a differentiated way for four reasons:

- To identify strengths and weaknesses in solutions, people, and the organizational framework;

- To recognize, acknowledge, and positively evaluate it;

- To encourage self-respect and the like in potentially creative individuals; and

- To achieve a good fit between organizations and individuals.

---

[1]The effect of the task on creativity is discussed in chapter 10.

The Need for a Multifaceted Approach to Diagnosing Creativity

The instruments available for diagnosing creativity have been criticized for their poor predictive validity. However, Milgram and Hong (1999) and Plucker (1999) concluded that creativity test scores are better predictors of creative life achievements than IQs or school grades. Plucker (1999) used sophisticated statistical procedures to reanalyze 20-year longitudinal data on predictive validity originally collected by Torrance. He concluded that composite verbal (but not figural) creativity scores on the Torrance Tests of Creative Thinking (TTCT) (obtained by averaging scores on three testings) accounted for about 50% of the variance of scores on the criterion of publicly recognized creative achievements and participation in creative activities obtained several years later, and predicted about three times as much of the criterion variance as IQs. This corresponds to a predictive validity coefficient of about .7.

Helson's (1996, 1999) studies are also informative here. Her findings are particularly important because: (a) they are longitudinal, stretching over more than 30 years; and (b) they use a criterion of creativity derived from real-life behavior, indeed behavior related to earning a living, rather than another creativity test or self- or observer ratings. Helson showed that almost all creativity scores obtained from female college students age 21 at the time of testing correlated with ratings of the degree of creativity of their occupations at age 52. These ratings differentiated among (a) conventional and realistic occupations (lowest level of creativity—1 point), (b) social occupations (an intermediate level—2 points), and (c) artistic and investigative occupations (highest level—3 points). People in an artistic or investigative occupation who had achieved substantial recognition as creative (sociocultural validation of acclaimed creativity) were placed in a higher category, receiving 4 or 5 points according to the level of acclaim. Examples include writers, artists, dancers and musicians. She reported correlations of .38 to .48 with the occupational ratings for measures of personality (e.g., originality), on the one hand, and self-ratings of interests on the other, obtained no less than 30 years earlier.

One possible problem with predicting creativity is that actual creative achievement requires more than simply the cognitive potential called in this book *creativity*. Other factors may well play a major role when it comes to real-life achievements, some of them psychological (mental health and ego-strength, diligence, technical skill, or knowledge of a field, presumably acquired via convergent thinking), some as mundane as sheer luck or opportunity or even something as apparently simple as good timing (see the discussion of convergent thinking and creativity in chap. 4). It is clear that a major psychological moderator of real-life creative achievement is noncognitive factors such as personality. Helson (1999) showed that youthful openness and unconventionality (typical characteristics emphasized in creativity tests) predict adult creative achievement only when they are associated with depth, commitment, and self-discipline. When accompanied by unresolved identity problems, lack of persistence, and self-defeating behavior, they do not. This finding brings out once again the need for psychological approaches to creativity to be multidimensional and differentiated in nature—in other words, the systems approach introduced in chapters 1 and 2.

SPECIFYING THE CREATIVITY OF PRODUCTS

The apparent diffuseness of the idea of *creativity* and the positive connotations associated with the term mean that there is a danger of "American pie": Any object, idea, or action that is thought to be good is praised as creative, and whatever is labeled *creative* has to be good. Under such circumstances, even when solutions really are creative, it is possible that neither the person whose work has just been judged creative nor the person making the judgment can specify what it was about the solution that was actually creative, why it was creative, how it could be made more creative, and so on. In educational settings, there is an obvious link (which is explored more fully in chap. 11) between foster- ing creativity and being able to say in what way a product is creative, where it could be made more creative and how, and so on.

Teachers at all levels are accustomed to analyzing the orthodoxy of prod- ucts—for instance, when they grade assignments for correctness and complete- ness of their factual content. In this section, we present a more differentiated approach aimed at making it possible to say more clearly how creative a solution is and what it is about it that is creative. We do this by building on chapter 2, where we attacked this problem by outlining a four-dimensional approach to defining the functional creativity of products: (a) relevance and effectiveness, (b) novelty, (c) elegance, and (d) generalizability. Of these, effectiveness and novelty seem to be more quantitative (concerned with the question: "How much?"), whereas elegance and generalizability seem to be more qualitative (to do with the question: "What kind?").

Scales for Assessing the Creativity of Products

The most straightforward way of determining the creativity of a product is to ask people who know about such things whether it is creative. This sensible idea is at the heart of the method of consensual assessment (for a summary, see Hennessey & Amabile, 1999). Amabile and her colleagues have developed and refined this approach, and the Consensual Assessment Technique (CAT) is now relatively well known among creativity researchers. The method frequently involves recruiting a panel of judges to rate the creativity of a product, often experts in the field to which the product belongs. However, we show herein that even people without expert knowledge of a field are capable of identifying creativity when they see it. Judges' ratings, whether they are experts or not, seem to relate to genuine differences between products (i.e., they are valid), and they are also reliable.

Although it involves assessing the creativity of products, paradoxically the CAT is most widely used as an instrument for identifying creative people. For instance, despite its suitability for focusing on an individual product made by a single person, possibly for private reasons, the CAT is often used by giving all members of a group, such as a class of students, the same standardized task leading to a closely specified product (such as a collage made from an egg carton, a sheet of writing paper, a paper clip, and as much string as they like). Judges then rate each person's product to identify the more (or less) creative members of the group. Subsequently, the people may be divided into subgroups on the basis of the score received by their product (e.g., the most creative third, the least creative third, and the people in the middle, or something similar). Thus, the CAT is often used more as a test for assessing the creativity of people rather than products, rather like the tests described later. Nonetheless, the CAT popularized an important principle for assessing the creativity of products: systematic ratings by observers.

Psychologists have developed instruments based on observers' ratings for systematically (but not objectively, it must be admitted) determining the creativity of products or, as we prefer to call them, solutions. An early example is Taylor's (1975) *Creative Product Inventory*, which measures the dimensions Generation, Reformulation, Originality, Relevancy, Hedonics, Complexity, and Condensation. The criterion of hedonics raises an interesting issue: It is reminiscent of Jackson and Messick's (1965) early distinction between external criteria of the effectiveness of a novel product (i.e., does it work?) and internal criteria such as logic, harmony among the elements of the product, and pleasingness (i.e., is it beautiful?). Taylor thus added to the definition of the functional creativity of solutions what are to some extent aesthetic criteria.

More recently, Besemer and O'Quin (1987) developed the *Creative Product Semantic Scale*, which is based on three dimensions: Novelty (the product is original, surprising, and germinal), Resolution (the product is valuable, logical, useful, and understandable), and Elaboration and Synthesis (the product is organic, elegant, complex, and well crafted). A later version of the Besemer and O'Quin scale has 43 items (Besemer & O'Quin, 1999). Besemer (1998) confirmed empirically that the scale measured three dimensions and demonstrated its ability to distinguish consistently among products (three chairs of quite different design). Reliabilities of the three dimensions ranged from 0.69 to 0.87 (alpha coefficients), with the majority of coefficients being in excess of .80. In the *Creative Product Semantic Scale*, these criteria are assessed by asking raters to rate something (in this case, a solution) on a bipolar dimension (e.g., *surprising–unsurprising, logical–illogical*, or *elegant–inelegant*). The raters' task is to indicate how close the object being rated is to one or the other extreme.

> Scales exist for rating the creativity of solutions. They focus on observers' ratings of external and internal aspects of creativity, and they also permit statements about both amount and kind of creativity.

It is true that the criteria mentioned earlier such as surprisingness, complexity, or germinality, seem to be highly intuitive or subjective. However, psychological research has shown that even untrained judges, working without knowledge of what other judges are saying, can reach much the same conclusions about the prominence of many of the criteria in a solution (interrater reliability) and can do this in a consistent (reliable) way, making similar ratings if they are asked to rerate the same products at a later date. Hennessey (1994) reported interrater agreement ranging up to .93 even among untrained undergraduates who rated geometric designs or Picasso drawings on Creativity of Product and Creativity of Process on a 7-point scale, simply applying their own subjective understanding of these qualities. Internal reliabilities of individual people's ratings of creativity ranged from .73 to .93. Vosburg (1998) reported that untrained judges who rated products on 7-point scales such as *very complex–not at all complex* or *very understandable–not at all understandable* achieved interrater reliabilities of about .90. In other words, people have a common and reliable understanding of novelty, complexity, elegance, and the like; can recognize them when they see them; and can express their judgments of the level of the characteristics in a quantifiable way.

> Creativity rating scales can be used by nonexperts and are reliable and valid.

The Cropley Solution Diagnosis Scale

The indicators of creativity of solutions assessed with the scales presented earlier are summarized in Table 8.1. We have combined the properties outlined in Table 8.1 with the four dimensions of functional creativity outlined in chapter 2 (relevance and effectiveness, novelty, elegance, generalizability) to develop a scale for assessing the creativity of solutions, whether a tangible product or an idea or approach (see A. J. Cropley, 2005, for an early version). This scale involves: (a) *principles of creativity* (relevance and effectiveness, novelty, elegance, generalizability), (b) *criteria* of the principles (possession and use of knowledge, problematization, adding to existing knowledge, going beyond existing knowledge, external elegance, internal elegance, going beyond the immediate problem), and

Table 8.1
Criteria of Creativity in a Solution

Kind of Criterion	Level of Creativity	Kind of Creativity
External	• differs from what already exists • leads to surprise • is generalizable • is seminal • is germinal	• relevant • valuable • effective • useful
Internal	• generates many ideas • leads to substantial reformulation of ideas • opens up new principles	• logical • elegant • understandable • well crafted • harmonious • complex

(c) *indicators* of the presence of the criteria (e.g., diagnosis, prescription, redefinition, reconstruction, convincingness, completeness, germinality, seminality, etc.). The latest version of this instrument is to be found in chapter 11, which also gives an example of the application of the scale to assessing two different models built by students in an engineering class. As is shown there, the scale can be used to assess (or diagnose) both amount and kind of creativity. It is intended as an instrument for teachers rating student assignments, managers evaluating proposed new products or other products, and as a self-assessment instrument for teachers, managers, students, and staff.

RECOGNIZING CREATIVE POTENTIAL IN PEOPLE

Psychological Dimensions of Creative Potential

In discussing creativity tests, a distinction made by Helson (1999) must be kept in mind. She distinguished between creative productivity and creative potential. In general, psychological tests, especially personality tests, measure only the latter. Consequently, a number of authors (e.g., Helson, 1999; Kitto, Lok, & Rudowicz, 1994) have suggested that creativity tests are best thought of as tests of creative potential, not of creativity. In recent years, this view has been presented with considerable force by Proctor and Burnett (2004). We concur, and in this section discuss procedures for diagnosing such potential.

In a recent comprehensive review, Proctor and Burnett (2004) brought out clearly that there is widespread (although not universal) agreement that measuring creativity requires more than simply testing thinking. Among other things, they quoted Sternberg's (1985) conclusion that thinking tests (especially tests of divergent thinking) run the risk of measuring only "trivial forms of creativity," and emphasized the need to take account of other aspects of the person, in addition to cognitive processes. We have already divided personal properties into knowledge, cognitive processes (thinking), motivation, and personality. A simple dichotomization of each of these four areas into favorable/unfavorable for creativity (+/−) would yield $2^4 = 16$ possible combinations.

The 16 theoretical possibilities are shown in Table 8.2, although some combinations are harder to imagine than others in practice. A plus sign indicates a favorable state for creativity, a minus sign an unfavorable one. This table shows that there are many combinations of circumstances in which people might possess some (or even most) of the characteristics necessary for creativity, but still fail to make creative achievements.

Column 1 depicts a person in whom all four elements are favorably developed and represents "fully realized" creativity; Column 2 describes a person in whom the knowledge base, thinking skills, and motivation are favorable, but the personal properties are unfavorable ("stifled" creativity, blocked by, for instance, rigidity or conformity). In Column 3, motivation is missing, although other psychological conditions are favorable ("abandoned" creativity—such people could be creative if they wanted to); and Column 4 shows a person without the necessary thinking skills despite the desire to be creative ("frustrated" creativity—the person wants to be creative, but lacks the necessary thinking ability).

People with different combinations of psychological prerequisites would require different forms of help to nurture their creativity. For example, "abandoned" creativity (Column 3) would require a different approach from "stifled" creativity (Column 2), despite the fact that both people possess appropriate thinking skills. Furthermore, in different phases of the process of production of a creative

Table 8.2
Possible Combinations of Psychological Prerequisites for Creativity

Prerequisite	Possible Combinations															
	1	2	3	4	5	6	7	8	9	10	11	12	13	14	15	16
Knowledge	+	+	+	+	−	−	−	−	+	+	+	+	−	−	−	−
Thinking skills	+	+	+	−	+	+	−	−	−	−	−	+	+	+	−	−
Motivation	+	+	−	+	+	−	+	−	−	+	−	−	+	−	+	−
Personal properties	+	−	+	+	+	+	+	+	−	−	+	−	−	−	−	−

product (see chap. 4), different combinations of personal prerequisites for creativity would have different consequences. For instance, lack of divergent thinking might not be a problem in the *Communication* phase, but would be fatal in the *Generation* stage. Thus, a diagnosis of creativity should not be based on thinking alone. The interesting question here is how to identify which characteristics are present, which absent, and to relate this to fostering creativity.

> There are many combinations of personal properties that could block creative achievement. Each of these would require different forms of support and encouragement ("remedial treatment").

Life History and Creativity

Csikszentmihalyi, Rathunde, and Whalen (1993) showed in a 5-year longitudinal study of adolescents that early absorption and fascination with an area successfully predicted later adult creativity. Milgram and Hong (1999) conducted 15- and 18-year longitudinal studies of the potency of predictors of later creativity and showed that teenage leisure activities predicted adult creativity much better than IQ or school achievement, although the latter were good predictors of undergraduate grades. Numbers of similar studies exist (see Cropley, 2001). On the basis of this connection among life circumstances, interests, hobbies, and so on and adult creativity, a number of procedures have been developed for assessing such factors.

Michael and Colson (1979) developed the Life Experience Inventory (LEI) for assessing potential creativity on the basis of early life experiences. The 100-item inventory concentrates on factual information (e.g., number of changes of address in childhood, composition of family, education, hobbies, and recreation). As the authors pointed out, this approach enhances reliability. In an initial study of 100 electrical engineers who had also been classified as creative or noncreative on the basis of whether they held patents, 49 items differentiated between creative and noncreative participants. An intuitive grouping of these items by the authors indicated that they cover four areas:

1. "self-striving or self-improvement" (e.g., enjoying competition, displaying curiosity, being committed to an area of interest),

2. "parental striving" (parental emphasis on getting ahead, perceived need to do well in order to satisfy parents),

3. "social participation and social experience" (membership of organizations, helping other students with their schoolwork), and

4. "independence training" (being allowed as children to choose their own friends, being allowed to set their own standards in judging their own accomplishments).

In a cross-validation study, again based on the real-life achievements of 98 engineers, a validity coefficient of .62 was obtained (criterion = possession—or not—of patents). No less than 83% of the engineers above the cutoff point on the inventory were indeed creative according to the criterion (i.e., correctly identified), although 29% of those not identified were, according to the criterion, actually creative (false negatives).

> A person's life history gives systematic clues about the likelihood of the person generating effective novelty in the future.

Measuring Divergent Thinking

Despite the prior conclusion that there is more to creativity than the cognitive aspects, the dominant approach to testing creativity has involved tests of divergent thinking. Such tests emphasize the underlying cognitive processes thought to be involved in production of novelty, with or without actual effectively novel products, and thus have the enormous advantage that they can be used with people who have not produced any acclaimed product in their life history. For our purposes here, the tests are interesting because they represent cognitive traits thought to be connected with creativity in concrete tasks, which means that they offer what is in effect an operational definition of creative thinking and give hints on how to recognize latent creativity. Research on the reliability (stability of scores) and validity (link between test scores and actual creativity) of the tests provides a degree of empirical support for the view that their representation of creative thought is useful. They thus offer a basis for a differential diagnosis of creativity.

Many of the tests are based on Guilford's concept of divergent thinking (see chap. 3). Conventional intelligence tests ask the people being tested to give the single, best, correct answer to a clear and concrete problem using existing knowledge, tried-and-trusted procedures, and conventional logic. Examples are: "What number comes next in the series 2, 4, 8, . . .?", "What is the capital of Venezuela?," and "What should you do if you are in a movie and you see smoke?" It is assumed that all intelligent people being tested would give the same answer because only one answer is regarded as correct or the best, and this answer exists independently of the people being tested (it is given in the test manual, and it would still be the best, correct answer, even if nobody were tested).

Tests of divergent thinking, by contrast, typically ask the people being tested to generate multiple answers to open-ended questions. There are no correct answers; there may be many equally good answers to the same test question, and the answers are sometimes unknown until the people being tested give them. Examples of items from divergent thinking tests are as follows: "Write down as many interesting and unusual uses as you can think of for a tin can." "What would the consequences be if it started raining and never stopped?" "What problems can you imagine in connection with birds nesting in a tree in your garden?" There are also nonverbal tests asking for unusual titles for pictures, for completion of partially completed drawings, or for interpretation of schematic drawings, to give a few examples. The people taking the tests are encouraged to give as many answers as possible and (usually) to produce unusual or unexpected answers.

> The first creativity tests of the modern era were based on divergent thinking and were heavily influenced by Guilford.

The best-known and most widely used of the tests based on divergent thinking are the TTCT. These tests were originally published in 1966 and have since been revised several times (e.g., Torrance, 1998). They are described in detail by Kim (2006) and subjected there to an extensive evaluation of their reliability and validity. The TTCT is most frequently used with children, despite the belief that it is suitable for a wide age range, probably because the test materials are more interesting for children. The test consists of a verbal section, "Thinking Creatively with Words," and a nonverbal or figural section, "Thinking Creatively with Pictures," both of them having two forms, A and B. There are six verbal activities (Asking Questions, Guessing Causes, Guessing Consequences, Product Improvement, Unusual Uses, and Just Suppose) and three figural activities (Picture Construction, Picture Completion, and Lines/Circles). The verbal activities yield scores on three dimensions (referred to by Torrance as "mental characteristics"): Fluency, Flexibility, and Originality (see the discussion of scoring divergent thinking tests in the next section). The nonverbal activities yield scores for five mental characteristics: Fluency, Originality, Elaboration, Abstractness of Titles, and Resistance to Premature Closure. In addition, the figural tests can be scored for 13 creative strengths (e.g., Storytelling Articulateness, Synthesis of Incomplete Figures, and Fantasy).

The test manual reports a median interrater reliability derived from a number of studies of the verbal activities of the TTCT of as high as .97, and other research (see e.g., Sweetland & Keyser, 1991) indicates that the figure is commonly greater than .90 for both parts. According to Treffinger (1985), test–retest reliabilities of the various subdimensions commonly lie between .60 and .70. Mumford, Marks, Connelly, Zaccaro, and Johnson (1998) asked judges to use a 5-point rating scale ranging from *low* to *high* to rate answers on a version of Guilford's *Consequences* test (similar to the *Guessing Consequences* subtest of the TTCT) on, among other things, "quality" (in essence, effectiveness), "originality," "complexity," and "realism." After a practice run and a meeting to discuss the basis of ratings, the judges achieved interrater reliabilities of .90 for quality, .86 for complexity, and .84 for originality. The figure for realism was somewhat lower at .65. Although the *Consequences* test is not identical with the TTCT, data from this test are highly suggestive of what might be expected of the TTCT.

Turning to validity, Plucker (1999) analyzed 20-year longitudinal data originally collected by Torrance and reported long-term predictive validity of the TTCT of about .7. The test scores differentiated well between students who subsequently went on to achieve public acclaim as creative and those who did not. In the study mentioned in the previous paragraph, Mumford et al. showed that the Originality scores of *Consequences* correlated .49 with the originality of over 1,800 U.S. Army officers of both sexes on simulated problem-solving tasks. These correlations remained almost unchanged when IQ and expertise were partialed out. The test scores for Originality also correlated .36 with real-life leadership achievement as estimated by the officers and .47 with job success as indicated by the level of seniority reached in the organization in question (the army).

Scoring Divergent-Thinking Tests

The most widely applied approach to scoring the tests focuses on three aspects of divergent thinking: *fluency* (quantity of answers), *flexibility* (variability of idea categories in the answers), and *originality* (uncommonness of answers). Fluency requires mere counting of the number of different answers given by a particular individual. Flexibility and originality, however, focus on the quality or style of answers. Flexibility involves the number of separate categories defined by the person's answers, whereas originality assesses the uncommonness of individual answers. Some tests extend scoring by including dimensions such as *elaboration* (complexity and completeness of answers) or *effectiveness* (link to the constraints of the real world).

To illustrate in a concrete way these dimensions of scoring, consider the following example: As a response to the test item, "Write down as many uses as you can think of for a tin can," the four answers "saucepan," "milk jug," "kettle," and "suit of armor for a mouse, to give it a fair chance in a fight with a cat" would each score one point for *fluency*, yielding a total of four. (It is merely necessary to count the number of answers.) However, there are two basic idea categories in the four answers: "container," on the one hand (saucepan, milk jug, and kettle), and "protective covering," on the other hand (suit of armor). Thus, the four answers would score two points for *flexibility*. Turning to Originality, the answers saucepan, milk jug, and kettle are commonplace and would score nothing, whereas suit of armor for a mouse to give it a fair chance in a fight with a cat is uncommon and would score several points, exactly how many depending on the particular scoring method used (e.g., two points using Torrance's [1998] approach, four points according to Cropley [1967]). The suit of armor answer is also obviously far more elaborate than kettle or saucepan and would score highly if this dimension were applied. Its effectiveness remains to be tested!

Fluency	=	number of separate responses
Flexibility	=	number of separate ideas in a list of answers
Originality	=	unusualness of answers

Scoring for originality can be laborious. Looking up the creativity of a person's answers in a test manual seems to be inappropriate because there is something inherently self-contradictory about having preexisting lists of novel answers—the essence of novelty is that an answer is *new*. Despite this, Torrance (1998) gives lists of common answers for his tests. Common answers receive no points. He also gives lists of fairly uncommon answers that receive some recognition (one point). All other answers that do not appear in the manual are regarded as original and worth two points. However, although this approach makes scoring for originality less tedious, it limits the usefulness of the tests in cultures other than the one where the word lists were compiled. To take a simple example, an Australian boy in a Canadian school made the extraordinarily unusual (for that country) suggestion for a use for a tin can, "Use it as the wicket for a game of cricket." Unsurprisingly, this answer was not included in the American test manual's list of common answers and received two points. However, in Australia (at least this was the case 50 years ago), a 4-gallon (5 U.S. gallons) kerosene tin is a highly favored wicket for a street game because it is just about the right size and makes an unmistakable sound when the ball strikes it, thus preventing arguments about whether the ball hit the wicket.

It is possible to deal with this cultural relevance of answers by explicitly incorporating it into the scoring procedures (e.g., Cropley, 1967). This process is done by calculating the relative frequency of each answer to a given item in a specific group—"saucepan," for instance, might appear on 30% of the protocols of a particular group of 200 people being tested on Tin Can Uses, "armor for a mouse," by contrast, on perhaps 0.5%. Answers given by only a few members of the group or only a single person (such as "armor") are regarded as original. It is possible to score answers in a more differentiated way by assigning different values to them according to their relative frequency/infrequency—for instance, zero for answers occurring on 15% or more of tests, one point for answers on from 7% to 14% of tests, two points for 3% to 6%, three points for 1% to 2%, and four points for less than 1%. These values correspond approximately to the proportions lying beyond half-standard-deviation (SD) intervals along the X-axis of a normally distributed trait—approximately 15% of scores lie beyond one SD above the mean, approximately 7% beyond one and a half SDs, approximately 3% beyond two SDs, and so on.

This approach defines Originality in the specific context of a particular group via a statistical procedure. The percentages for a given answer may be quite different in different groups. In an Australian sample, for instance, the "wicket" answer for the use of a tin can might be given by 20% of children and receive zero points, whereas in a Canadian group, it might occur only rarely and receive four points. The Originality score of a particular answer given by a specific child depends on the answers of the rest of the group, which makes intuitive sense if the social definition of creativity is borne in mind (see chap. 6), but is unsatisfactory if novelty is looked at in a universal way.

This procedure is laborious and time-consuming, because each protocol has to be assessed twice, once to tally the relative frequency within the entire group of each suggestion for each item, a second time to assign to each answer in the specific protocol the value calculated for that answer by means of the first step. These values would obviously change from group to group and have to be recalculated every time. This approach also has the disadvantage that it cannot be used to score a small number of tests, because calculating the relative frequencies of answers requires a substantial pool of participants. A third disadvantage is that the values assigned to answers are dependent on the makeup of the group tested and cannot be transferred to other groups unless they closely resemble the first one. However, the scores reflect the unusualness of answers in a specific context and thus take account of the fact that the context is one of the determining factors in the creativity of a product. The scoring system is also based on a model of the distribution of the capacity for producing novelty (it assumes that it is normally distributed) and differentiates between answers that have been shown empirically to be not at all novel, those that are mildly novel, rather novel, very novel, or almost (or completely) unique. What is not assessed in this procedure is effectiveness.

> Scoring of divergent thinking tests using norms is logically questionable, because novelty by definition lies outside norms. Otherwise, however, it is very time-consuming and arithmetically laborious—and requires testing a large sample of people.

A CREATIVITY QUOTIENT?

Although scores for the other dimensions tend to correlate substantially with fluency, it was demonstrated quite early (e.g., Cropley, 1972) that the various dimensions are not the same. Some people taking the tests produce only a small total number of answers, of which many are highly original (low fluency, but high originality). Others produce large numbers of answers of which few or none are original (high fluency, low originality). Still others produce a consistently high proportion of original answers throughout a large number of answers (high on both fluency and originality) or a consistently low level of originality in a small number of answers (low on both). From the point of view of differential diagnosis, this kind of information is useful, although the problem remains of how to summarize and compare the different possible combinations of high and low fluency, flexibility and originality.

Snyder, Mitchell, Bossomaier, and Pallier (2004) suggested dealing with this situation by calculating what they called a creativity quotient (CQ), using a calculational procedure derived from information theory. Focusing on fluency and flexibility, they analyzed the real example of two people, one of whom gave 23 uses for an object, the other 19. However, the first person's 23 answers involved seven separate categories (flexibility = 7), whereas the second person's 19 answers were clustered in only two categories (flexibility = 2). The first person obtained a CQ of 14 (rounded), the second a coefficient of 6 (also rounded). But what about a third person who gave only eight uses, but spread these equally over four separate categories, two examples in each? Intuitively, when compared with the scores of the second person above, the higher flexibility (distribution of uses over four categories as against two) might balance out the lower frequency (only 8 uses suggested as against 19). Indeed, the Snyder et al. procedure yields a CQ of approximately 6 for this constellation too (i.e., the same CQ score as for the second person), a result of greater variability in the smaller number of suggestions. A fourth person who also gave eight responses in four categories, but with five exemplars of one category and only one in each of the remaining three, would obtain a CQ of approximately 5.5, the massing of uses in one category (as against spreading them evenly over categories) reducing the CQ.

A multidimensional approach suggests the possibility of comparing people with different combinations of fluency, flexibility, and originality and also offers prospects for diagnostic statements. In an example given earlier, for instance, one person suggested 19 uses (fluency = 19) in two categories (flexibility = 2). The person did not lack in inventing answers (favorable for creativity), but stuck to a small set of ideas (unfavorable). This person would be advised to look beyond the immediate horizon. Another person gave eight answers (fluency = 8) in eight categories (flexibility = 8). This person's scores showed a higher level of generation of surprise, but suffered because of the small number of answers: varied answers (favorable), but only a few of them (unfavorable). The advice here would be to generate more answers (greater quantity) without dropping the quality.

Other Tests of Creative Thinking

A frequently cited creativity test of the foundation period in the 1960s was the Remote Associates Test (RAT; Mednick, 1962). This test is now out of print, but because of its seminal influence on creativity testing, it is discussed here. One important technical characteristic of the test is that it involves correct or incorrect answers, meaning that it can be administered to a single person and is quick and straightforward to score. It is based on the fact that some people are more successful than others at finding remote associates to stimulus words: These people are rated more creative. Each of the 30 items, for which 40 minutes are allowed, consists of three apparently unrelated words (e.g., *moon*, *cheese*, and *grass*), and the task is to find a fourth word that links these words, the more remote the better (in the case of the example just given, "blue" would be appropriate). The score is the number of correct solutions.

Mednick reported internal consistency coefficients of .91 and .92, respectively, when the test was administered to samples of male and female undergraduates. The correlation with instructors' ratings on a university-level design course was .70, and the scale distinguished significantly between psychology students rated as creative researchers and those rated as low on creativity. Scores on the RAT also distinguished between students with liberal social attitudes and those with conservative attitudes, as well as between those with artistic and those with mechanical-agricultural vocational interests. However, as Kasof (1997) summarized relevant findings, the RAT has not shown more than moderate correlations with creative behavior in nontest situations.

Guilford developed a series of tests derived from his complex model of intellectual ability known as the structure of intellect (SI) model (e.g., Guilford, 1976). Based on this approach, the Structure of the Intellect Learning Abilities Test: Evaluation, Leadership, and Creative Thinking (SOI: ELCT) (Meeker, 1985) measures eight cognitive activities connected with creativity, all of them involving divergent thinking (see chaps. 3 and 4): divergent symbolic relations, divergent symbolic units, divergent figural units, divergent semantic units, divergent semantic relations, divergent semantic transformations, divergent figural relations, and divergent figural transformations. Factor-analytic studies support the construct validity of the test (i.e., it seems to measure what it claims to measure), and interrater reliabilities are often as high as .99 (different people scoring test responses reach identical conclusions).

Another influential creativity test to appear in the early period was that of Wallach and Kogan (1965), whose major contribution was perhaps their emphasis on a game-like atmosphere and the absence of time limits in the testing procedure. This test contains three verbal subtests (Instances, Alternate Uses, and Similarities) and two subtests consisting of ambiguous figural stimuli (Pattern Meanings, Line Meanings). Probably the most widely applied subtest is Alternate Uses, which, as the name suggests, asks respondents to give as many unusual uses as they can for various common items (e.g., newspaper, knife, car tire, button, shoe, key). Originally, the test was scored by counting the number of responses (fluency) and identifying responses that were unique to a specific person within the group being tested (uniqueness).

Nowadays, some users also score the test for flexibility, originality (statistical uncommonness), and usefulness (practicality and relevance to reality). Fluency and flexibility require merely counting, but originality and usefulness involve rating answers on a 7-point scale (*not original–very original*; *not useful–very useful*). Kogan (1983) listed many studies supporting the validity and reliability of this test. More recently, Vosburg (1998) reported interrater reliabilities of .92 for originality ratings and .83 for usefulness. An overall alpha (internal consistency) reliability of .86 was reported by the same author (i.e., people taking the test a second time obtain scores similar to those they achieved the first time).

The Test of Creative Thinking–Drawing Production

Perhaps the most convenient test of creative thinking ability is the Test of Creative Thinking–Drawing Production (TCT–DP; Urban & Jellen, 1996). The name of this test suggests that it is a divergent thinking test, and its acronym (TCT–DP) makes it easy to confuse with Torrance's TTCT. However, it is based on an approach that differs substantially from divergent thinking (Torrance) or divergent production (Guilford)—a Gestalt-psychology theory of creativity. The test has two forms, A and B, on each of which respondents are presented with a sheet of paper containing incomplete figures. Their task is to make a drawing or drawings containing the fragments in any way they wish. Scoring assesses what the authors call *image production*: Respondents' drawings (productions) are rated not according to statistical infrequency of occurrence, but according to dimensions such as "Boundary Breaking," "New Elements," and "Humor and Affectivity." These are properties of a particular test answer sheet and do not depend on other people's drawings for their points tally. The test can thus be given to an individual person if desired.

Studies in a number of different countries indicate that the interrater reliability of the test is above .90, while test-retest reliability is .70 to .75. The test manual reports correlations up to .82 with teacher ratings of creativity, and correlations with real-life criteria show that TCT–DP scores distinguish between people who follow acknowledged creative pursuits and those who do not. Our practical experience (e.g., Cropley & Cropley, 2000) confirms that TCT–DP is also suitable for administration to university students—it is readily accepted by them, is easy to administer and score, and can be used for counseling purposes. The scores can be used either at the highly and perhaps artificially differentiated level of the 13 dimensions suggested in the handbook or by combining subtest scores to form the three more complex dimensions "Productivity," "Novelty," and "Unconventionality," which have been demonstrated factor-analytically (Cropley & Cropley, 2000):

- *Productivity* involves continuation of what already exists in an existing direction: It produces novelty, but only in the sense of "more of the same." The only difference between two people's responses is the amount of additional material, and the only difference between highly and less "creative" protocols is found in the amount of material produced.

- *Novelty* involves addition of new elements to what already exists, but along existing lines. The new material may differ from person to person, but is a logical and predictable extension of the source material.

- *Unconventionality* occurs when new, surprising elements are added. They may differ sharply from person to person, and the main difference between people is the degree of surprisingness of responses.

Thus, the TCT–DP makes it possible to differentiate novelty even further by distinguishing between novelty through extension of what exists and novelty via generation of previously unknown elements. Focus on a multidimensional concept of creativity, on assessment of potential, and on the use of tests as a basis for differentiated counseling makes this procedure worth using in higher education and applied settings. Cropley and Cropley (2000) used the test in counseling engineering students (see chap. 10).

> The TCT–DP is based on a theory of image production and can be scored without reference to the statistical commonness of answers. It can also be used to assess not only amount of creativity, but also kind.

Tests Based on Problem Solving

Runco, Plucker, and Lim (2000–2001) argued that ideas are, in effect, products yielded by creative thinking. They went on to suggest that it should be possible to specify observable, relatively objective behaviors that indicate the extent to which a person gets ideas and infer from these the presence of creative thinking. In other words, they aimed at measuring the effects of creative thinking, not the thinking. They argued that such a test would provide a criterion against which to validate tests based on assessing thinking. They set out to construct the scale, and the result was the Runco Ideational Behavior Scale. This scale has 23 items, such as "I often have trouble sleeping at night, because so many ideas keep popping into my head" (large number of ideas), "I am good at combining ideas in ways that others have not" (unusual combinations of ideas), or "My ideas are often considered 'impractical' or even 'wild'" (unexpected ideas). The reliability of the scale was .91 and .92 in two college student samples. Its factor structure suggested that it measures one or two dimensions. Test scores correlated scarcely at all with GPA, indicating that production of ideas is not related to academic achievement.

In examining creative thinking, Mumford and coworkers (for a summary, see Mumford, Supinski, Baughman, Costanza, & Threlfall, 1997) focused on problem solving. They developed tests of Problem Construction, Information Encoding, Category Selection, and Category Combination and Reorganization. The category combination test, for instance, involves problems consisting of sets of four exemplars of each of three categories. To take an example in the style of Mumford et al. (1997), a problem could consist of the following three sets of exemplars: (a) table, chair, lamp, bed; (b) banana, pineapple, orange, peach; and (c) telephone book, search warrant, marriage certificate, map. These are given without naming the categories defined by the exemplars. The respondents' task is to identify the categories defined by the exemplars; to combine these categories to create a new superordinate category; to provide a label for the new category and write a brief, one-sentence description of it; to list as many additional exemplars of the supercategory as possible; and to list additional features linking the exemplars combined in the new category. A respondent might identify the three subordinate categories in the example above as *furniture, fruit,* and *printed documents* and might then combine these to form the supercategory of forest products, supporting this with the explanatory sentence, "All the furniture could be made of wood, all the documents of paper (which is made from wood), and fruit and wood come from trees, which grow in a forest."

In the Mumford et al. (1997) study, five judges rated the respondents' products on a 5-point scale for *quality* and *originality* of solutions. After a brief discussion to iron out discrepancies, interrater reliabilities of .84 and .81 were achieved for quality and originality, respectively. When Category Combination scores were compared with a criterion consisting of originality of solutions to simulated management and advertising problems, correlations of .32 and .40 were achieved. Similar coefficients were obtained for Problem Construction, Information Encoding, and Category Selection with the same criteria. When Problem Construction, Information Encoding, Category Selection, and Category Combination scores were combined in a regression approach, the multiple correlations with originality of the solutions to the advertising task was .45, with originality on the management task .61.

A second test based on problem solving, but one that adopts a novel approach, is the Creative Reasoning Test (CRT; Doolittle, 1990). This test has two levels: Level A for Grades 3 to 6 and Level B for secondary and college levels. There are two forms of each level (Form 1 and Form 2), each with 20 items. A novel aspect of this test is that the problems to be solved are presented in the form of riddles. At Level A, for instance, these take the form of four-line rhymes, in which some animal or object gives clues to its identity, and respondents must work out what the animal or object is. An example in the style of this test would be: I grow in the park, / where I stand tall and green./ For birds I am home./ When the wind blows I lean. Respondents are required to find the correct answer, and a scoring key is provided that contains these answers. According to Doolittle, the test, which is in some ways reminiscent of the RAT, requires associative, inductive, and divergent thinking. Because answers are specified in the scoring key, interrater reliability is not an issue. The author reported split-half reliabilities of .63 to .99 for Form A and .90 for Form B, and validity (correlations with scores on the RAT) of .70, the latter scarcely surprising in view of the similarity of contents.

Perhaps the most obvious way of looking at creativity as an aspect of innovation is to focus on using creativity to solve problems. Test procedures exist that assess the way people go about attacking problems, especially Problem Construction, Information Encoding, Category Selection, and Category Combination and Reorganization.

Special Personal Properties

A different approach to the study of the creative person involves identifying not thinking, but personal characteristics whose presence is thought to increase the likelihood of creativity or even to be essential for its appearance. The Creativity Checklist (CCL; Johnson, 1979) can be used for rating people at all age levels, including adults in work settings. On a 5-point scale ranging from *never* to *consistently*, observers rate the behavior of the people being assessed on eight dimensions. In addition to the by now familiar cognitive dimensions Fluency, Flexibility, and Constructional Skills, personal properties such as Ingenuity, Resourcefulness, Independence, Positive Self-Referencing, and Preference for Complexity are assessed. Interrater reliabilities ranged from .70 to .80, and the test correlated between .51 (RAT) and .56 (TTCT) with other tests.

Colangelo, Kerr, Huesman, Hallowell, and Gaeth (1992) developed the Iowa Inventiveness Inventory, initially by studying inventors who held industrial or agricultural patents. The final instrument consists of 61 statements (e.g., "Whenever I look at a machine, I can see how to change it") with which respondents indicate level of agreement on a 5-point scale. The inventory distinguished significantly between acknowledged creative individuals and other people—for instance, sorting into the expected order acknowledged inventors, "young inventors" rated as inventive by teachers, and noninventive, academically talented adolescents. The test–retest reliability of the inventiveness score reported by Colangelo et al. was .66 and internal consistency was .70.

Basadur and Hausdorf (1996) emphasized a somewhat different aspect of the personal correlates of creativity: attitudes favorable to creativity (e.g., placing a high value on new ideas, believing that creative thinking is not bizarre). The 24-item Basadur Preference Scale consists of statements with which respondents express their degree of agreement/disagreement on a 5-point scale ranging from *strong agreement* to *strong disagreement*. Items include "Creative people generally seem to have scrambled minds," "New ideas seldom work out," or "Ideas are only important if they impact on major projects." Factor analysis yielded three dimensions when the scale was administered to university students and young adults working in business settings: Valuing New Ideas, Creative Individual Stereotypes, and Too Busy for New Ideas. Test–retest reliabilities of the three dimensions ranged from .58 to .63, while alpha coefficients ranged from .58 to .76. Basadur and Hausdorf reported validity coefficients involving correlations with other creativity tests of about .25.

Creative Types

The Creatrix Inventory (C & RT; Byrd, 1986) is of considerable interest because it integrates both cognitive (thinking) and noncognitive (motivation) dimensions of creativity. It is based on the concept of *idea production*, the ability to produce unconventional ideas, creativity being regarded as the result of an interaction between creative thinking and the motivational dimension of risk-taking. The test consists of two blocks of 28 self-rating or attitude statements, one block measuring creative thinking and the other risk-taking. These are answered using a 9-point scale ranging from *complete disagreement* to *complete agreement* (e.g., "I often see the humorous side when others do not," "Daydreaming is a useful activity"). Scores on the items of each dimension are summed, and the total score for the dimension is rated as high, medium, or low. Each person's scores are then plotted on a two-dimensional matrix (creativity vs. risk-taking) and the person assigned to one of eight styles: *Reproducer, Modifier, Challenger, Practicalizer, Innovator, Synthesizer, Dreamer,* and *Planner.* The innovator is high on both creative thinking and risk-taking, the reproducer low on both, the challenger high on risk-taking but not creativity, the dreamer high on creativity but not risk-taking, and so on. Byrd reported a 1-week test–retest reliability of .72 for this scale. He argued that the scale possesses face validity, but provided no data on other forms.

Self-assessment: What is your personal style?
Reproducer?
Modifier?
Challenger?
Practicalizer?
Innovator?
Synthesizer?
Dreamer?
Planner?

Another procedure based on properties of the individual is the Myers-Briggs Type Indicator (Myers-Briggs & McCaulley, 1992), a test that has achieved considerable popularity in business circles in recent years. This procedure measures four bipolar personality types: Extraversion (E) versus Introversion (I); Sensing (S) versus Intuiting (N); Thinking (T) versus Feeling (F); and Judging (J) versus Perceiving (P). A dimension, let us say Sensing versus Intuiting, is a bipolar scale on which some individual people are rated as falling at one pole (let us say, Sensing) and some at the other (i.e., Intuiting). For present purposes, Extraversion involves being more attentive to external stimuli, whereas Introversion involves attending more to internal information; Sensing involves focusing on information delivered by the senses, whereas Intuiting involves internal hunches and the like, Thinking focuses more on thinking about evidence, whereas Feeling gives greater weight to things feeling right; and Judging involves weighing up and evaluating, whereas Perception leads to proceeding on the basis of the way things look.

People are rated on each dimension according to the pole to which they are closer. Four bipolar dimensions produce 16 possible combinations or types (e.g., "pedagogue," "field marshall," "inventor," or "administrator"). These types are presented and discussed in an interesting way at the www.ibiblio.org/pub/academic/psychology/alt.psychology. personality/FAQ.almost. Of the various possible combinations, the profile I–N–F–P involves looking into oneself and not constantly checking what others think or are doing, playing hunches and the like, being open to what feels right regardless of logic, and taking in all available information without censoring some out. This profile is referred to as that of the *questor*, and is thought to be most favorable for production of variability, whereas I–S–T–J (*trustee*), which involves being dominated by the way things are always done, looking to others for information and feedback, concentrating on hard information and knowledge, and puzzling things over and intellectualizing, favors production of orthodoxy or singularity.

Many writers have reported that creativity is particularly related to the Sensing–Intuiting dimension, with creative people frequently being intuiters (N), although it has also been shown (e.g., Walk, 1996) that creative graduate students showed a strong tendency toward the N–P combination (open for uncensored information and inclined to interpret it in terms of intuitions) as against S–J (inclined to focus on concrete information and process it on the basis of strict logic, correctness, and the like).

Self-assessment: What type are you?
Extraverted (E) or Introverted (I)? Senser (S) or Intuiter (N)? Thinker (T) or Feeler (F)? Judger (J) or Perceiver (P)?

Kirton's (1989) Adaptation–Innovation Inventory (KAI) does not mention creativity in its title, but is frequently cited in creativity research and is becoming particularly well known in organizational settings. This test distinguishes between people who seek to solve problems by making use of what they already know and can do (adaptors) and people who try to reorganize and restructure the problem (innovators). Kirton's view is that both adapting and innovating are involved in generating novelty, but the innovative style (which is accompanied by greater motivation to be creative, higher levels of risk-taking, and greater self-confidence) leads to higher productivity.

The scale consists of 32 items (e.g., "Will always think of something when stuck," "Is methodical and systematic," "Often risks doing things differently") on which respondents rate themselves, indicating how difficult it would be for them to be like this on a 5-point scale (*very easy–very hard*). The procedure yields an overall score and scores on three subscales: Originality, Conformity, and Efficiency. Kirton reported KR20 reliabilities of .76 to .82 for the subscales and .88 for the total score, and test–retest reliability over 7 months of .82 for the total score. Puccio, Treffinger, and Talbot (1995) reported alpha reliabilities for the total score of .86 to .88, and from .61 to .83 for the subscales. The same authors reported correlations ranging from .25 to .47 for the subscale Originality with the rated originality of products.

CREATIVITY-FACILITATING ASPECTS OF ORGANIZATIONS

The final element in the complex of factors involved in production of effective novelty is the organizational environment in which people operate, whether this is an institution of higher education or a business, factory, financial institution, or other organization. What this environment needs to be like was discussed in chapter 7. The issue here is whether it can be assessed or, as we prefer to say, diagnosed.

Tests of Organizational Conditions

Mathisen and Einarsen (2004) reviewed four organizational climate inventories and summarized their psychometric properties (see Table 8.3). The scale KEYS: Assessing the Work Environment for Creativity (Amabile & Gryskiewicz, 1989) has been used in organizations in many fields, including electronics, high tech, pharmaceuticals, manufacturing, and banking. It consists of 78 statements about the organization, such as "The tasks in my work are challenging," "I feel challenged by the work I am currently doing," "A great deal of creativity is called for in my daily work," and "I believe that I am currently very creative in my work." Respondents rate their own organization by answering *never or almost*

Table 8.3

Overview of a Number of Tests of Workplace Environments

Test	Items (N)	Level	Aspects Tested	Notes
Situational Outlook Questionnaire (English language version of "Creativity Climate Questionnaire"—Swedish) (Isaksen, Lauer, Ekvall, & Britz, 2000–2001)	50 statements about the organization. Participants agree/disagree on 4-point scale from *not at all applicable* to *applicable to a high extent*	Engineers and scientists	Nine scales: • Challenge • Freedom • Idea support • Trust/Openness • Playfulness/Humor • Debates • Conflicts • Risk taking • Time for ideas	Only available after taking training from The Creative Problem Solving Group Inc Contact: http://www.cpsb.com/contact.html
KEYS: Assessing the Work Environment for Creativity (Amabile & Gryskiewicz, 1989)	78 statements about organization. Participants respond on 4-point scale from *never or almost never in this organization, sometimes, often, to always or almost always*	Many organizations including electronics, high tech, pharmaceuticals, manufacturing, and banking	Ten scales: • Organizational encouragement • Supervisory encouragement • Work group supports • Sufficient resources • Challenging work • Freedom • Organizational impediments • Workload pressure • Creativity • Productivity	Protocols must be sent to the Center for Creative Leadership for scoring. Contact: http://www.ccl.org/leadership/pdf/assessments/keys.pdf
Siegel Support for Innovation Scale (Siegel & Kaemmerer, 1978)	61 items. Participants respond on 6-point Likert scale: *strongly agree to strongly disagree*	Schools, engineering firms, university school of nursing	Five dimensions, including: • Leadership (Support of ideas, diffusion of power, support of workers' individual development) • Ownership (of ideas, procedures and processes)	All 61 items are found in Siegel and Kaemmerer (1978). Most readily available but not as well supported by research as other scales.

Instrument	Items/Scale	Organizations	Dimensions	Availability
Team Climate Inventory (Anderson & West, 1994)	38 items. Sometimes responses on 7-point Likert scale from *not at all* to *completely*, sometimes 5-point scale from *strongly disagree* to *strongly agree*	Health services, University staff, Oil companies, TV production company	• Norms for diversity (Being different is accepted, workers choose ways to solve problems, creativity is rewarded) • Continuous development (Fundamental assumptions of the organization are constantly questioned, its goals change, and its methods change)	Test and manual can be purchased from ASE Psychometric Tests Contact: http://www.ase-solutions.co.uk/index.asp
Lipman-Blumen Organizational Achieving Style Inventory (Lipman-Blumen, 1991)	45 items: Participants respond on 7-point Likert items from *never* to *always*.	Many different organizations	Four dimensions: • Vision (clearly defined goals, shared goals, attainable goals) • Participative safety (safe to present new ideas) • Task orientation (shared concern with excellence) • Support for innovation (approval and practical support of attempts to introduce novelty). Three broad domains, each with three more specific styles (nine styles in all): • Relational Style (vicarious, contributory, collaborative) • Direct Style (intrinsic, competitive, power) • Instrumental Style (entrusting, social, personal)	Can be accessed on the Internet. The Achievement Styles Institute processes inventories accessed and submitted on the Internet, and provides results for downloading. Contact: http://www.achievingstyles.com/ Can be administered to assess organization and individuals, and assess the degree of match between relational styles of individual people and those of the organization.

never in this organization, sometimes, often, or *always or almost always.* The scale rates the organization on 10 dimensions: Organizational Encouragement, Supervisory Encouragement, Work Group Support, Sufficient Resources, Challenging Work, Freedom, Organizational Impediments, Workload Pressure, Creativity, and Productivity. The subscales have reliabilities (alpha coefficient) between .70 and .85, and their validity is supported by factor-analytic studies, as well as some applications in real organizations.

A second scale is Isaksen, Lauer, Ekvall, and Britz's (2000–2001) Situational Outlook Questionnaire, an English-language version of a rating scale originally published in Sweden. It consists of 50 statements about the organization. People rating the organization agree or disagree with these statements on a 4-point scale from *not at all applicable* to *applicable to a high extent.* The scale has been applied mainly in scientific and engineering organizations, as well as large manufacturing and business firms. It yields scores for the organization on nine scales: Challenge, Freedom, Idea Support, Trust/Openness, Playfulness/Humor, Debates, Conflicts, Risk Taking, and Time for Ideas. Alpha coefficients of .62 to .90 are reported for the various subscales, with most of them being above .80. Factor-analytic studies have confirmed that the scale measures nine dimensions.

Siegel and Kaemmerer's (1978) Siegel Support for Innovation Scale consists of 61 items with which respondents agree or disagree on a 6-point Likert scale ranging from *strongly agree* to *strongly disagree.* It has been used in, among other organizations, schools, engineering firms, and a university school of nursing. It assesses five dimensions of the organization: Leadership (support of ideas, diffusion of power, and support of workers' individual development), Ownership (of ideas, procedures, and processes), Norms for Diversity (being different is accepted, workers choose ways to solve problems, and creativity is rewarded), Continuous Development (fundamental assumptions of the organization are constantly questioned, and its goals and methods change), and Consistency (people work together toward common goals).

The Team Climate Inventory (Anderson & West, 1994) has been used to assess health services, university staff, oil companies, and a TV production company. It consists of about 40 items depending on the version being used. On some items, the people rating the organization respond on 7-point scales ranging from *not at all* to *completely,* sometimes on 5-point scales from *strongly disagree* to *strongly agree.* This scale yields scores on four dimensions: Vision (the organization has clearly defined goals, shared goals, and attainable goals), Participative Safety (it is safe to present new ideas), Task Orientation (members of the organization have a shared concern with excellence), and Support for Innovation (within the organization, there is approval and practical support of attempts to introduce novelty).

The idea of achieving a good fit between the characteristics of the people in an organization and the psychological characteristics of the organization has already been mentioned. Lipman-Blumen (1991) specifically incorporated this into her assessment procedure, the Achieving Styles Questionnaire (ASI), for which there are two versions, one for organizations and one for individual people. The two forms can be administered and then used to make a diagnosis based, in essence, on goodness of fit. The individual version consists of 45 statements (e.g., "Faced with a task I prefer a team approach to an individual one" or "I achieve by guiding others towards their goals") to which participants respond on a 7-point Likert-type scale ranging from *never* to *always*. These define nine achieving styles such as *collaborative, competitive, vicarious,* or *personal*. Lipman-Blumen (1991) reported reliabilities (alpha coefficients) ranging from .82 to .91 for the nine subscales, and construct validity was demonstrated by means of factor-analytic studies as well as correlations with data on variables like task accomplishment, gender roles, or leadership styles.

STOCKTAKING

As in earlier chapters, Summary Table 8 maps the subject matter of the chapter onto the phases of creativity and the subproducts. The entries in the table are attributes and properties that are measured by tests and scales reviewed in this chapter. It is interesting to note that certain cells are almost empty or entirely empty, which may to some extent reflect our own interests because the tests reviewed here are only a selection. However, an examination of which cells are underrepresented is informative. For instance, *Validation* is more or less ignored by test constructors, as are motivational and personal aspects of *Illumination*. However, a look back at Summary Table 4 shows that *Validation* is largely a matter of convergent thinking, so that it is scarcely surprising that tests of divergent thinking have not focused on this phase.

PRACTICAL GUIDELINES

We are not advocating here that teachers and managers should engage in wide-spread creativity testing. Despite this, there may well be a place for the use of the tests, especially in educational settings. There might be limited call for the use of tests to identify students with high creative potential (e.g., to help in selection of students for special programs where emphasis is to be placed on creativity). One example is to be seen in the selection of students for honors programs, where professors are particularly looking for creativity (e.g., Cropley, 1967b). However, this idea can be criticized as using creativity to restrict access to education. Creativity tests would be better used to increase access (e.g., by widening the criteria for admission to university). In an early study in England

Summary Table 8
Aspects of Creativity That Can Be Identified Through Tests

Product (According to Criterion of Creativity, not Phase)	Phase	Process (Thinking)	Motivation	Personality	Organization (Press)
Relevance and effectiveness: • Valuable • Useful	Preparation	• Uncensored perception and encoding of information	• Goal-directedness • Fascination for a task or area	• Curiosity • Ability to restructure problems	• Challenge • Freedom • Encouragement • Tolerance of questioning of goals
	Activation	• Fluency of ideas (large number of ideas) • Problem recognition and/or construction	• Willingness to ask many (unusual) questions	• Trust in one's own senses • Ability to abstract from the concrete	• Time • Resources • Idea support • Debates
Novelty: • Original • Surprising	Generation	• Adding new elements • Unusual combinations (remote associates, category combination, symbol combination, boundary breaking, nonstereotypical linking of fragments) • Transformation and restructuring of ideas • Construction of broad categories (accommodating) • Combining symbols	• Desire to go beyond the conventional • Resistance to premature closure • Risk-taking • Preference for asymmetry • Preference for complexity • Resistance to premature closure	• Active imagination • Flexibility • Tolerance for ambiguity • Openness to subconscious material • Ability to work on several ideas simultaneously	• Encouragement of intrinsic achieving style • Playfulness • Support of risk-taking • Encouragement to find own ways of solving problems

Internal elegance: • Logical • Organic • Complex • Well crafted • Condensed • Complete	Illumination	• Image production • Making connections • Thematic construction • Recognizing solutions (category selection) • Seeing implications • Gaining a new perspective • Synthesizing ideas			• Encouragement of setting own goals • Flexible institutional goals
	Verification	• Self-directed evaluation of ideas • Elaborating and expanding ideas • Completion of ideas	• Drive for closure	• Trust in one's own sense	• Granting ownership of ideas to individual • Intrinsic achieving style
External elegance: • Pleasing • Understandable • Attractive	Communication	• Articulation of ideas	• Willingness to display results • Willingness to consult other people (but not simply to carry out orders) • Urge to "sell" own ideas	• Independence • Acceptance of own differentness • Relational style	• Atmosphere of trust and openness • Safe environment for those who think differently • Social achieving style
Generalizability: • Generative of new ideas • Reformulates existing ideas	Validation	• Flexibility, ability to recognize the value of other people's ideas • Ability to adapt	• Desire for a good solution	• Openness to the new • Tolerance for criticism	• Group and team support • Feedback on idea • Provision of rewards for creativity

(Hudson, 1968), students were admitted solely on the basis of creativity test scores, ignoring their level of success (or lack of it) in the traditional matriculation examination. The students obtained grades in the course of their 3-year program of undergraduate studies that were similarly to those of students selected on the basis of traditional high conventional grades, although some of them would not have been admitted had their high school grades been the sole criterion.

It is also possible to imagine the use of creativity tests in personnel selection in a way analogous to the one just outlined in educational settings. Tests could help in selecting people for special training or special duties or could widen the criteria for employing people in the first place. An informal survey of the personnel selection policies of a number of leading accountancy firms in England several years ago indicated that all the firms insisted that applicants have high grades at university. When approached by mail, all the firms that were willing to respond indicated that they would not even look at the *curriculum vitae* of a candidate who did not have high grades or, indeed, one from an atypical background.

The earlier discussion of the effects of external rewards raises an interesting point in this regard. As was pointed out, Eisenberger and Armeli (1997) stressed the importance in promoting creativity of specifying to both teachers and students what they were expected to do differently to be creative. The whole issue of the effect of what it is that students and instructors think they are doing in learning settings has been related to creativity by Reid and Petocz (2004). They gave examples from the widely varying fields of music, design, and statistics of the differences among students and staff members—highly relevant for creativity—in what they thought they were teaching and learning. For instance, music could be conceived of as, on the one hand, acquiring (or, in the case of teachers, of imparting) high levels of technical skill or, on the other hand, as developing the ability to express one's concept of the meaning of a particular composition and communicate it to listeners. Statistics was sometimes conceived of as acquiring useful techniques that would lead to passing an exam, but sometimes as understanding how variables, even apparently unrelated ones, hang together in ways that reveal previously unnoticed meaningful structures in the world.

An important practical contribution of creativity tests and assessment procedures can then be seen not as exercising some kind of gatekeeper function, but as providing what is in effect an operational definition of creativity, and thus making it possible to specify in a common language what is being taught and learned. This theme is taken up again in more detail in chapters 10 and 11, where among other things, an instrument for assessing the creativity of student assignments (grading) is presented. The crucial thing about this instrument for present purposes is that it provides criteria of what is required to be creative (novelty, elegance, etc.), indicators for recognizing the presence or absence of the criteria (e.g., diagnosis, incrementation, reinitiation), and summary descriptions of how to recognize the indicators (e.g., "shortcomings in what already exists are revealed," "the known is extended in an existing direction," "thinking begins at a radically different point from the current one").

A further noncustodial use of creativity assessments is to provide what Cropley and Cropley (2000) called *creativity counseling*. They discussed with students in a university engineering class the personal and social conditions thought to be favorable for production of effective novelty (see chaps. 5–7). Students' scores on the TCT–DP were then used to construct a personal profile for each student and each student interviewed (counseled) about strengths and weaknesses in areas thought to be of relevance to creativity (e.g., "You produced a large number of responses, but they were mainly extensions of existing ideas. Remember from the creativity lectures that not just number of ideas but also quality, especially novelty, is needed"). Students also prepared reports on social factors in groups in which they worked and their effects on novelty generation and the like.

Creativity counseling presupposes the ability to differentiate personal properties relevant to creativity in different people. Creativity tests provide the means for doing this, thus making it possible to construct individualized programs for fostering creativity. A number of the important characteristics that may need to be strengthened in different individuals can be identified with tests. A selection of these characteristics is summarized in Table 8.4.

Table 8.4
Test-Defined Characteristics That Are Favorable for Creativity

Motivation	Personality
• Goal-directedness	• Active imagination
• Fascination for a task or area	• Flexibility
• Resistance to premature closure	• Curiosity
• Risk-taking	• Independence
• Preference for asymmetry	• Acceptance of own differentness
• Preference for complexity	• Tolerance for ambiguity
• Willingness to ask many (unusual) questions	• Trust in own senses
• Willingness to display results	• Openness to subconscious material
• Willingness to consult other people (but not simply to carry out orders)	• Ability to work on several ideas simultaneously
• Desire to go beyond the conventional	• Ability to restructure problems
	• Ability to abstract from the concrete

Techniques, Packages, and Programs for Fostering Creativity

Training creativity in individual people can be approached in two ways: (a) focusing on creative potentials that already exist and eliminating blockers that inhibit the expression of these potentials, or (b) focusing on what people do not already possess (e.g., knowledge and skills, favorable attitudes, values, etc.) and helping them acquire these. An intermediate position involves training people to express what already exists in new ways. A substantial number of techniques and programs for training creativity now exist, ranging from simple loosening-up exercises, through systematic training procedures, to organized programs involving sequences of lessons, special materials, and practice activities. Some of the latter are published on a commercial, rather than a scientific, basis. Despite doubts that have been expressed by researchers, creativity training does have beneficial effects, especially when it satisfies four requirements. It is based on general, cognitive principles such as problem recognition, it is prolonged and demanding, it involves real-life examples (e.g., case studies), and it includes practice exercises that are domain-specific. Thus, it needs to be simultaneously general and specific.

FOSTERING CREATIVITY

In an insightful paper from early in the modern era, Olken (1964) identified the major factor blocking efforts to establish creativity training in the immediate post-Sputnik years—the belief, even among engineers (an occupational group where divine inspiration is not typically seen as particularly active), that creative people are born, not made. This theory leads to the assumption that creativity cannot be fostered or promoted through training. More recently, Edwards (2000–2001) confirmed that many creativity researchers still do not believe that creativity as a psychological characteristic of individual people can be inculcated where it is not already present. Indeed, because personality is known to be partly dependent on biological factors and is, in any case, substantially formed early in life, it is reasonable to question the ability of training to make people, let us say, more open or flexible, or of teaching them to enjoy, let us say, risk-taking.

Nonetheless, there is now widespread agreement that creativity is not the expression of a divine spark found only in a handful of chosen ones and leading to occasional blinding achievements. On the contrary, for the practical purpose of teaching people how to do it, creativity is best thought of as a not extraordinary or superhuman (although statistically uncommon) characteristic of products. This is the view of, for instance, Amabile (1983). Indeed, authors such as Richards, Kinney, Bennet, and Merzel (1988) showed that, in the course of everyday life, ordinary men and women frequently produce effective novelty in fine arts, the sciences, the humanities, handwork, and so on. Cropley (2001) gave a number of examples of everyday creativity, including generation of effective novelty in a housewives' weekly sewing circle or in a pee-wee soccer team.

This position is optimistic in that it implies that many people can produce effectively novel products (i.e., be creative), provided that the circumstances are right. In this book, we explicitly reject the born-not-made approach to creativity. Generation of effective novelty is not something for a small group of the unusually talented, who must be identified and forced on to ever higher achievements, but involves—in principle at least—everybody. Nichols (1972) went further. He argued that creativity is a normally distributed trait like intelligence and emphasized the importance of creativity in people who have never received public acclaim and never will. This is not to say that everybody can be expected to become a creative genius, just as not everybody performs astonishing feats of intelligence, but that even in ordinary settings people can be encouraged to generate effective novelty consistent with their level of knowledge, ability, skill, talent, experience, and the like.

> Creativity is not the preserve of a small band of people chosen by nature. All individuals can be encouraged to increase the extent to which they generate effective novelty.

Domain-Specificity of Creativity

In earlier chapters, we called for a differentiated understanding of creativity. In the main, however, creativity-training procedures assume that: (a) a single, general approach will foster all kinds of creativity in all kinds of people; and (b) the appropriate approach is cognitive (i.e., training in thinking). To what extent is such an undifferentiated approach useful? Dow and Mayer (2004) looked at the issue in a limited way (solving insight problems), but still made an interesting point. They argued in effect for a differentiation into verbal, mathematical, and spatial creativity. They concluded in three studies that training in solving spatial insight problems (which they specifically referred to as *creativity training*) was the only form that consistently fostered creativity. Furthermore, all in all, spatial training only clearly improved the solving of spatial problems. Thus, they showed that not all approaches to training creativity are equally effective and that the effects of training are domain-specific.

Baer (1998) pointed out that *domain* can be understood in terms of "cognitive content domains" such as linguistic, mathematical, or musical, but also in terms of "task content domains" such as poetry writing or collage making. He summarized findings of a number of studies and reported that individual people's levels of creative performance in different domains (e.g., verbal, mathematical, mixed) were highly variable, with correlations between scores in different domains not uncommonly being negative. This idea was true for both cognitive and task content. He also reported that creativity training showed similar domain-specificity, with benefits found only on tasks resembling the original training.

Both these reports suggest that (a) creative performance is domain-specific (i.e., a person may show dramatically different levels of creativity in different domains), and (b) creativity training is narrow in its effects.

This supports our call for differential diagnosis of creativity and subsequent differentiated training. However, a substantial diagnostic system accompanied by a wide range of specific programs would no doubt be expensive and difficult to administer. A defensible, one-size-fits-all training approach would cover a number of domains and teach a range of creativity skills. This approach would achieve effects that transcended a single domain, and thus deliver general benefits, even if the effects of creativity training really are specific. Baer (1998) strongly supported this view, advocating use of a wide variety of tasks from different cognitive content domains as well as different task content domains.

> At least in the case of problem solving, creativity training should not aim at fostering creativity in general, but at teaching groups of problem-solving skills that are general within a domain, but specific to that domain. To achieve broader effects, it should incorporate a range of material from different cognitive and content domains.

Generality of Creativity

Plucker (1998), however, defended a general approach and made the interesting point that claims of domain-specificity, which seem to be highly differentiated, may in fact be too sweeping. Using our terms, the domain-specificity approach would, paradoxically, be undifferentiated! Plucker's review suggests that (a) amount of originality may be general, and (b) quality may be domain-specific. This makes sense if we return to the earlier division (introduced in chap. 2) of creativity into two components: (a) generation of novelty, and (b) exploration of the novelty to identify effective aspects. Although generation may be nonspecific (general), exploration may require knowledge, skills, ability, attitudes, values, a self-image, and social support that are (a) specific to particular task content, (b) more affected by the specific setting (see chap. 6), and (c) more dependent on convergent factors (see chap.4).

The general-but-yet-specific approach is also consistent with our division of creativity of products into amount of creativity (more general) and kind of creativity (more specific), suggesting that general creativity-facilitating techniques would help to encourage increases in the amount of novelty generated, but that more specific approaches are needed to improve the quality of this novelty. Related to the Phases of creativity, broad and general creativity training may tend to focus on *Generation* at the expense of *Verification* and *Validation*, for which more specific training is necessary.

> In some phases creativity is general, in others specific: Generating novelty is general, exploring it is more specific.

Creativity in Different Domains

The idea that creativity can be trained by means of a general procedure implies that creativity is the same in all content domains (i.e., that creativity in, let us say, engineering is the same as creativity in philosophy). To what extent is this true? On the basis of an analysis of over 1,000 eminent creators in various fields, in which he analyzed creativity in terms of the psychological demands of the field (in other words, he looked at the problem's effects on creativity; see chap. 11), Ludwig (1998) concluded that the relationship between creativity and field of endeavor is governed by the mathematics of fractal geometry. This is the geometry of self-similar objects that are characterized by a structure that repeats itself again and again at progressively smaller scales.

Ludwig identified four central dimensions for describing these demands. Different fields differ by being: (a) impersonal versus emotive, (b) objective versus subjective, (c) structured versus unstructured, and (d) formal versus informal. He then divided fields of activity into two kinds: investigative and artistic. The characteristics of these two broad categories are summarized in Table 9.1.

The examples in the table are arranged hierarchically, with mathematics the most impersonal, objective, structured, and formal; medicine and art history in the middle; and visual arts the most emotive, subjective, unstructured, and informal.

Ludwig went on to show that the four-dimensional framework just outlined applies not only to the broad division into investigative versus artistic, but that it also applies within fields. Thus, it is possible to use the same four criteria to divide investigative fields once again into natural sciences, such as mathematics

Table 9.1
Differences Among Academic Fields

Field			
Investigative		Artistic	
Characteristics	Examples	Characteristics	Examples
Impersonal	Mathematics	Emotive	Art history
Objective	Engineering	Subjective	Writing
Structured	Biology	Unstructured	Composing
Formal	Medicine	Informal	Visual arts

or physics (which are more impersonal, objective, structured, and formal), versus social sciences, such as economics or psychology (which are more emotive, subjective, unstructured, and informal). This subdivision can continue, always on the basis of the four dimensions, yielding ever finer differentiations. For instance, natural sciences could be divided into physical sciences that are more impersonal, objective, structured, and formal than life sciences; and physical sciences could be subdivided in turn into theoretical versus applied sciences, the former being more impersonal, objective, structured, and formal than the latter. An applied field such as engineering could be divided into different subfields ranging from those that are extremely impersonal, objective, structured, and formal (e.g., structural engineering) to those that are (in comparison) more emotive, subjective, unstructured, and informal (e.g., environmental engineering).

Although writing in a literary sense, Joseph Conrad suggested a taxonomy for distinguishing different forms of creativity that has something in common with Ludwig's approach, although he emphasized the products rather than the requirements of the field. In the foreword to his own novel, *Nigger of the Narcissus*, Conrad argued that writers, poets, artists, and the like produce effective novelty through production of beautiful objects, philosophers through production of novel ideas, and scientists and engineers through production of novel facts. The progression from generation of beauty, through ideas, to facts shows a progression in products similar to the one described by Ludwig in terms of demands of the field. Production of beauty is intuitively more emotive, subjective, unstructured, and informal than production of novel facts, which would be expected to be more impersonal, objective, structured, and formal, whereas production of novel ideas intuitively lies between production of beauty and production of cold facts.

Ludwig's analysis suggests that if we wanted to train people to be creative in fields that are structured, formal, objective, and impersonal, a different training would be necessary than for fields that are personal, subjective, unstructured, and informal. We have already argued that fostering creativity has both general aspects, connected mainly with quantity of novelty generated, and domain-specific aspects, which are more relevant to quality of novelty. Ludwig's research yields guidelines for the nature of domain-specific training.

There is a link between field (the kind of problem and the way problems are attacked) and creativity. Creativity training needs to take account of this link.

FOSTERING CREATIVITY IN INDIVIDUAL PEOPLE

We turn now to the question of how to help individual people become ready and able to generate effective novelty—creativity training.[1] Much of what is known on this topic was developed in discussions focused on schoolchildren. Nonetheless, the material is informative for our topic, and is included here. In broad terms, there are two approaches to creativity training: (a) helping people acquire knowledge, skills, ways of working, attitudes, values, and personal properties that are necessary for creativity, but that they do not possess; and (b) removing blocks—such as fear of the unknown, lack of self-confidence, or belief that generation of novelty is strange—that block people from manifesting creativity that they already possess. The first approach assumes that something needs to be put into people that is not there at present, which leads to a concentration on "assisters" or facilitators of creativity (see chap. 7). In other words, the emphasis is placed on organizing the environment in such a way as to develop or promote the acquisition of knowledge, skills, motives, and personal characteristics necessary for generation of effective novelty. A substantial armory of procedures exists that can be applied for this purpose, and a number of these is discussed more fully herein.

By contrast, some theorists argue that all people already possess the potential to be creative. According to this view, creativity will emerge naturally, provided that it is not inhibited or blocked (e.g., by conditions in organizations). The basic idea is that people already know how to think divergently, fantasize, make remote associations, and so on. In other words, they already possess the cognitive skills necessary for generation of variability, possibly because these are part of the functioning of the central nervous system. They are also capable by nature of being open to the new and flexible and having the courage to take risks, develop a drive to break away from the well known and a fascination for the

---

[1]This section focuses on individual people. Thus, we do not discuss organizational factors except in terms of their effect on properties of individuals.

new, and so on, at least as potentials. However, in the otherwise highly desirable process of socialization (for a discussion of this process, see chap. 6), most people learn to suppress or hide these properties, which are thus blocked, possibly to the point where they are close to being completely lost. Fostering creativity is then seen as eliminating blocks, principally in the areas of motivation and personal properties (e.g., fear of taking a risk, desire to avoid uncertainty, intolerance of ambiguity, fear of complexity, etc.).

> There are two approaches to creativity training: Inserting what is not there via learning and practice or releasing what is already there by eliminating blockers.

Eliminating Blockers

The blocking factors are partly properties of the environment, both physical (e.g., facilities and resources) and social (e.g., organizational status afforded people who generate novelty, approval/disapproval offered by other people), but also personal (e.g., personality and motivation). For a more detailed discussion, see chapters 6 and 7. Blockers block not because they involve lack of ability to get ideas and the like, but because they inhibit people from doing what they actually already can—for instance, by making them frightened to do so (a personal or social blocker) or by channeling their thinking into an unproductive pathway (a cognitive blocker). Typical blocks in the *social climate of an organization* include:

1. exaggerated success orientation,

2. strict distinction between work and play,

3. intolerance of questioning,

4. crushing conformity pressure,

5. rigid maintenance of strict sex roles, and

6. intolerance of differentness.

Because environmental and social factors are not part of the individual person (although they may have profound effects on personal properties), they are not discussed any further here, where the focus is on training individual people.

Typical blocks located in a person's own mind include;

1. inability or unwillingness to relax control and let ideas flow,

2. inability to handle a flow of ideas when it occurs,

3. fear of letting the imagination loose, and

4. fear of giving the wrong answer.

Blocks also have cognitive aspects. Some of these are more general, for instance:

1. excessive emphasis on speed,

2. reliance on external evaluation,

3. one-sided emphasis on analytic thinking,

4. inability to break an existing set,

5. heavy reliance on verbal communication.

Other cognitive blocks are more specific, such as:

1. assuming that new problems must be attacked from existing perspectives;

2. imposing limits on the way a problem is looked at, more or less from habit;

3. assuming that there is always a single, best answer, if we can only spot it; and

4. assuming that the solution can only take a certain form.

It seems that many of these blocks can be eliminated with the help of simple, general procedures. Cropley (2001) summarized studies showing, for instance, that merely giving people examples of unusual responses seemed to increase their scores on a divergent thinking test. Other researchers he mentioned reported higher scores on creativity tests brought about simply by allowing people (admittedly, children) to play with test materials, watch a video of a comedian, or watch a film of a person solving a creativity test.

There are also activities more specifically designed for releasing blocked creativity. Cropley (1992b) gave a number of examples of simple games and game-like activities for breaking blocks: These include "bridge building," "idea production," or "creative connections." Many activities are based on simple thinking techniques such as: (a) reversing the problem, (b) considering the end result, (c) focusing on the dominant idea, and (d) discarding irrelevant constraints. Procedures such as these aim, in essence, at loosening people up. They seek to encourage expression of what is already there. Hence, creativity trainers often start training sessions with such games. The idea is to get what is already there flowing, and it is done at the personal level by breaking through unwillingness to relax control and let ideas flow, reducing fear of letting the imagination loose, encouraging people to break existing mind-sets, encouraging their confidence in their own ability to handle a rush of ideas when it occurs, or reducing fear of giving the wrong answer. At a more cognitive level, the activities help to escape from stereotypical patterns of thinking, break down barriers against unusual ideas, avoid imposing self-generated limits on thinking that are not inherent in the task, and so on. The definitive term describing what is required in this area of creativity facilitation is *flow* (Csikszentmihalyi, 1996).

> Breaking down blocks is usually carried out with simple, often general, even everyday activities. These are usually seen as encouraging people to let go or go with the flow, to use a popular (if unscientific) expression.

Inculcating What Was Not Previously There

The opposite approach to removing blocks (so that creativity that is already there can emerge), involves helping people develop skills and propensities that they do not already possess. In fact, this is the dominant approach to fostering creativity. Treffinger, Sortore, and Cross (1993) reported in excess of 250 published materials that can be regarded as resources for training people in how to generate novelty. Huczynski's (1983) encyclopedia of methods listed dozens, including "buzz groups," "flexastudy," "lateral thinking," and "mathetics." The website (www.mycoted.com/creativity/techniques/) lists more than 200 procedures, including some of those just mentioned. What is striking about these programs is that they focus overwhelmingly on training the cluster of thinking skills summarized in chapter 3 as belonging to the family of divergent thinking. This notion is neither surprising nor foolish in view of Scott, Leritz, and Mumford's (2004) conclusion that divergent thinking has been shown by 50 years of research to contribute to "many forms of creative performance."

> Inculcating creativity differs from removing blocks by assuming that people need to be taught how to generate effective novelty. This kind of training relies heavily on teaching thinking skills, especially skills related to divergent thinking.

Both the discussion of the interaction between creativity and intelligence in chapter 4 in terms of creativity as a style of application of ability and Ludwig's fractal geometry analysis contain the essence of an alternative conceptualization of positive encouragement of creativity (as against simply removing blocks). An important effect of creativity training may be not teaching people thinking skills that they did not possess before, but teaching them how to apply what they already have in a way with which they were not previously familiar. Creativity training based on the style approach would aim at encouraging people to use their existing ability to generate novelty, rather than focusing exclusively on orthodoxy, and giving them practice in doing so, as well as encouraging them to place a high value on generation of novelty, feel good about themselves when they do it, and respect it in others (noncognitive aspects of creativity).

Focusing on the demands of a field, Ludwig's analysis gives even more emphasis to noncognitive aspects. Training aimed at getting people to generate novelty in their field (versus continuing to generate what is orthodox in that field) would focus on impersonality versus emotivity, objectivity versus subjectivity, structure versus lack of structure, and formality versus informality. People in highly impersonal, objective, structured, and formal fields such as requirements engineering would benefit from creativity training that helped them work in a more emotive, subjective, unstructured, and informal way, whereas those in *avant garde* theater would benefit from training in the opposite facets (although the idea of training people to be more impersonal, objective, structured, and formal does not fit well with most discussions of creativity). Ludwig's work suggests that a differentiated approach to creativity training would need to diagnose not only the characteristics of individual people, but of individual fields too.

Contrary to what at first seems to be the case, creativity training aimed at developing what is not there may not be a matter of training missing abilities, skills, and the like, but of encouraging people to change the way they give expression to what they already have. This may involve noncognitive factors and may also require consideration of the demands of the field in which they work in.

SPECIFIC CREATIVITY-FACILITATING TECHNIQUES

Some authors (for a brief overview, see Cropley, 1992b) have emphasized the need to learn special thinking techniques, such as: (a) reversing the problem, (b) considering the end result, (c) focusing on the dominant idea, and (d) discarding irrelevant constraints. Other procedures for training specific thinking skills are game-like, including: (a) producing, (b) analyzing, (c) elaborating, (d) focusing, (e) associating, (f) combining, (g) translating, (h) breaking out, and (i) recognizing the new. All of these are specific thinking techniques, almost tricks, that can be learned quickly and then applied in a wide variety of settings as a help to generating novelty.

Some procedures are more formal, broader, and based on at least a rudimentary theory of the nature of creativity. An example is the *SCAMPER* procedure, originally developed by Osborn (1953) in the advertising industry. This approach assumes that production of novelty essentially involves changing what already exists and includes seven change techniques: **S**ubstituting, **C**ombining,

Adapting, Magnifying, Putting to a different use, Eliminating, and Rearranging/ Reversing. Another procedure in this category is *Bionics*, which involves seeking out instances in nature where a solution to the problem at hand already exists and transferring this solution to the human problem. For instance, a dirt-resistant paint was developed by noting that the underside of the lotus plant's leaves allow virtually nothing to stick to them and reproducing the method used by the lotus plant in paint. The procedure involves three steps:

1. Analyze the essence of the problem to which a solution is being sought

2. Find examples in nature where this problem has already been solved.

3. Transfer as much as possible of the solution to the human problem.

Some procedures are more elaborate and may have a formal, organized set of steps, although they still consist of fairly specific procedures that can be learned and then applied in different situations, usually to get ideas—that is, to generate variability (e.g., *Synectics, Brainstorming, Morphological Analysis, Imagery Training, Mind Maps*, the *KJ Method*, the *NM Method*). Most of these are described by Torrance (1992) or Michalko (1998). Although they are mostly suitable for use with schoolchildren, they are also often applied with adults (e.g., in business product development or advertising). A few of these are discussed here in somewhat greater detail.

Brainstorming (Osborn, 1953) is probably the best known of all idea-getting procedures and has become the prototype for a number of related techniques. In the early 1940s, Osborn, an advertising executive, came to the conclusion that business meetings often blocked generation of new ideas. He proposed a set of rules for interactions among people in groups that would eliminate the blocking effect and encourage participants to come up with ideas for solving a specific problem on which the group was working. The core of brainstorming is unrestricted production of ideas. Although this can be done alone, "classical" brainstorming is a group activity in which all members of the group are encouraged to put forward ideas without any constraints, such as fear of looking foolish, no matter how implausible the idea. There are four key principles:

- Quantity of ideas, rather than quality. is what counts.

- Criticism is not permitted because of its inhibitory effect.

- "Hitchhiking" by attaching one's ideas to those of others is encouraged.

- Wild or exaggerated ideas are welcome.

There are various procedures for recording, selecting, testing, and otherwise ultimately relating ideas to reality (i.e., although the approach emphasizes generating novelty, *Verification* and *Validation* are not ignored). According to the website (www.brainstorming.co.uk), brainstorming has been used successfully in a vast range of different settings, including planning advertising campaigns and developing marketing strategies, as might be expected, but also in developing new products, making investment decisions, designing better insurance policies, developing government policy, and, particularly interesting in a higher education context, designing research projects and planning written documents and reports.

Morphological analysis is a technique for finding new combinations of conditions that define a novel product, let us say a novel kind of pencil. The person or people using morphological analysis (it can be done in a group or alone) start by listing all the attributes of the product they are attempting to expand, improve, or build on in a creative way. Attributes are parts, properties, qualities, and the like. For example, attributes of a pencil would be the material it is constructed of, the material that does the actual writing, hardness/softness of lead, color, thickness, and so on. In the next step, a table is drawn up with each attribute as the heading for a column in the table. All the possible imaginable variations of the attribute in question are then entered into the respective column: Thus, for a pencil, the column "material" might have the entries "wood," "plastic," "glass," "metal," "clay," "blue tack," and so on. The column "material that actually does the writing" might have "graphite," "dry paint," "mud," "tree sap," and so on. The table now contains all possible variations of each attribute that you can think of independently of each other. Finally, in a kind of automated *Generation*, one entry from each column is selected (i.e., one kind of material, one kind of writing substance, etc.) and these are combined (e.g., metal shaft + tree sap, plus one further attribute from each of the other columns). The selections from the columns can be done randomly or on the basis of some kind of heuristic. Each set of combined elements, one from each column, defines a new kind of pencil, although which are practicable designs (if any) is a matter for the *Verification* and *Validation* phases.

The KJ Method was developed in Japan. Like Brainstorming, it is based on generating large numbers of ideas and is also usually a group procedure. Individual members of the group write on cards their ideas about what constitutes the core of the problem at hand (one idea per card). The cards are then sorted into sets (i.e., groups of cards containing statements that define the nature of the problem in a similar way). The different sets are given labels that summarize the essence of the problem as it is defined in a particular set. For instance, a group applying the method to designing a revolutionary new form of public transport might come up with sets of cards that focus on the categories

- How could it be financed?
- What energy source could be used?
- How should routes be planned?
- How could safety levels be raised?
- What special staff training would be needed?

Sets of solutions can then be constructed via a similar procedure.

Mind Maps were originally developed in the 1960s, but have been substantially developed since (e.g., Buzan, 2003). This procedure is usually carried out by individuals working alone. Mind Maps retain the idea of unhindered generation of variability, but go beyond simple blind generating of ideas. The central theme is written down and then a "spray" of associations recorded, without pausing to evaluate, judge, or edit. Each association functions as the possible beginning of a new spray of further associations. Solutions are found by identifying patterns or threads in the masses of associations. To continue with the earlier example, the theme "public transport" might produce a spray of associations, including "passengers," "schedules," and "vehicles." Among the associations to "passengers" might be "complaints," "peak hour masses," "fare evasion," and "security." "Schedules" might evoke among others "frequency," "reliability," and "routes," and associations to "vehicles" might include "comfort," "safety," and "power source." Solutions are found by identifying patterns or threads found in the masses of associations. One thread running through the (entirely fictitious) prior sprays of associations is "Increase numbers of passengers by providing frequent services in comfortable vehicles, using socially acceptable sources of energy and running frequent schedules on high density routes." (This solution is banal, of course, but it was constructed purely to illustrate the nature of the procedure, not to solve mass transit problems.) The mechanics of the procedure have been systematized in recent years, and mindmapping software is available from a number of sources (e.g., www.visual-mind.com).

The Hierarchical Method (e.g., Butler & Kline, 1998) involves an even stronger element of organization and structure. Although the core idea of generating large amounts of variability (possible solutions) is retained, this approach is based on the idea that a hierarchical organization of ideas (rather than simple clusters of related ideas or associational chains) produces solutions of better quality. Suggested solutions are sorted into classes on the basis of common content. Subsequently, hierarchies are formed by combining lower level classes into superordinate classes or, by contrast, by breaking down higher order classes into lower level categories. In the public transport example already introduced, a higher order, general category might be "energy source." At the next lower level in the hierarchy, this category might be broken down into the somewhat more specific categories ("forms of energy" and "methods of harnessing energy"). The category "forms of energy" could have subcategories lower in the hierarchy and more specific and concrete such as "cost," "availability," "environmental impact," and "practicability." Methods of harnessing would have similar more specific and concrete subcategories. At a still more specific and concrete level, "cost" could have categories such as "impact on passenger numbers," "impact on national economy," and "alternative ways of covering costs." It is then possible to work downward through the levels—for instance, identifying the questions that will have to be answered to achieve relevance and effectiveness or identifying answers in one category at a particular level that also apply in another category, possibly being obvious in one pathway through the hierarchy but novel in another.

Formal Training Programs

Even more organized and formalized are a number of creativity-training programs that consist of a package of tutorials or lessons arranged sequentially in order and accompanied by exercises, practice sessions, and the like, often supported by print materials such as handbooks, audio- and videotapes, and so on. To take two examples, Brainstorming and Mind Maps have been formalized in this way and are available commercially on the Internet (e.g., www.brainstorming.co.uk; www.mindsystems.com.au).[2] We listed them above, however, because they can also be applied less formally and used as helpful techniques, rather than formal training programs. Several of these are described herein.

The Purdue Creative Thinking Program (PCTP; Feldhusen, 1988) is based on Torrance's divergent thinking concepts. It is intended for use with elementary-school children, but is included here because it illustrates so clearly the degree of organization and formalization of what we call *programs*. It is also true that the general approach seems to be readily transferable to higher education. The third edition of the program consists of 36 lessons of 14 minutes duration on audiotape. In each lesson, a principle for enhancing one of the aspects of divergent thinking is presented for 3 to 4 minutes, then demonstrated in action through a case study of an individual person lasting about 10 minutes. Finally, each lesson is accompanied by three or four exercises in print form that provide practice in applying the principle demonstrated in the lesson. The case studies are of major contributors to American history, either traditional figures like Christopher Columbus or George Washington, or popular modern figures such as Martin Luther King, Jr. However, the case studies would easily be adaptable to world figures, people from another culture, people from specific fields, and so

---

[2]We are not suggesting that other procedures are not available commercially or on the Internet, or that Brainstorming and Mind Maps cannot be found on other sites. The purpose of the references here is to draw attention to the possibilities via examples.

on. In chapter 10, we describe a university-level engineering course conducted in Australia in which case studies were used as a teaching medium.

Synectics emerged at about the same time as Brainstorming (Gordon, 1961). Gordon worked in the Invention Design Group of Arthur D. Little Inc, a consulting firm that helped companies develop new products. He noticed that some groups were highly productive, whereas others were less productive, and concluded that the differences in productivity derived from the way members of a group interacted, not from ability, knowledge, and so on. In 1960, he founded the firm Synectics. Synectics is available in a formal form online (www. synecticsworld.com). Like Brainstorming, it is based on unfettered production of ideas to solve a problem. However, the essence of Synectics goes beyond simply generating novelty. At its core is the principle of seeing connections between things not normally regarded as connected. Such unexpected links (we called them *remote associates* in chap. 3) generate novelty. They require making analogies—seeing aspects of the other thing that are like aspects of the present problem. Analogies are frequently based on metaphors and are frequently made with living organisms (e.g., a vacuum cleaner is like a pig because both ingest garbage). Synectics is a group procedure. Ideally, one person states a problem, the group helps to define the essential core of the problem, and group members begin generating remote associates by looking at what already exists. They do this, however, by seeing both the present object (let us say, a new kind of vacuum cleaner) and the remote associate (in this case, a pig) in a new way—making the strange familiar/the familiar strange. Seeing a vacuum cleaner as a garbage eater makes the familiar (a vacuum cleaner) strange. Seeing a garbage eater as a pig makes the strange familiar. Such analogies are constructed with the help of special techniques, including Subtracting, Adding, Transferring, Empathizing, Animating, Superimposing, Changing size, Substituting, Fragmenting, Isolating, and Distorting, to give a number of examples. Subsequently, the people in the group identify the link between the new way of looking at the situation and the desired solution to the problem, and work out the value of the analogy in practice (i.e., in our terms, they explore the novelty and verify and validate its relevance and effectiveness). For instance, the group might suggest the idea of a vacuum cleaner with teeth that grind dirt. An example of a synectic approach to generating effective novelty is to be seen in the way the engineer Isambard Kingdom Brunel is said to have hit on the method of tunneling he adopted to build the Thames Tunnel, completed in 1843. He saw his problem as the same as that of the ship's worm, which tunnels through timber by chewing a layer of wood off the surface in front of its mouth and passing the chewed-out wood back along the length of its own body, excreting it behind itself. It then advances by the amount chewed off the surface of the wood and chews off the new surface, repeating the whole process over and over again until it has tunneled right through the wood.

CoRT Thinking Lessons, devised and marketed by Edward de Bono (www. edwarddebonofoundation.com), are based squarely on the view that thinking cannot simply be picked up on the side as a result of academic work such as studying a particular, "challenging" discipline, but has to be taught directly and explicitly. It consists of six sections, each containing 10 lessons; the lessons consist of teaching materials, teacher's notes, and student's notes and are available in print form or as videos. The section most directly relevant to this book is the section on creativity, which is based directly on de Bono's concept of lateral thinking (see chap. 3) and teaches principles for changing the way people look at things. These principles include first important priorities (FIP), consider all factors (CAP), and alternatives, possibilities, choices (APC). It is suitable for use with children and adults.

TRIZ (Altshuller, 1988; Savransky, 2000) is based on the idea that all inventions (i.e., creative solutions to problems) display the same pattern of emergence of ideas. These patterns were identified in an analysis of thousands of successful patent applications. Training in TRIZ is commercially available (e.g., www.Altshuller.ru). It consists of 29 lessons in print form. Training consists essentially of learning 40 inventive principles and how to apply them in one's own thinking. Examples of the 40 principles are:

- Segmentation (an object is divided into parts or the existing degree of division is increased);

- Extraction (the necessary properties must be defined and "extracted");

- Asymmetry (symmetrical objects must be made asymmetrical, already asymmetrical ones even more asymmetrical);

- Consolidation (elements of an object that belong together in time and/or space must be brought together); and

- Reversing (do the opposite of what seems to be required; e.g., make movable parts fixed, fixed parts movable, etc.).

Creative Problem Solving (CPS) is based on Wallas' stage model (see chap. 3). In its "classical" form (Parnes, 1981), it involves five steps that can be applied in a systematic way to finding, investigating, and solving problems. Treffinger, Isaksen, and Dorval (1995) added a preliminary stage at the beginning, with the result that CPS is nowadays understood as having six steps: mess finding, fact finding, problem finding, idea finding, solution finding, and acceptance finding. In his book, Parnes (1981) goes through a large number of problems with readers to make the steps automatic so they can be reapplied over and over again with new problems. Treffinger (1995) extended understanding of CPS by emphasizing that it is not a purely cognitive exercise. He drew attention to the role of other people in the acceptance finding phase, both assisters and resisters. The CPS Group (www.cpsb.com) offers training in CPS.

POPULAR AND COMMERCIAL PROCEDURES

In addition to more scientific work on fostering creativity, there is a substantial number of semiscientific or popular publications with essentially commercial goals aimed at organizations (business/commerce, the armed forces, government) and individuals (adults interested in self-help, teachers, parents). Many of these were developed by practitioners, not necessarily researchers or even traditional educators. Probably the best known are de Bono's publications, in which he has elaborated the concept of *lateral thinking* (e.g., de Bono, 1993). Originally a medical practitioner, he developed not only a graphic and picturesque terminology (e.g., *water* and *rock logic*), but has also published the *CoRT Thinking Program* (de Bono, 1993), a set of strategies for creative thinking that has been widely applied in business and education. Michalko (e.g., 1996, 1998), a former officer in the U.S. Army, has recently become prominent in the United States, with programs such as *Thinkertoys* (aimed at nurturing business creativity) or *Cracking Creativity* (self-training).

Such books are often based on scholarly findings even if the connection is sometimes loose. They are frequently technically well produced, extremely readable, easy to understand, and plausible. In addition, they often contain sensible and humane advice with which few people would disagree, and many of them are undoubtedly capable of bringing benefits. However, there are problems with much of this popular literature, and these were summarized by Hruby (1999, p. 327)—he was reviewing a specific book, but his comments are pertinent and can be applied here in a more general way.

Hruby (1999, p. 327) complained that enthusiasm for fostering creativity can "run away with itself." Among other weaknesses, he identified: presenting speculations, conjectures, and hypotheses as established facts; confusing correlations with causal relationships; making unjustified sweeping generalizations that are either not unequivocally supported by research or contradicted by some findings; drawing unwarranted conclusions about the implications of research findings for practice; and failing to understand the factors that inhibit conversion of admirable recommendations into practice. Some popular books proclaim incompletely digested research findings as containing a revolutionary panacea that can be applied in a set way in any and all situations, without taking account of the individuals involved, the special characteristics of the situation, or the personal or structural factors facilitating or impeding implementation of good practice. We recommend moderation, flexibility, and sensitivity in their use.

THE EFFECTIVENESS OF CREATIVITY TRAINING

But does creativity training work? From almost the beginning of the modern era, doubts have been expressed about whether it actually achieves what it sets out to do, which is to foster creativity (e.g., Mansfield, Busse, & Krepelka, 1978). It is true that that Torrance (1972) analyzed 142 studies of creativity training and concluded that about three quarters of them had been successful, mainly it must be admitted, in improving scores on Torrance's test battery (TTCT; see chap. 8). Despite this, Wallach (1985) argued that the effects of creativity-facilitating programs are narrow and specific, and scarcely generalize to behavior in settings other than those closely resembling the training procedure. Dow and Mayer (2004), for instance, found that spatial training led to improved scores on spatial tasks only.

Scott, Leritz, and Mumford (2004) listed a number of methodological objections that cast doubt on the convincingness of reports that support the usefulness of creativity training. Treffinger, Sortore, and Cross (1993) came to the conclusion that it has not been shown that there are clearly definable effects of creativity training on specific cognitive or personal characteristics, that particular programs foster specific aspects of psychological development, or that people with one particular psychological profile benefit from a specific program, whereas other people need a different one.

Although later programs include knowledge, problem solving, and decision making (Treffinger, Sortore, & Cross, 1993), creativity training has concentrated overwhelmingly in the past, and continues to do so, on the cognitive aspects of creativity even if factors such as self-concept or positive attitudes to problem solving are sometimes considered. Cropley and Cropley (2000) criticized this narrowness in the conceptualization of creativity inherent in the programs and called for an integrative, holistic approach, as did Urban (1997). Such a call is consistent with the position adopted in this book that creativity should be looked at in a differentiated way, and the wide range of components leading to production of effective novelty, cognitive, personal, motivational, and social, all taken into account.

A Meta-Analysis of the Value of Creativity Training

In a comprehensive recent study, Scott, Leritz, and Mumford (2004) reached a more positive verdict about the usefulness of creativity training on several counts. They identified 70 studies published in or after 1980, in which the effects of creativity training were tested empirically. The studies had to meet strict methodological criteria that eliminated some of the criticisms of earlier studies reporting favorable effects of creativity training. There had to be a specific focus on creativity training, the procedure employed in the training had to be clearly described, the measures used to assess the effectiveness of the training had to be clearly identified and described, and statistical data on effectiveness had to be provided. There also had to be some kind of control condition, either a control group or at least a test–retest design. The effects of creativity training were tested statistically by calculating effect strengths.

Effects of Training on Different Domains.   Scott et al. (2004) found that creativity training was effective. The strongest effects were obtained when the criterion was cognitive processes (i.e., improvements in people's divergent thinking and problem solving after training). Within the cognitive domain, the single largest effect of creativity training was on originality of thinking, as defined in chapter 8, although training also enhanced fluency, flexibility, and elaboration. Thus, after training, people produced a greater number of surprising ideas—what we call *generation of novelty*. The second strongest effects of training were on creative performance (i.e., creative products people produced after training). There were also noteworthy effects on attitudes. The effects of creativity training were strong in both children and adults in both educational and noneducational organizations and were found in both gifted and nongifted samples. There were sizable effects for both males and females, but the effects were larger for males, especially with regard to divergent thinking.

> Creativity training does have beneficial effects. In particular (but not exclusively), it promotes generation of novel ideas (original thinking).

Effectiveness of Different Kinds of Training.   Of great interest is that some forms of training worked better than others—there were differences between training procedures in the strength of the effects obtained. When cognitive, social, personality, motivational, and combined training procedures were compared, it was found that the cognitive approach had by far the largest effect. Scott et al. (2004) then divided cognitive training procedures according to the particular process that each procedure emphasized and found that training in problem identification (*Activation*), idea generation (*Generation*), and conceptual combination (*Illumination*) was most effective.

The best way to foster these processes was to give participants opportunities to analyze novel, ill-defined problems, whereas mere unfettered expression of unexplored ideas was actually negatively related to the effectiveness of training. It was also found that highly organized and systematic training based on realistic examples and involving substantial periods of structured, focused practice (i.e., relevant to a field or domain) was most effective, not short bursts of unstructured work on an *ad hoc* collection of activities that might or might not be connected with the setting in which people were to become more creative. Finally, training that started by introducing specific, relevant concepts and basic principles, then moved to targeted practice aimed at acquiring specific skills, achieved stronger effects than holistic training. In connection with the intrinsic versus extrinsic motivation debate, it should be noted that provision of evaluative feedback positively affected improvements in problem-solving and relevant performance criteria, but inhibited improvement in divergent thinking.

The four characteristics of good creativity training according to Scott, Leritz, and Mumford (2004):

1. Training should be based on a cognitive model of creativity (see chaps. 3 and 4).

2. Training should be lengthy and challenging and should involve presentation of discrete cognitive skills whose relevance to creativity should be explicated.

3. Presentation of the material in 2 should be followed by illustrations of their application in the real world.

4. After presentation of the prior material the training should move onto exercises appropriate to the domain in question that give the people being trained practice in applying them in their field.

10

A Case Study of Creative
Instruction in Higher Education

A broad concept of creativity was adopted in an engineering class. Teaching and learning were oriented toward providing a practical concept of creativity, promoting appropriate thinking skills, encouraging positive attitudes to creativity, developing a positive self-image, increasing motivation to be creative, and becoming aware both of the effect of other people on one's own creativity as well as of one's own effects on their creativity. Creativity was not treated simply as an abstract principle, but students were also encouraged to change their actual behavior on an assignment resembling the real-life work of engineers. This task formed part of their assessment in the class (i.e., it was subjected to external evaluation). An evaluation of the effects of the class showed that students had become more creative in both thinking and behavior.

A CREATIVITY-FACILITATING ENGINEERING CLASS

In this chapter, we present a case study of a class in engineering that put into practice a number of the principles for fostering creativity spelled out in earlier chapters. Engineering seems to be a particularly appropriate discipline. At least since the Sputnik shock, university-level teaching of engineering has been widely regarded as indifferent or even hostile to creativity, and empirical studies over the years have supported this view (see Cropley & Cropley, 2005, for a summary). For instance, students at an American university who preferred trying new solutions dropped out of engineering courses three times more frequently than those who preferred conventional solutions, whereas no correlation was found between creativity and grade point averages (GPAs) in engineering courses. Attempts to train engineering students in problem solving have met with only limited success. For instance, it has been shown that emphasizing divergent thinking increases students' interest in generating new solutions, but this is not accompanied by changes in actual behavior.

227

There are other reasons for the appropriateness of engineering as the domain from which to draw the case study to be presented in following sections. The original Sputnik shock was widely interpreted as resulting from a failure of engineering education to foster creativity (i.e., the problem of lack of creativity in this discipline has already been identified and was linked to education). There are some grounds for believing that engineering is a particularly difficult discipline in which to arouse interest in creativity, and engineering creativity is particularly important for the maintenance of national prosperity. Engineering is also an appropriate field because, in addition to being an academic discipline, it is an area of practice that is relevant to the real work of many organizations. Furthermore, it is an area into which scientific and technological creativity is often inserted in practice, so that innovation is of great concrete importance.

> Engineering is a particularly appropriate discipline from which to take a case study of creativity-facilitating instruction.

ORGANIZATION OF THE CLASS

Overview

Participants in the case study were enrolled in a second-year undergraduate course, "Engineering Innovation and Practice" (EIP) in a large engineering school. Contents and form of instruction were adapted to the goal of fostering creativity, as well as learning activities and assignments, and assessment too. The aim was to encourage undergraduates to generate effective novelty—not simply in an abstract sense, but also in a practical exercise of a kind resembling the real-life work of the discipline the students were studying. The core of the class was the assignment: "Build a wheeled vehicle powered by the energy stored in a mousetrap." The students' work on this assignment was assessed on the basis of its creativity, not its correctness, using a scoring scheme based on principles enunciated in chapter 2, referred to briefly in chapter 7, and described in detail in the next chapter. The class was taken for credit as a normal part of the participants' undergraduate program, and they received grades based on assessments of their assignments (i.e., there was a strong element of extrinsic motivation, theoretically fatal for creativity; see chap. 5). In addition, an attempt was made to foster positive attitudes toward creativity as well as to encourage tolerance for other people's ideas or willingness to resist group pressure (chap. 6).

Because of the importance in fostering creativity of making plain to students in a practical and readily understandable way where there are discrepancies between what they are doing and what is needed, we introduced what we called *creativity counseling* into our teaching. A creativity test (the Test of Creative

Thinking–Drawing Production [*TCT–DP*]; see chap. 8) was administered to students, as well as creativity counseling based on test scores.[1]

> The class was eclectic, covering not just knowledge, but also personal and interpersonal factors.

Organization of the Class

During the first week of the semester, the purpose of EIP was explained to the students enrolled in it, as well as the various activities involved in the course. Of particular interest here are the creativity testing, the creativity counseling, the orientation of lecture contents to creativity, and the construction of the mousetrap-powered vehicle. In the second week of the semester, students took Form A of the TCT–DP. In the third week, students were counseled individually by a psychologist. In the second, third, and fourth weeks of the semester, all students in EIP received three lectures about creativity and its link to engineering from a psychology specialist. For the remainder of the semester, all students received normal lectures from an engineering instructor, although these were also oriented toward engineering creativity. In the eighth week, the students who had taken the TCT–DP were retested. Table 10.1 summarizes the organizational steps in the project.

INSTRUCTIONAL ASPECTS OF THE CLASS

The Lectures

The program of instruction involved two kinds of lectures: creativity lectures by a psychologist and engineering lectures by the regular instructor, an engineering professor. The three creativity lectures were aimed at encouraging:

1. appropriate thinking skills;

2. positive attitudes to creativity and creative performance;

3. motivation to be creative;

4. perception of oneself as capable of being creative;

---

[1]Participation in the testing and counseling was voluntary. The result was that we had some students in the class who had been tested and counseled, others who had not, which presented an opportunity for an evaluative comparison of the performance of the two groups. Results of this phase are presented later.

Table 10.1
Organization of the Class

Date	Action	Purpose	Comment
Week 1	Explanation of the structure and purpose of the class Clarification of what they would be required to do.	—to make sure that students understood what they were going to be required to do	*Preparation* phase (students gather knowledge about the problem)
Week 2 (Lab period)	Administration of Form A of the creativity test	—to provide a baseline estimate of students' creative potential —to provide a psychological profile for the creativity counseling	Such data make it possible to evaluate students' work in a formative (and not simply a summative) way
Week 3 (Lab period)	Creativity counseling	—to help students understand in a more concrete way what was meant by behavior and personality traits favorable for creativity —to help students relate these ideas to themselves —to help students understand what they should do differently	*Activation* phase (This information is of crucial importance)
Weeks 2, 3, and 4	"Creativity" lectures	—to open students' minds to the idea of creativity —to provide students with relevant basic concepts —to persuade students that they were capable of being creative	*Generation* phase (contents of these lectures are summarized later)
Week 5 to end of lectures	"Engineering" lectures	—to provide role models of creative engineers —to give examples of creative thinking by engineers	(contents of these lectures are summarized later)

Weeks 4 to 7 (Lab period)	Group work on designing and building the wheeled vehicle	—to give students experience of the effects of working in a group —to enable students to observe and experience how groups affect creativity	*Illumination phase* (we conceptualize group effects in terms of blockers and facilitators)
Week 8 (Lab period)	Retesting with the creativity test	—to ascertain whether the creativity counseling and lectures had had a measurable effect on creativity as a psychological trait	*Verification phase* (criteria for the evaluation are given in chap. 10)
Week 8	Groups handed in their wheeled vehicles, which were evaluated	—to ascertain whether the counseling and lectures had had an effect on practical behavior on an "engineering" task	The social setting in which creativity is to occur is full of blockers and assisters; students need to identify these.
Week 8	Individuals submitted reports on work in their groups	—to test whether students were able to use psychological concepts to analyze thinking processes and interpersonal factors operating within their group that facilitated or discouraged creativity (metacognition) —to test whether students had developed insights into factors within themselves that affected their own or other people's creativity (self-evaluation)	
Week 9 (Lab period)	Students demonstrated their models to other participants in EIP and received feedback from a "jury"	—to foster willingness to reveal ideas to other people (courage) —to encourage students' pride in their own creativity —to give students experience of public evaluation of their creativity —to have some fun (joy of creativity)	*Communication phase* (see expanded-phase model)

continued on next page

Table 10.1
(Continued)

Date	Action	Purpose	Comment
Week 10 (Lab period)	The instructor [the instructor] discussed the vehicles with the students during the laboratory, particularly emphasizing aspects related to creativity	—to encourage evaluation of products —to make the basis of evaluation transparent —to show students what they could have done better	*Validation* phase (an expert [the instructor] publicly judges the creativity of the models)
Week 13	Students handed in a log listing their contribution to the work of their group and evaluating what they had added to the group's work	—to encourage self-evaluation —to promote understanding of group processes in creative work	This log helps to detect "freeloaders" when looked at in combination with reports on the way the group functioned.

5. positive mood in problem-solving situations;

6. recognizing and placing a high value on the creativity of other students, as well as their own; and

7. reduction of anxiety about creativity.

The content of the lectures focused on providing students with a practical, down-to-earth concept of creativity, and thus reducing their skepticism about this topic as something that is not for engineers. The lecturer's intention was that students would transfer ideas from the lectures to working out and evaluating their own assignments. The main topics dealt with were:[2]

1. What has creativity got to do with engineers?

2. Why do engineers have problems with creativity?

3. What are the psychological elements of creativity?

4. What are the characteristics of a creative product?

5. How can you solve problems creatively?

6. What blocks creativity?

These lectures thus provided students with an understandable, practical model of creativity that stressed cognitive, motivational, affective, and social aspects (for greater detail on contents, see chaps. 2-6, of this volume). They emphasized that creative products must not only be novel, elegant, and generalizable, but must also reflect a high level of engineering knowledge (i.e., be effective and relevant). As discussed later, this stress on building a model that really worked, but at the same time displayed novelty, caused difficulty for some students.

The engineering lectures were given by the regular instructor for the course and focused on specifically engineering content. They emphasized the importance of creativity in modern engineering practice and as a factor in developing a career in the field. One of the main forms of content consisted of case studies of innovations in engineering, such as insulin pens, Kevlar, disposable contact lenses, Gore-Tex fabric, Xerox, the GE, Rolls Royce and P&W aero engine maintenance concept, and the development of EBay (online auctions). The purpose of these lectures was to foster:

1. perception of engineers as capable of being creative,

2. understanding of the pressures and rewards of engineering creativity,

---

[2]Specific contents for topics 3 to 6, which are capable of being adapted to any academic discipline, are contained in chapters 1 to 5 (this volume).

3. familiarity with role models of engineering creativity,

4. understanding of the kind of thinking involved in real-world generation of effective novelty,

5. acquisition of positive attitudes to creativity and creative performance, and

6. motivation to be creative.

It is apparent that this list goes beyond simply thinking and encompasses attitudes, motivation, self-image, and similar factors.

In addition, there was a 2-hour laboratory session each week. In the first 8 weeks of the semester, students worked on designing and building their models during the labs, while the lab was also the site of both the public presentation of the completed models and a forum in which the products were discussed and the class evaluated.

Instruction was based on case studies of real-world creativity in engineering.

It emphasized aspects of the work of the people in the case study that demonstrated principles of creativity in practice.

CREATIVITY COUNSELING

Administration of the Creativity Test

Urban and Jellen's (1996) TCT–DP was used to develop a creativity profile for each student who wished to participate in this aspect of the class. The wisdom of referring to procedures such as the TCT–DP as creativity tests is unclear (i.e., their validity has been questioned). Recently, Helson (1999) distinguished between creative potential and creative productivity, pointing out that the former—measured by tests—may or may not lead to the latter. For this reason, we prefer to write "creativity" in quotation marks when referring to the tests or to label them "tests of creative potential." This test is presented in detail in chapter 8, where its rationale, format, administration and scoring procedures, and technical details such as reliability and validity are discussed.

The tests were scored by three graduate students of psychology according to the procedures outlined in the test manual. These raters had been trained to score the test in a half-day workshop. Protocols were identified by code numbers only, and the raters were not informed which group the men whose work they were rating belonged to. In the eighth week of the semester, the students took Form B of the test, and their protocols were once again scored blind by the same raters. Later, a random sample of test protocols were rescored by a fourth rater, also a graduate student in psychology, and an interrater reliability of .94 was obtained, suggesting that test scores were not dependent on which rater scored the protocol in question.

On the basis of scores on 13 of the subtests of the TCT–DP (time taken was excluded from this analysis because it is not clear that it is connected with creativity), a profile was constructed for each of the 37 EIP students who had taken Form A of the test. The profiles focused on three dimensions: Productivity, Originality, and Unconventionality.

Initially, these dimensions were established by means of an intuitive grouping of subscales that experience with the TCT–DP suggested belong together. Subsequently, however, the dimensions were empirically confirmed by a factor analysis of the Form A protocols of 111 male, second-year engineering students (the men who completed Form A in connection with the present study, regardless of the group they belonged to or whether they also completed Form B, plus additional students who took EIP in the next semester). These three factors accounted for about 90% of the accountable variance of the test.

Each participating student was subsequently invited to attend a creativity counseling session, which typically lasted 15 to 30 minutes. The counselors were psychology graduate students who had scored the test protocols. They had also received training in using the test for creativity counseling during the workshop mentioned earlier. Each participant was shown his own profile, and attention was drawn to areas of relative strength and weakness, not in a normative, but in an ideographic fashion. This step was performed without reference to the actual test or scoring criteria. To take a concrete example that illustrates what the procedure was like, a student with high Productivity but low Unconventionality and Originality might be advised, "You produced plenty of ideas. However, only a few of them were novel or unconventional." The student might then specifically thematize issues such as unwillingness to risk doing something "foolish," whereupon the counselor would encourage the participant to distinguish between prudence and excessive caution. If such material were not introduced spontaneously, the counselor would ask the student how he saw the situation or why he was productive but unoriginal. In these sessions, counselors used the language of the creativity lectures (i.e., "divergent thinking," "creativity blockers," etc.).

THE ASSIGNMENTS

The Wheeled Vehicle

The course outline indicated that one of the assignments to be completed and scored as part of the assessment for the course was to build "a wheeled vehicle powered by the energy stored in a mousetrap," and it had to be submitted in the eighth week of the semester. For this practical assignment, students were required to form groups. Each group was given the task of designing and building its own vehicle. Although a passing grade was guaranteed if the vehicle proved to be capable of moving at least a short distance under its own power, assessment emphasized the importance of obtaining a high grade of novelty, elegance, and generalizability (all of which had been explained to the students in the creativity lectures and demonstrated in a practical form in the engineering lectures with the help of the case studies). If students asked for an elaboration of the assignment, they were told that from the point of view of the instructor the problem was sufficiently defined by the words, "Design and build a wheeled vehicle powered by the energy stored in a mousetrap," although they were reminded that the class was about engineering innovation. Some students expressed annoyance at this, in essence demanding what we have called overdefinition of the problem, and the instructor was regarded by some as hard or unreasonable or unhelpful. Such is students' love for overdefined problems.

After the vehicles were demonstrated in action in the lab and then handed in to the instructor, they were rated on four dimensions according to the subjective judgment of the rater: Effectiveness (whether or not they traveled the required distance), Novelty (originality and surprisingness), Elegance (understandability and workmanlike finish), and Germinality (ability to make people think about the whole idea of "wheeled vehicle," "powered by," ability to open up new perspectives).[3] These four dimensions are a fusion of categories from existing scales for assessing creativity of products (see chap. 8). In addition, each vehicle was awarded points for the overall impression it made, bearing in mind that the students had been urged to make their vehicles as creative as possible. In all five categories, a vehicle could receive from 0 to 5 points, with intervals of 0.25 points between ratings being possible (i.e., scores such as 3.50 or 2.75 could occur). The machines were assessed blind (without knowledge of the group to which a particular student belonged) by an engineering instructor. Unfortunately, because the models were part of the students' exams and had to be returned to them quickly, there was only time for a single rater to assess them, so that the level of agreement between raters (interrater reliability) could not be determined.

Reports on Group Functioning

Creativity is often viewed as something best done in groups, the group being regarded as a source of novelty and a forum in which variability can be explored in search of effective novelty. However, as pointed out in chapter 7, it is well

---

[3]Subsequently, we have modified the scoring system subtantially, although it is still based on these dimensions. Chapter 11 contains a more detailed discussion of the more recent scoring procedure, including an example.

known that the group can inhibit creativity by intimidating people who might otherwise have generated novelty. To make such positive and negative group influences explicit, each student was required to submit a written report on the effects of the group on him and on his estimate of his effect on the group. In particular, students were expected to examine cognitive, personal, motivational, and social effects of the group. At the end of the semester, students were required to hand in a log summarizing concrete details of their own work in the group (e.g., "I attended group meetings on the following days . . ."; "I was given the task of finding suitable materials for building our vehicle and reported back on . . ."). They were also required to analyze and evaluate their own contribution to the conceptualization and construction of their group's vehicle.

THE EVALUATIVE PHASE

Case studies of changes in instruction are frequently confined to a description of the procedures and enthusiastic comments about their effects. When we introduced EIP, we wanted to evaluate its effects on students in a formal way, and not simply rely on our subjective feelings about the class. For this reason, we incorporated an evaluative phase into the project. Because of well-known gender differences in creativity test scores and effects of creativity training, possible confounding of the results of the evaluation of the project by gender needed to be controlled. The small number of female students in EIP meant that this could most easily be done by confining the evaluative phase to males. However, all female students who wished to take part in the class did so and participated fully in creativity testing, counseling, and model-building.

From the beginning, it was emphasized that participation in the testing and counseling was voluntary. About 60% of the 64 male students in the course did in fact volunteer ($N = 37$). They are referred to in the following as the "counseled" group. Of these people, 3 did not complete the class, leaving a reduced group of 34. The remaining 27 EIP students (the men who declined to volunteer for the evaluation phase) attended the lectures and submitted the vehicle, but did not complete the test or receive counseling. They comprise the "lecture" group. Male volunteers were also recruited in a different engineering course that included none of the elements of EIP. These students ($N = 21$) did the creativity test with the EIP students, but did not attend EIP lectures, receive counseling, or build a wheeled vehicle. They formed the "control" group.

The 85 men in the three groups ranged in age from 18 to 25 years. It is important to note that the counseled and control groups were self-selected, whereas the men in the lecture group, who simply attended lectures and built the model, were "refusers." Thus, the possibility cannot be discounted that the counseled and control groups contained men particularly receptive to material on creativity, whereas the lecture group men were particularly unreceptive. Indeed, the TCT–DP scores of counseled students and controls were considerably higher than scores for similar groups given in the test manual, thus supporting the view that our participants in the evaluation phase were positively disposed to creativity. Subsequently, creativity test scores of the counseled and control group students were compared. In addition, and more interesting from a practical point of view, it was possible to compare the models built by students who had been counseled and those who "merely" attended lectures in EIP.

WHAT HAPPENED?

What emerged from all of this is presented in two parts: on the one hand, results relating to TCT–DP scores and involving comparisons of the counseled group with the control group; and on the other hand, results relating to the assessment of the vehicle and involving comparison of the counseled group with the lecture group.

Changes in Test Scores

The first results are derived from a comparison of the test scores of the counseled group with those of the control group. The members of both groups were tested with the TCT–DP and retested 6 weeks later. At the time of the second testing, the counseled group's members had received counseling based on their creativity profiles and had attended the lectures on creativity. The control group had simply waited 6 weeks. Both groups consisted of volunteers, a fact that is likely to have reduced the possible confounding effects of self-selection, because both groups' members had opted in. Indeed, because the controls were not even in EIP, but responded to a general appeal in second-year courses, the volunteer effect may well have been stronger in their case than in that of the counseled, and would thus have acted conservatively as far as any possible counseling effects were concerned (i.e., it would have reduced the chance of creativity differences in favor of the counseled).

The TCT–DP scores of the counseled and control groups, both total scores and also scores on the various dimensions, were compared. The statistical analysis indicated that there was a large increase in the mean creativity score of the counseled from the first testing to the second, whereas the mean of the controls remained almost unchanged. Thus, it can be concluded that simply waiting 6 weeks for the second testing had no effect on the mean score of the controls, precisely as common sense would suggest, whereas participation in lectures and counseling led to a significant increase in the scores of the counseled. The lectures and counseling had "worked," so to speak.

The subdimensions of the TCT–DP on which the participants in EIP obtained significantly greater increases on retesting than the controls were in essence tasks requiring either (a) producing something fundamentally new (as against extending or altering something that already existed), or (b) using the materials in a radically unconventional way. Some controls drew figures on the second testing that were more novel than they had been on the first testing, but these mainly remained within the existing framework. For instance, on the retest, they elaborated existing figures in a freer fashion than before, which can be attributed to the fact that on the second occasion the test materials were familiar and the unstructured nature of the task less inhibiting. By contrast, the EIP students went further. As a group, they were more prepared to introduce new material out of their own heads or to change the existing structure. The untrained students increased their scores, but did so by being less inhibited, whereas the people taking EIP increased their scores by being more innovative.

This interpretation is supported by the fact that the variance of the EIP group decreased at the second testing, whereas that of the control group increased. In the treated group, weaknesses were reduced, thus homogenizing performance, whereas in the untreated group, those with higher initial scores became more adept with experience of the test, whereas those with lower scores to start with remained limited in their answers. Thus, the quantitative differences between the counseled students and the control group seem to reflect a qualitative effect of counseling on behavior: Both groups produced more novelty at the second testing (quantitative difference), but lectured and counseled students did this through introduction of novelty, whereas the control group did it through becoming less inhibited.

Creativity of the Product

The second set of results focused on the mouse trap-powered vehicles submitted by the students. Models built by members of the counseled group (who had taken the test, been counseled, and received the lectures) were compared with those of the lecture group—who had not taken the test and had not been counseled, although they did receive the lectures. All participants, regardless of whether they had received counseling, succeeded in constructing a vehicle that met the minimum formal requirements (it had wheels and was capable of moving itself). Several of the resulting models were elegantly designed and well finished. However, most students, regardless of the group they belonged to, assumed that the vehicle had to be four-wheeled and had to run on the ground like a car or truck. In addition, most focused on the energy stored in the trap's spring as the source of power, as well as consciously opting for a vehicle that was effective (in that it could move) and socially acceptable (in that it looked like existing motor vehicles).

Only a few groups were able to achieve a dramatic breakaway from conventional thinking. One group built a large hollow wheel set rolling by a weight mounted in its interior and wound into position by the mousetrap's spring, thus redefining *wheeled vehicle* (see Fig. 10.1). This approach involved synthesis of known elements, the traditional mechanical energy of the spring being combined with the effects of gravity on the mass of the mousetrap to propel the vehicle.

An even more surprising solution was achieved by one group that constructed a car that was thrown by a catapult powered by the mousetrap's spring. The car flew more than a meter through the air and had wheels, even if it did not run on them. This model introduced a novel principle: The power source did not travel with the vehicle. It is shown in Figure 10.2.

More radical in some ways was a wheeled cart attached to the mousetrap by a string. When the mousetrap was thrown off the table on which the vehicle stood, its weight pulled the vehicle along as the trap fell to the floor, thus using the gravitational force acting on the mousetrap's mass as the source of energy. The only limit on the distance this method could propel the vehicle was the height of the surface from which the mousetrap was thrown and the length of the string. This group redefined the idea of "energy stored in a mousetrap," seeing the mass of the mousetrap in a new way as a source of energy, whereas most others focused on the mechanical energy of the spring. Another group that redefined "energy stored in a mousetrap" set fire to the mousetrap and used the heat generated by the flames to produce steam that moved the vehicle

FIG. 10.1.   A redefinition of *wheeled vehicle.*

FIG. 10.2.   A novel application of the energy stored in the mousetrap.

a short distance, thus using the chemical energy stored in the wooden base of the mousetrap. A final group used the mousetrap's spring to compress a bellows and inflate a balloon, which then deflated violently and drove the vehicle by its jet action.[4]

> Students were able to build effective models (they worked), but generating novelty was less common. Nonetheless, some groups succeeded in redefining existing materials or synthesizing elements not usually linked together.

Comparison of Groups

Comparison of the means of the scores assigned to the models built by counseled and uncounseled students showed that the mean of the counseled group on Elegance was significantly different from the mean of the group that "merely" received lectures on creativity. The difference between the mean of the counseled students on Overall Impression and that of the lecture group was also statistically significant. In all other cases (Novelty, Germinality, and even Effectiveness), the means of the counseled students were numerically higher than those of

---

[4]Two additional vehicles are presented in chapter 11, where they are evaluated in detail.

the lecture group (i.e., it is possible to speak of a tendency for the counseled group to surpass the group without counseling on the various assessments of their vehicles).

> Students who had received more creativity training achieved more novelty.

WHAT DOES THIS ALL MEAN?

The results show that, in addition to producing more novelty in the test setting, the counseled students transferred this to the actual building of a vehicle. This finding is of considerable interest because it involves a criterion intuitively resembling the actual work of engineers, raising the hope that the effects obtained in this study might persist in real-life settings. This was achieved despite the fact that the students were working for grades (extrinsic motivation) and supports the position of Eisenberger and Armeli (1997) rather than Amabile (1983). The "counseling" described here gives practical hints on implementing Eisenberger and Armeli's recommendation for concrete feedback to students on what they need to do differently to behave more creatively.

When their instructors ask engineering students to create novelty, they expose them to a dilemma. Engineering requires high levels of expertise—mastery of basic knowledge, skills, and techniques. The public wants machines to work and bridges to continue standing. Thus, mastery of what already exists has a high value for students, and production of novelty runs directly counter to this tradition. Paradoxically, however, production of novelty is highly prized. Somehow a compromise must be found between two apparently contradictory ways of behaving. Some researchers have discussed the problem of encouraging people who possess a high degree of expertise to retain the ability to break out of the straitjacket of their own expertise and look at their subject with the openness and freshness of beginners. The present study can be seen as looking at this issue from the other end of the scale: It is concerned with how to encourage beginners to develop expertise, but at the same time remain capable of creating novelty.

Subjective reports from students taking EIP indicated that their reactions were mixed. Some thought that the whole thing was mere tomfoolery, whereas others were highly enthusiastic. Some students marched out of the administration of the TCT–DP, but others announced that they had been waiting for such an opportunity ever since starting at university. By and large, it can be said that the large majority of students could see the sense of such a class and found building the vehicle an interesting and stimulating task.

One problem with the group work was that most of the work was done by one or two enthusiasts, other members enjoying a free ride. This issue was discussed in later class sessions, where the point was made that having passengers in the group can be a problem in real life. Chapter 7 discussed factors associated with teamwork in the context of the institutional environment. One partial solution to this problem in the case of the particular class, if not in everyday life, was to require each individual participant to submit a log showing his contribution to the work of the group in terms of time, ideas, and completion of concrete tasks, and insisting on concrete examples. This log was discussed with the full group and eventually graded. Of course, a log showing no contribution or rejected by the balance of the group as a fabrication was graded zero, thus reducing the freeloader's overall grade substantially.

It is scarcely conceivable that the brief training provided in the present study would bring about profound and long-lasting changes in participants' ability or personality structure. However, it was possible to show them a different way of solving an engineering problem that they found enjoyable, as well as to give them a convincing demonstration of their own ability to come up with ideas. In this sense, the study offers hints about how to influence the emergence of attributes such as specific knowledge about creativity, divergent cognitive strategies, and a positive attitude to novelty. However, there seems little likelihood that such attributes will persist unless they are further developed by appropriate follow-up activities.

> The training had effects of the hoped-for kind, although the question of how persistent they would be or how much they would generalize to other areas remains open.

GENERALIZATION TO OTHER CLASSES AND DISCIPLINES

The four characteristics of effective creativity training (according to Scott, Leritz, & Mumford, 2004) are summarized earlier: It should be cognitive, challenging, linked to the real world of the discipline in question, and followed by practical exercises. The best way to implement these principles is to give students necessary concepts for understanding creativity, base their training on realistic examples relevant to their discipline, provide opportunities to develop their own structure for novel ill-defined problems, and require them to carry out substantial periods of structured practice focused on their discipline. Training should start by introducing specific relevant concepts and basic principles, and then move to targeted practice aimed at acquiring specific skills. These principles seem to be sufficiently general to be transferred to other disciplines.

Although the class described in this book was not designed on the basis of prior knowledge of Scott, Leritz, and Mumford's principles, it went a considerable way toward satisfying them, and thus can be seen as a general example. The practical exercise was preceded by an introduction to relevant creativity theory, the relevance of creativity for students' future work as engineers was stressed, many practical examples of creativity in engineering were given, the assignment involved an "engineering" problem (as against general creativity exercises of some kind), the problem was only loosely defined and attempts by students to extract more information from the professors were resisted, and they were given the opportunity to work on their project for several weeks.

Three questions are of great importance at this point:

1. To what extent can the approach to teaching and learning demonstrated here be applied in other engineering classes?

2. To what extent can the approach be transferred to other disciplines in higher education?

3. To what extent can the approach described here be transferred to other institutional and organizational settings?

Although the case study in this chapter is a case study of an educational action aimed at fostering creativity, to some extent conditions prevailed that resemble those of real-life work in organizations:

- a task requiring creativity was identified,
- design work was carried out in a team,
- an actual working product had to be constructed,
- the product had to be communicated to others, and
- there was a risk of sanctions if the creativity went wrong.

It seems to us that it offers insights into fostering creativity in other settings too, such as in industry, administration, finance, and the like. However, we focus here on the first two questions.

In other publications, we have argued against consigning creativity to a specific class and returning to business as usual in the rest of the curriculum. What is needed are general principles with which the entire curriculum can be infused. Which elements of the present class can be generalized in this way?

Contents

If they are to generate effective novelty, students (and workers too) need to acquire a systematic understanding of creativity and a set of concepts and terminology for evaluating their own work, understanding what they are trying to do, and understanding their supervisors' comments (see e.g., Eisenberger & Armeli, 1997). The contents of EIP sought to provide the necessary information. A general case for the necessity of creativity is easy to make nowadays because this is so widely accepted (see chap. 1). Instructors could return to this theme in classes in many disciplines. Material on the nature of creativity in a particular discipline, criteria of creativity in the particular discipline, and concrete examples of creative work could also be introduced in a wide variety of disciplines.

Creativity-related content that is relevant for classes in all disciplines:

- what has creativity got to do with this discipline?
- characteristics of a creative product, both in general and in this discipline
- psychological elements of creativity in the individual (thinking, personality attitudes and motivation) both in general and in this discipline
- social factors in creativity, especially as they influence this discipline
- the way creativity manifests itself in the actual practice of this discipline
- how to solve problems creatively, both in general and in this discipline
- what blocks creativity, both in general and in this discipline

---

Methods

Case studies of actual events in the discipline in question could be used to organize and unify content in all classes, with emphasis on, for instance, the domain-relevant problems besetting the person in the case, the process of production of relevant novelty, the source of motivation, the effect of the social environment, and so on. Consider the cases of, for instance, Semmelweiss or Galois, who introduced effective novelty only to have it rejected by the people around them, albeit for different reasons. The provision of creativity counseling is more problematic. Among other things, ethical issues may need to be considered, as students may feel that their privacy is being invaded or that they are being used as guinea pigs. In this case study, we offered the counseling as a helpful teaching and learning activity, but emphasized that only students who opted in would be involved. Some students did in fact decline, and this decision was accepted without any comment or pressure. However, many students welcomed this aspect of instruction. Furthermore, when the whole concept of the class was explained, many of them saw the testing as a necessary prerequisite for specific counseling targeted at their personal strengths and weaknesses.

Assessment

In discussing assessment, chapter 11 distinguishes between the setting of assignments that foster creativity and criteria for grading such assignments. Essentially, what is recommended are open assignments involving an activity similar to what people actually working in a particular domain normally do and requiring the exercise of imagination and fantasy for good grades. The assignment in the present case study is an example that is suitable for engineering classes. The general idea, however, is readily transferable to both other engineering classes and completely different disciplines.

For instance, take education aimed at fostering creativity in music, a field that seems to have little in common with engineering. In an interesting analysis, Odena (2001) saw it as involving promotion of:

- working reflectively and spontaneously;

- adopting and developing ideas;

- using thinking skills such as analysis and evaluation;

- selecting and combining resources within *existing* musical structures and genres, styles and traditions; and

- carrying out practical musical activities, such as improvisation and composition.

These principles are highly consistent with the ones spelled out earlier in an engineering context.

To apply such principles in, for instance, a history class, the instructor might set as an assignment: "Suppose that the South had won in the American Civil War. Analyze the causes of their victory as a modern historian might do it." A mathematics professor might ask: "What would be the consequences for mathematics if parallel lines were found, in fact, to meet." In a law class, the assignment might be: "Prepare a football rule book as it would look if it were written by a senior judge." Experience indicates that it is necessary to remind students that pseudocreative flights of fancy are not what is desired, but reasoned arguments showing deep knowledge of the relevant facts (relevance and effectiveness) that nonetheless succeed in generating effective novelty and show elegance and generalizability.

STOCKTAKING

In chapters 1 to 9, we laid down a framework for fostering creativity based on relevant theory and research. In the case study described in the present chapter, we have given an example of what our principles could look like in practice. We now turn to a discussion of how the class in the case study represents a realization of a number of the principles sketched out in earlier chapters. Summary Table 10 highlights the key principles from earlier chapters and demonstrated in the case study that we believe foster creativity. As a result, the case study makes it possible to see in a concrete way what is meant by the principle in question.

Summary Table 10
Principles for Fostering Creativity Demonstrated in This Case Study

Recommendation
The activity should be sustained over some time.
The activity should be demanding.
The activity should involve a clear concept of creativity.
The activity should involve a product and require not only novelty, but also relevance and effectiveness.
The activity should involve *general* cognitive content, but simultaneously, *specific* domain content.
The activity should emphasize links with the real world.
It should be made clear to students what they are expected to do differently.
The activity should go beyond thinking and include motivation and personality.
The activity should go beyond thinking and include social aspects.
The activity should go beyond thinking and include attitudes and values.
The activity should take account of the demands of the field.
The activity should aim at all students, not just a chosen few.
The activity should require knowledge of the field.

Assessment and Creativity:
A Problem-Solving Approach

In keeping with the differentiated approach to creativity and innovation adopted in this book, we look at assessment of creativity from the point of view not only of the **P**roduct (or, as we prefer to say, *solution*), but also from the perspective of one of the new **P**s that we have added to the traditional four **P**s of creativity—**P**roblem. Related directly to assessment in higher education, this means that we regard assignments as problems that students have to solve, and treat their responses as solutions. This process makes it possible to apply the material in earlier chapters to working out guidelines for using assignments to foster creativity. Three aspects are important: (a) the statement of the problem (i.e., the form in which assignments are set), (b) the processes of problem solving (i.e., what people have to do to generate answers), and (c) the criteria for assessing solutions. Overdefined problems (i.e., narrowly and concretely defined ones) inhibit creativity, whereas under-defined problems encourage it. Processes such as finding problems, generating novelty, defining solutions, and recognizing solutions yield effective novelty. Products need to display relevance and effectiveness, novelty, elegance, and generalizability. These can be identified with the help of indicators such as "diagnosis," "redefinition," "surprisingness," "harmoniousness," and "germinality."

PROBLEM SOLVING AND CREATIVITY

Guilford (1950), the initiator of the modern creativity era in psychological thinking, described creativity as problem solving, and defined it (Guilford, 1959) as having four stages:

- recognition that a problem exists,
- production of a variety of relevant ideas,

- evaluation of the various possibilities produced, and

- drawing of appropriate conclusions that lead to the solution of the problem.

This approach has been the object of considerable attention over the years since Guilford (e.g., Newell, Shaw, & Simon, 1962) and has a well-established place in creativity research. More recently, Rabinowitz and Glaser (1985) also adopted a problem-solving approach, emphasizing the importance of effective internal representation of information, rapid information processing, and flexible use of information-processing strategies. Boden (1994b, p. 113), using the language of artificial intelligence, stressed the importance in creativity of "representation of structural features" of a domain. These authors may be regarded as examples of the current problem-solving approach to creativity theory—one based on information processing, often using the language of information technology and cognitive science. Mumford and his colleagues have applied this approach in practice in a series of research studies, in which they looked at various aspects of problem solving and creativity: problem construction (Mumford, Baughman, Threlfall, Supinski, & Costanza, 1996) or category combination (Mumford, Supinski, Baughman, Costanza, & Threlfall, 1997).

The four aspects of problem solving listed previously correspond well to the seven phases of the expanded-phase model presented in chapter 4. Table 11.1 maps the steps in problem solving onto the phases of the extended-phase model. In this chapter, we stay close to Guilford's approach.

We regard assignments set by teachers as problems and students' essays, term papers, lab reports, and similar work as solutions. We then adapt the problem-solving approach to work out guidelines for setting assignments and assessing the results (e.g., grading assignments or evaluating proposals) in such a way as to promote creativity.

Table 11.1

Relationship Between Problem Solving and the Phases of Creativity

Phase	Mental Action in Problem Solving
Preparation	Knowing enough to recognize that a problem exists
Activation	Defining the problem and redefining it
Generation	Producing many candidate solutions
Illumination	Recognizing promising novel solutions
Verification	Recognizing an effective solution when one occurs
Communication	Making the solution available to other people
Validation	Working out the implications of the solution for effective application in practice (i.e., for innovation)

The Components of Creative Problem Solving

In working out guidelines, we distinguish between *creative* and *ordinary* problem solving. Our approach is based on creative problem solving (for a more detailed discussion, see Marvszewski & Noscal, 1995). For present purposes, the crucial thing about creative problem solving is that creative problems allow various ways of understanding what the core of the problem is, allow for differing ways of setting about solving the problem, and permit a variety of solutions. Put in a somewhat more practical way:

- the problem is not specified exactly,
- the nature of the solution is largely open,
- the pathway to the solution is not specified, and
- the criteria for recognizing a solution are open.

To return to the phase approach, in creative problem solving, the *Preparation* and *Activation* phases are not curtailed or, in the case of educational settings, virtually eliminated for the problem solvers (students working on assignments) by teachers who specify the results of their own *Preparation* and *Activation* phases as part of the problem description. The problem solver's task begins at an earlier phase. This focus emphasizes the importance of a number of components of problem solving, and these are discussed in more detail in following sections.

Knowledge.   We already emphasized that problems cannot be solved by people who know nothing of the contents of a domain, except perhaps via blind luck or accident. This point was discussed at length in chapter 3. Sternberg (2006), Savransky (2000), and Altshuller (1988) elaborated on the processes through which existing knowledge is applied to solve problems creatively. However, as important as it is for problem solving, knowledge of the domain is not specifically a characteristic of creative problem solving, because it is also important in ordinary problem solving. For this reason, knowledge plays only a subordinate role in forms of assessment aimed at fostering creativity. Clear identification of the problem as well as knowledge and understanding of its elements and dimensions are essential for relevance and effectiveness, but not enough for a creative solution. Nonetheless, knowledge is indispensable and cannot be ignored. We regard it as a prerequisite, rather than the central issue. Although its importance must be kept in mind, it is not elaborated on any further in this chapter, the emphasis of which is to bring out the special characteristics of creative problem solving.

> Conventional knowledge is important for creative problem solving, but is mainly to be regarded as a prerequisite for creativity.

Problem Finding.   At least until the dawning of the modern creativity era, the idea of problem solving was encapsulated in intelligence testing. The person being tested is presented with a clearly defined problem, for which there is a known answer that the person either already knows and need only recall from memory store or else can work out by applying known techniques or logic. The examiner merely has to check whether the person has given the one and only correct answer (which is to be found in the test manual). Becoming good at this was, by and large, what was regarded as the purpose of teaching and learning and, of course, was emphasized in setting and marking assignments.

However, from the beginning of modern interest in creativity, some writers argued that the special thing about creative problem solving is that it departs from this paradigm and involves not solving well-defined problems that have already been constructed by somebody else, but finding or defining your own problems (e.g., Torrance, 1965). Creativity researchers spoke of "problem aware-ness," "problem recognition" and the process of "problem finding" or "problem definition." As Dillon (1982) pointed out, it is possible to distinguish between recognizing problems that are already evident in the present organization of available information and are obvious to any qualified observer, discovering hidden problems, and, finally, inventing problems. Merely recognized problems may well be solvable without creativity, or solving them may even be inhibited by creativity, as we argue later. In modern times, it has been recognized that invented problems have most to do with creativity (Jay & Perkins, 1997), and Mumford and coworkers (1996) identified problem construction as one of the main cognitive processes involved in creative problem solving.

CASE STUDY: Defining the Problem in a Creativity-Facilitating Way

In a civil engineering setting, it was necessary to drill a large number of holes in hard, prefabricated concrete slabs. The drill bits kept snapping un-der the excessive load, delaying the work considerably and causing extra costs. A group of engineers was given the task of solving this problem. They conceived the problem as successfully drilling holes and the solution as developing bits to do this. They tried using special steel and also making the bits sharper, but without success. Only when finding a solution proved much more difficult than expected did they redefine the problem: They now saw it not as drilling holes, but as avoiding the need for the holes that were causing all the problems. They redesigned the concrete slabs in such a way that they slotted together without holes.

> The first step in creative problem solving is defining the problem yourself.

Finding Good *Problems.*   However, simply finding any problem is, although presumably better than nothing, not enough. Tardiff and Sternberg (1988) not only stressed the importance in creativity of sensitivity to problems, but went further and emphasized an additional element: finding good problems. Getzels and Csikszentmihalyi (1976) concluded that this is as much the case in artistic as in scientific creativity. A striking example of both these aspects of creative problem solving is Einstein's recognition that existing theories of electrodynamics were inadequate in dealing with moving bodies. He (a) invented a problem where many others saw none, and (b) identified the good aspect of this problem, which quickly led to the special theory of relativity, revealed the need for a general theory of relativity, and ultimately resulted in lasting fame. Good problems are those that not only provoke a helpful answer to a specific situation, but also yield or even require elegant and generalizable solutions (i.e., they lead on to new things that go beyond the present situation). In the previous case study, the new design of prefabricated slabs was transferred to many other building sites. Solutions to the best problems lead to Nobel prizes and similar awards.

> Creativity is enhanced by finding good problems.

Problem-Awareness.   However, problem finding is not as straightforward as might be thought. Sosa and Gero (2003, p. 25) recently argued that many creative products are developed "to satisfy the needs of . . . social groups." As we see it, the needs may be concrete and down to earth, such as cheaper power or a cure for a particular disease, but they may also be more general, such as better educational methods or more beautiful ways of combining colors on canvas, or more abstract, such as improved ways of expressing feelings through music. Generally, the social groups whose needs must be satisfied are (a) people who are knowledgeable in a domain—specialists or experts, or (b) users of the domain—people who are in some way affected by it. The people who are motivated to solve the problem are most commonly active in the domain as practitioners, experts, researchers, and the like. In general, only such people are sufficiently engaged with a domain to notice problems. Those who have no contact with an area seldom (although perhaps not never) experience the need for solutions to problems or produce solutions in that domain. Such people lack problem awareness or, in terms of the expanded-phase model, have not passed through the *Preparation* and *Activation* phases.

> Problem awareness is a central element in creativity.

Creative Solutions

Even creative solutions to problems must be "appropriate," "correct," "useful," or "valuable," as Amabile and Tighe (1993, p. 9) put it. Poincaré (2003[1908]) made the same point nearly 100 years earlier, and Bruner (1962) referred to the necessity of *relevance* and *effectiveness*. But appropriateness and correctness are required in conventional solutions too. You do not get large numbers of points on an IQ test or on a conventional school achievement test for irrelevant, incorrect answers, nor in the real world either. At the practical level, this notion is particularly obvious in domains such as engineering, where usefulness and similar properties are easy to define and are uncompromisingly expected (with a few exceptions, as in the example of the Sydney Opera House already given). How, then, does creativity go beyond correctness, appropriateness, usefulness, or value to expand the idea of a solution?

As we have seen already, the first special characteristic of a creative solution to a problem (vs. a routine solution) is novelty. However, novelty, unexpectedness, surprisingness, and the like are not required for ordinary problem solving and, indeed, are likely to be rejected or punished. Creativity thus expands the idea of *solution* by adding the criterion of novelty. In discussing the creativity of products, however, we have already gone beyond novelty in chapter 2. Other authors too have done the same; Taylor (1975), for instance, focused on generation, reformulation, originality, relevancy, hedonics, complexity, and condensation. Besemer and O'Quin (1999) added resolution (the product is valuable, logical, useful, and understandable) and elaboration and synthesis (the product is organic, elegant, complex, and well crafted). We have already summarized some of these characteristics in the criteria of elegance and generalizability proposed in chapter 2 as additional criteria of creative problem solutions in addition to effectiveness and novelty, as well as in chapter 8.

> The main characteristic of noncreative problem solutions is correctness (relevance, effectiveness). Creative solutions, by contrast, are characterized (in addition to correctness) by properties like generation, reformulation, originality, relevancy, hedonics, complexity, condensation, elaboration, and synthesis.

The hierarchical organization of products shown in chapter 2 introduced an important principle into the discussion of problem solving: Creativity is not an all-or-nothing quality of a solution. There are levels and kinds of creativity. It is not something that solutions either have or do not have. Different solutions can have creativity to greater or lesser degrees or can display different kinds of it. We already suggested different labels for different kinds of creative solutions ("original," "elegant," "innovative"), whereas the hierarchical organization of these kinds of creativity means that there are also levels of creativity (innovative solutions are more creative than elegant ones, whereas elegant solutions are more creative than original ones).

> Creative solutions can display both greater and lesser amounts of creativity (quantitative difference between solutions), as well as different kinds of creativity (qualitative differences).

Defining the Solution

The traditional model of problem solving sketched out earlier presupposes that the solution is known and can be recognized by a knowledgeable observer—in our experience, this situation is precisely the one that teachers and, above all, students like best. However, where problems are loosely defined and the solution pathway involves branching out, making unexpected connections, trying unlikely possibilities, taking a risk, being tolerant of uncertainty, using nuanced judgment, and the like (see chap. 3), it may be difficult to say just what constitutes a solution or to recognize a solution when one is at hand. Indeed, Ghiselin (1955) argued that recognizing solutions is the key to creativity.

The case study of the pathologist who did not realize that he had discovered penicillin (see chap. 4) is a striking example of failure to recognize a solution. A simple example from the business world is seen in the report that Victor Kayam declined the opportunity to purchase the rights to Velcro because he could not see any practical application for it. Both Eugen Semmer and Victor Kayam had an extremely important, novel, effective, elegant, and generalizable solution in their hands, but did not see it. These two examples can be contrasted with the case of Antoine Henri Becquerel, who did recognize a solution when he saw one and subsequently shared the 1903 Nobel Prize for physics with Marie and Pierre Curie.

> Because of their novelty, unexpectedness, and the like, as well as people's commitment to a particular way of conceptualizing a situation, creative solutions may be difficult to recognize when they occur.

THE EFFECT OF THE PROBLEM ON CREATIVITY

One way of showing the relationship of creativity to problem solving is to focus not on creativity, but on the problems. Sticking to the three dimensions introduced at the beginning, problems can be divided according to:

- their degree of definition,

- the degree to which the solution pathway has already been defined, and

- the clarity of the criteria for recognizing a solution.

Clearly defined problems that are solvable by means of standard techniques and for which there are obvious and well-known criteria identifying the solution constitute routine problems. They can often be solved without the need to generate novelty, although when existing knowledge is applied in settings where it has previously been treated as irrelevant, a certain technical or inventive creativity occurs. Nonetheless, creativity is not absolutely necessary and is probably not usual. By contrast, some problems require (a) becoming aware that there is a problem at all and finding a way of defining it, (b) working out techniques for solving the problem, and (c) developing criteria for recognizing a solution. Such loosely defined problems often demand a high level of creativity.

Hence, certain kinds of problems (routine problems) may actually inhibit creativity (see also earlier discussions of high expertise and creativity). It also seems that a too highly defined definition of the solution may hinder problem solving. We have already argued (Cropley & Cropley, 2005) that this was the case with the new Collins class submarines built for the Australian navy in the 1990s, where the desired result was so narrowly defined (even down to the exact nature of the design of the propeller and the materials from which it was to be constructed) that little creativity was possible, and the constructers were almost condemned to build a beautifully designed and finished boat with a high level of physical comfort for the crew, but only limited combat capacity. The submarine is reminiscent of the Ferrari case study presented later in this chapter. Applied to setting assignments in higher education, the effect of highly defined problems on the creativity of solutions means that care is required in the way problems are presented to students. Inappropriately stated problems can block creativity from the start. Table 11.1 makes some suggestion for how to set assignments in an appropriate way.

Overdefined problems inhibit creativity. In education, for example, overdefined assignments are bad for creativity (although they are easier to correct and assess, and are therefore well liked by both professors and students).

It is also conceivable that the reverse could occur: Creativity could inhibit the solving of routine problems, for instance, by making the solver overlook perfectly effective and obvious (but not novel) solutions and look for obscure (novel) ones, or by encouraging the solver to go beyond the actual problem at hand and define it in an excessively complex fashion. In the case of loosely defined problems, in contrast, creativity may be indispensable. However, although loose problem definition may facilitate or even demand creativity, it does not guarantee creative solutions (because it is possible that no effective solution may be achieved), but merely opens the doorway for them. Furthermore, because, as we have argued, creativity is not an all-or-nothing phenomenon, although there are different forms of creativity, loosely defined problems may elicit different amounts of creativity or creativity in different aspects of the solution, according either to the aspects that are loose or the predilections of the problem solvers. This idea is demonstrated by the following evaluation of the mousetrap-driven cars described in the previous chapter.

Existing Approaches to Problem-Setting in Education

A simple example of the first kind of problem, which inevitably leads to the one and one only correct answer and is unsolvable for people without the necessary (specifiable in advance) knowledge and/or reasoning skills, is to be seen in standardized achievement tests. The instructions to these tests often contain elaborate details that exclude any uncertainty about what is required. In our terms, the tester's intention is to exclude the possibility of any test candidate discovering or inventing a problem. There is a payoff to defining the problem in a circumscribed manner and precluding problem finding (i.e., in concentrating on ordinary problem solving—it simplifies the search for a solution and standardizes the kind of solution likely to be reached). In education, such problems are greatly admired by testers and examiners, because all relatively knowledgeable persons being tested quickly recognize what is required by the problem and confine themselves to the limited range of possible solutions implied by the problem's definition—indeed, it is quite possible, or even usual, that there may only be a single answer. Even those who do not possess sufficient knowledge to solve the problem play by the rules, often acknowledging their lack of knowledge and behaving as good losers.

Thus, scoring and grading are simplified and arguments about the accuracy of assessment are eliminated. However, such problems stifle creativity. From the point of view of creative problem solving, they are overdefined. Nonetheless, it is extremely hard for teachers to break away from the habit of overdefining the problem. Furthermore, students like such problems, because there is always a specifiable answer—the teacher knows it, knows how to find it, and can give appropriate guidance on request. The learners' task is clear-cut (learn the facts by heart) even if many of them do not relish the idea of doing the necessary work. In effect, the solution too is overdefined.

In all probability, an answer is to be found for any overdefined problem somewhere on the Internet. The solution can be obtained with sufficient searching and copied down, without the need for too much thinking. This notion raises one of the concerns of some teachers at various levels of education—the trend toward students coming into possession of massive amounts of raw information that they can download without the effort of making notes and retyping, but about which they understand little. We have already emphasized the need for extensive information and do not wish to seem to be complaining that students know too much. However, from our point of view, blind regurgitation of facts—straight from the screen to the student's assignment, without going through anybody's brain on the way—is the opposite of what we want to achieve. The decisive pedagogical device for inhibiting blind regurgitation of information is the way assignments are stated and assessed. The purpose of this chapter is to show how this can be done even if students do not like underdefined problems that require them to define the problem, indicate the criteria for identifying a solution, recognize solutions when they see them, and so on, and teachers do not know how to evaluate them.

> Students and teachers like overdefined problem statements because they are easier to prepare for and assess. Both groups need to learn about loosely defined problem setting: How to set and assess them.

PREFERENCE FOR OVERDEFINED PROBLEMS— A CASE STUDY

A case study of the reactions of teachers and pupils based on grading practice at the University of Adelaide in South Australia at two points 100 years apart is informative here.

CASE STUDY: "Le plus ca change, le plus c'est la meme chose"

In 1904, there was an unusually high failure rate among Western Australian high school students taking the matriculation examination for admission to the University of Adelaide (there was at that time no university in Perth). This led to an intense public discussion (e.g., Morning Herald, 1904). The complaint was straightforward: The university had changed its assessment criteria and made the exams too difficult.

The problem was that the university had suddenly set assignments such as "Make an evaluation of the historical accuracy of Sir Walter Scott's historical novels," whereas what the parents and protesting teachers had expected was "List three examples of anachronisms in the novel Ivanhoe." The complainants specifically criticized the fact that it was not possible to learn the answer to the "Make an evaluation..." example by heart, and students would have had to use their own judgment with the associated risks. Protesting parents and educators made it plain that they were not demanding an easy examination, but one that they saw as predictable, objective, and fair (and solvable by means of earnest hard work).

Almost 100 years later, in 1996, the same university changed the criteria for admission to medical school—as a rule, students in Australia enter medical school directly from high school, and the number of applications exceeds by far the number of places available. As a result, students are traditionally awarded places on the basis of their high school grades—high grades mean admission, regardless of other properties that may be relevant to being a doctor. The new criteria involved a combination of high school grades, scores on an aptitude test, and results of an interview. Among other things, the latter two procedures assessed problem-solving ability, communication skills, and ability to work in teams.[1]

There was a public outcry. Some candidates with extraordinarily good high school grades did not obtain a place, and the university was depicted in the press as being anti-academic. Some parents even went to the South Australian ombudsman (without success), although the procedure had been judged by educational theorists to be "based on cogent reasoning."

In 1996, too, the thrust of the objections was that (a) problem-solving ability and the like are ill defined and subjective, (b) the new approach meant that what students needed to know could not be reduced to predefined factual knowledge that teachers know in advance and can pass on to students, and (c) the necessary qualities (problem solving, teamwork) cannot be acquired through honest toil over textbooks, whereas "the facts" of physics, chemistry, and biology can. In both cases, the call was for assignments that were, in our terms, overdefined, with highly defined solutions, and a clearly defined pathway to the solution (learning by heart).

It seems that the liking of teachers and students of overdefined problems had not changed much during the course of an entire century! In fact, in October 2006, the university announced that from 2007 greater emphasis would be given to traditional criteria.

---

[1] Our intention here is neither to criticize nor praise the new procedure. What is important is the contrast between the old and new approaches.

SETTING ASSIGNMENTS

What does all this mean for practice? Although it would be possible to tease out from these thoughts practical suggestions for business, we concentrate here on education and, in particular, on classroom teaching. The link between the university classroom and creativity has a substantial history in Sputnik-era thinking. From the beginning of the era, the modern creativity discussion focused on education. Immediately following the Sputnik shock of 1957, the perceived defeat of American engineers in the first event of the space race was attributed to defects in their education, and the now familiar call for education to foster creativity arose. We turn first to the question of how to set assignments that encourage creativity.

The first practical requirement is setting tasks that permit, facilitate, provoke, or even demand creative solutions: in our terms, underdefined problems. These require knowledge, to be sure, but encourage or require application of knowledge to find good problems and construct novel and effective solutions. In our opinion, the key difficulty here is the one already referred to: Not only do teachers like overdefined problems or even have difficulty breaking away from them, but students like them too because they are so clear-cut. Both parties know how to prepare themselves and what is expected of them, even students who do not make any particular effort to prepare well. As a university student, Cropley Sr. was a master at predicting what questions would be on the final (through an analysis of past papers) and focused on preparing only for what he knew was coming. Overdefined examinations were vital to his ability to pass, and ill-defined problems would have represented a disaster for him.

Setting Underdefined Assignments

Our position is that, from the point of view of fostering creativity, the new versions of the 1904 assignments and the new 1996 selection procedure were preferable to the more traditional forms of assignment that protesters demanded. Table 11.2 offers more general guidelines for setting assignments of a kind that would have defeated Cropley Sr. and have caused fury in Perth in 1904 or Adelaide in 1996. The rows in the table are derived from earlier sections of this chapter; the columns represent a progression from more general, abstract guidelines to increasingly specific specifications; and the entries in the cells are derived from ideas developed in earlier chapters of this book. The thrust of these guidelines is to set assignments that encourage problem finding and solution definition, while providing enough structure and definition to block wild speculation and blind idea production (i.e., pseudo- and quasicreativity).

Table 11.2
Guidelines for Setting Assignments

Domain	General Principle	Practical Guidelines
Problem finding	Do not overspecify the problem	• Set "open" or ambiguous problems • Set assignments in the form of open issues such as gaps in existing knowledge, conflicts of opinion, etc. • Set varied, even apparently conflicting source material
	Encourage finding good problems	• Encourage students to state "the problem" as they see it • Emphasize the importance of selecting problems that have the potential for elegance and/or generalizability • Encourage students to discuss the "goodness" of the problem as they have defined it
Finding solutions	Do not overspecify the solution	• Set tasks with multiple, even conflicting answers • Set tasks without a set answer • Encourage students to test the limits of the acceptable in their solutions
	Encourage solution recognition	• Encourage students to state what they would regard as a satisfactory solution, and why • Encourage students to evaluate how well what they have done matches the solution definition given by the instructor • Encourage students to evaluate how well what they have done matches their own solution definition • Encourage students to look for and specify "wrong way barriers"

EVALUATING ASSIGNMENTS

A closely related aspect of practice that is of considerable concern to many teachers is that of evaluation or grading. Teachers at all levels are nowadays expected to state in advance, in relatively concrete and objective terms, the criteria they will employ in grading students' assignments, and to show in actual grading practice how these criteria were applied. Under such conditions, teachers need to be able to specify criteria in an understandable way and, in the case of poor, or even less than perfect grades, to show how things should have been done differently. Although the call for clear criteria is linked by some teachers with a general, undesirable climate of dissatisfaction and unwillingness to accept authority, the idea that assessors should state what they are looking for and show where students' performances have failed to meet expectations is not simply a political/legal issue and has much to recommend it from the point of view of fostering learning.

The Effects of Evaluation on Creativity

In real life, even people in aesthetically creative areas (such as literature, music, or fine art), where, we argued earlier, pressure for concrete effectiveness may be less than in medicine, business, engineering, and the like, are usually subject to external evaluation of their work. We suspect that the idea of completely intrinsically motivated creators, who produce novelty for no one but themselves and care nothing for other people's opinions, is not an accurate representation of the majority of creative people. We have already drawn attention to the widely held view that creativity is actually in the eye of the beholder (i.e., the external assessor), and that a product is only creative when knowledgeable people apply this label. We have also called for an expanded-phase model of creativity that includes, among other things, phases of communication to other people and external evaluation by those people.

Turning to education, it is often assumed that evaluation is inherently inimical to creativity. Amabile's (1996) research is frequently taken to have established that extrinsic rewards inhibit creativity and thus to have shown that grades (because they are given by the teacher, not by students themselves, and are thus extrinsic) are bad for creativity. However, Eisenberger and Armeli (1997) showed that the giving of grades can promote creativity, even in such intrinsically creative areas as music, provided that: (a) instructors know what it is that they are trying to promote, and (b) students know what it is that they are expected to do differently to be creative. Although it must be admitted that the area is still beset by differences of opinion (e.g., Joussemet & Koestner, 1999), what seems to be important for teachers is that they are familiar with what it is that they want students to do in assignments and they can:

1. show students how to evaluate their own work from the point of creativity,

2. recognize aspects of students' work that can be said to be creative,

3. show students where any creativity lay,

4. show them where they have fallen down, and

5. give guidelines on how to do better.

> Despite an impression to the contrary, appropriate forms of assessment can encourage creativity, even in aesthetic areas.

Guidelines for Creativity-Facilitating Assessment

In Table 11.3, we have derived from earlier sections of this book a generalized set of guidelines for assessing solutions in a way that encourages creativity—represented as the Cropley Solution Diagnosis Scale (CSDS). The material can be used for assessing both the amount of creativity and also the kind (i.e., both quantitatively and also qualitatively). The rows in the tables (novelty, elegance, and generalizability) are derived from the criteria of a creative product summarized in chapter 2. As in Table 11.2, the columns represent a progression from more general, abstract criteria to increasingly specific and concrete indicators, and the entries in the cells are derived from ideas developed in this and earlier chapters. These guidelines and criteria are not meant to be treated as exhaustive, but only as an indication of what is needed and a first step toward establishing concrete criteria.

It might be thought that judging such properties is so subjective as to run the risk of becoming arbitrary, thus defeating the purpose of constructing the table. However, Hennessey (1994) reported interrater agreement ranging up to .93 even among untrained undergraduates who rated aspects of creativity simply by applying their own subjective understanding of these qualities. Other studies also suggest that judging properties connected with the creativity of products such as novelty, effectiveness, or understandability is not as difficult as might be supposed. Vosburg (1998) reported that untrained judges who rated products on 7-point scales such as *very understandable—not at all understandable* achieved interrater reliabilities of about 0.90.

APPLYING THESE GUIDELINES

What is needed now is a practical example that shows how the criteria function when applied to a specific assignment. The example that follows is taken from the case study in chapter 10. The actual wording of the assignment was to "construct a wheeled vehicle powered by the energy stored in a mousetrap that is capable of moving at least a short distance."

Table 11.3

Guidelines for Assessing the Creativity of Solutions:
Applying the Cropley Solution Diagnosis Scale (CSDS)

Principle	Kind of Solution	Criterion	Indicator
Relevance and effectiveness	Routine solution	Satisfying requirements in the problem statement	*correctness* (solution accurately reflects conventional knowledge and/or techniques)
			effectiveness (solution does what it is supposed to)
			appropriateness (solution fits within task constraints)
Novelty	Original solution	Problematization	*diagnosis* (solution draws attention to shortcomings in what already exists)
			prescription (solution indicates how what already exists could be improved)
			prognosis (solution indicates likely effects of changes)
		Adding to existing knowledge	*replication* (the known is transferred to a new setting)
			redefinition (the known is seen or used in a new way)
			combination (generation of new mixtures of existing elements)
			incrementation (the known is extended in an existing direction)
			reconstruction (an approach previously abandoned is shown to be useful)
		Developing new knowledge	*redirection* (the known is extended in a new direction)
			reinitiation (solution indicates a radically new approach)
			generation (construction of fundamentally new—but at least potentially effective—solutions)

Elegance	Elegant solution	External elegance: Effect on other people	*recognition* (the beholder sees at once that the solution has something)
			convincingness (the beholder is convinced by the solution)
			pleasingness (the beholder finds the solution "beautiful")
		Internal elegance: Ideas are well worked out and hang together	*completeness* (the solution is well worked out and "rounded," not just fragmentary)
			harmoniousness (elements of the solution fit together in an internally consistent way)
Generalizability	Generalizable solution	Ideas go beyond the immediate problem	*foundationality* (solution lays down a general basis for further work)
			transferability (solution offers ideas for other, apparently unrelated problems)
			germinality (solution suggests new ways of looking at existing issues or problems)
			seminality (solution draws attention to previously unnoticed problems)

Setting the Assignment

The problem was open, even ambiguous. This ambiguity exposed students to the danger of interpreting it to mean that they had to design a conventional car or truck and assuming that the source of power had to be the mousetrap's spring (i.e., of defining the problem in a conventional way). The assignment offered opportunities for solutions capable of eliciting a "Now why didn't I think of that?" reaction from observers (i.e., of elegant solutions even if few students took advantage of this possibility). The greatest strength of this assignment is that it did not overdefine the solution. It involved a task with multiple, even conflicting solutions, without a set answer, and offered an opportunity for students to test the limits of the acceptable, as indeed several of them did (see chap. 10).

Grading the Assignment

The grader's task is to distinguish among widely differing models in a systematic way that students can understand and that provides not only a summative evaluation from both quantitative and qualitative viewpoints, but also offers hints on how to do better on future tasks of this kind. Two examples of differing solutions are graded next using the indicators in Table 11.3.

The first example is a well-constructed conventional vehicle that met the formal criteria (it was a wheeled vehicle, it was powered by a mousetrap, and it moved). This model is shown in Fig. 11.1 and is henceforth referred to as the "Ferrari." It is quite attractive and ingenious and shows that the students involved went to a considerable degree of trouble to design and build it. It also worked

FIG. 11.1. The "Ferrari" mousetrap-powered vehicle.

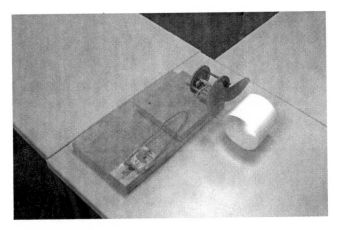

FIG. 11.2. The "Fan" mousetrap-powered vehicle.

in the sense that it covered the required distance. However, it is immediately apparent that it is quite conventional (e.g., understanding *wheeled vehicle* as a four-wheeled vehicle in the general form of an automobile).

This vehicle can be contrasted with an alternative solution that involved a redefinition of *wheeled vehicle* and a novel means of propulsion, although it retained the potential energy stored in the mouse trap's spring as the source of power (see Fig. 11.2). The spring was used to drive a fan, and the wind created by the action of the fan was used to propel an ultralight cylinder (a large wheel). Again, it is immediately apparent that there is a dramatic difference between the two models. *Wheeled vehicle* is understood quite differently (and unconventionally) in comparison with the Ferrari model, as is *powered by*, while the method for transferring the energy stored in the mouse trap also differs from the Ferrari, as well as being unexpected.

What is now needed is a system for analyzing these solutions that brings out sharply how much they differ (with regard to criteria of creativity) and in what way they differ, doing so in a way that is readily understandable and readily communicable to people, such as the students who built the models, and can be applied by different raters in a consistent way. In the next section, we do this using the system presented in Table 11.3.[2] A summary of the scoring is given in Table 11.4.

---

[2]For simplicity's sake, we award points only on a "Yes" or "No" basis: If a criterion is satisfied, one point; if it is not, zero points. In practice, it would be possible to grade on, let us say, a 5-point basis such as: *pronounced, obvious, easily observable, weakly present,* and *absent,* thus providing more differentiated feedback.

Table 11.4

Assignment of Points to the Ferrari and the Fan on CSDS

Principle	Criterion	Indicator	Ferrari	Fan
Relevance and effectiveness	Satisfying requirements in the problem statement	• *correctness* (solution accurately reflects conventional knowledge and/or techniques)	—	—
		• *effectiveness* (solution does what it is supposed to)	—	—
		• *appropriateness* (solution fits within task constraints)	—	—
Generation of novelty (i.e., aspects of the process)	Problematization	• *diagnosis* (shortcomings in what already exists are revealed)	0	—
		• *prescription* (points at which what already exists could be improved are indicated)	0	—
		• *prognosis* (broad suggestions are made for how to carry out improvements)	0	—
	Adding to existing knowledge	• *replication* (the known is transferred to a new setting)	—	—
		• *redefinition* (the known is seen or used in a new way)	—	—
		• *combination* (generation of new mixtures of existing elements)	—	—
		• *incrementation* (the known is extended in an existing direction)	—	—
		• *reconstruction* (an approach previously abandoned is shown to be useful)	0	0
	Developing new knowledge	• *redirection* (the known is extended in a new direction)	0	—
		• *reinitiation* (thinking begins at a radically different point from the current one)	0	—
		• *generation* (construction of fundamentally new—but at least potentially effective—solutions)	0	—

Elegance (i.e., aspects of the solution)	External elegance: Effect on other people	• *surprisingness* (the beholder is "surprised" by the solution)	0	1
		• *convincingness* (the beholder is convinced by the solution)	1	0
		• *pleasingness* (the beholder finds the solution "beautiful")	1	1
	Internal elegance: Ideas are well worked out and hang together	• *completeness* (the solution is well worked out and "rounded," not just fragmentary)	1	0
		• *harmoniousness* (the elements of the solution fit together in an internally consistent way)	1	0
Generalizability (i.e., aspects of the solution)	Ideas go beyond the immediate problem	• *foundationality* (the solution lays down a general basis for further work)	0	1
		• *transferability* (ideas are offered for other, apparently unrelated problems)	0	0
		• *germinality* (the solution suggests new ways of looking at existing issues or problems)	0	1
		• *seminality* (the solution demonstrates the existence of previously unnoticed problems and/or suggests solutions)	0	0
		TOTAL SCORE	11	17

The Ferrari

The Ferrari was a wheeled vehicle and moved at least a short distance. Thus, it successfully takes the first hurdle of relevance and effectiveness and could be evaluated for creativity. It displayed knowledge of existing principles and facts (correctness, effectiveness, appropriateness), but did not in any way show concern about problems with existing approaches or improve them in any way (no points for Problematization). It displayed a certain degree of novelty in that Lego is not usually used in classroom assignments, although the use of Lego to make models is commonplace. Thus, it scores a point for *replication* (see Table 11.4). The mouse trap was also used in a new way (*redefinition*), and there was a *combination* of existing elements (model building with Lego and mousetrap), while there was perhaps *incrementation* (use of the mouse trap spring was extended, but in an existing way, because the well-known "snapping shut" action of the mousetrap was retained). Thus, the Ferrari scores four points for adding to existing knowledge. However, it did not develop any new understandings of lego, mousetrap, or wheeled vehicle, and no points for developing new knowledge. Thus, there was some Generation of Novelty—four points in all. In the area of Elegance, this model scores well. It is unsurprising, to be sure, but is *convincing, pleasing, complete,* and *harmonious*—four points. In the area of Generalizability, however, it offers no basis for further work, suggests nothing that can be transferred, and offers no new way of looking at "wheeled vehicle," and thus scores zero, yielding a total score of 11, largely obtained via elegant and effective use of the known. The Ferrari group would be praised for their workmanship, but advised to introduce more novelty.

The Fan Vehicle

In some ways, the fan-driven vehicle suffers by contrast with the Ferrari, but overall it obtained substantially more points. It was a wheeled vehicle and moved some distance, and was thus relevant and effective. It also shows knowledge of the basic facts (one point). Unlike the Ferrari, it receives points for *diagnosis, prescription,* and *prognosis,* because it draws attention to the need to change from vehicles with a power source that travels with the vehicle, indicates a possible line of improvement (ultralight vehicle), and shows roughly how these two ideas might be combined: three points for Problematization. The lever action of the trap's spring is used to drive a fan (*replication*); *wheeled vehicle* is defined in an unusual way (*redefinition*); the combination of mousetrap, fan, and wheeled vehicle is uncommon (*combination*); and the already known ability of fans to impart movement to light objects is extended from air or smoke to a wheel (*incrementation*). The known fan action is used in a new way by using it to drive a vehicle (*redirection*); "propelled by" and "wheeled vehicle" are existing concepts, but are taken in a new direction (*reinitiation*); and the whole results in a solution that suggests a new line of attack: an ultralight vehicle that does not carry the power source with it (*generation*). Thus, the fan car receives 10 points for Generation of Novelty.

In the case of Elegance, the fan vehicle is surprising and elicits a feeling that it is clever (*pleasingness*), but is perhaps not convincing. It is also only fragmentary and rather crude and scores zero for internal elegance: two points only for Elegance. Finally, the fan vehicle suggests where further work could be done (ultralight vehicles, stationary power source, use of moving air as a driver—*foundationality*) and suggests putting the vehicle inside the wheel instead of the reverse (*germinality*): two points for Generalizability. Thus, the fan car receives 17 points.

The Fan lost points to the Ferrari for its roughness and lack of detail, but gained more than the Ferrari for new ideas and generalizability. The pluses of the Fan in these areas considerably outweighed its minuses in the area of Elegance. In discussing their work with them, the Fan group would be praised for their divergent thinking, nonconformity, and courage in the introduction of effective novelty, but advised to work out their ideas more fully and build a more finished prototype. The Ferrari group would be praised for the elegance of their design, but urged to think more divergently and have more courage.

CASE STUDY: The Cropley Solution Diagnosis Scale (CSDS)

The creativity assessment scale was tried out in a small study in which it was used by 13 school teachers (9 women and 4 men) with a wide age range (20–50) to rate the Ferrari and the Fan vehicle. They did this on two occasions separated by a 2-hour training in how to recognize the creativity of products (this was based on chap. 2 of this book). On the second occasion, the mean score for the Ferrari was 11.50 (SD = 2.87) and for the Fan vehicle 16.07 (SD = 2.25). These scores correspond closely to our own ratings made prior to meeting the teachers: We gave the Ferrari 11 points and the Fan 17. (It seemed more appropriate to compare the teachers' second assessment with ours because we had already had experience with the use of the scale.)

The Ferrari ratings on the second occasion correlated 0.79 (Pearson *r*) with the initial ratings. The Fan ratings, however, correlated only 0.42 with the initial ratings. In other words, the Ferrari ratings were only moderately affected by the training session, whereas the Fan ratings changed considerably. What caused this? The means for both vehicles were numerically lower on the second rating than on the first (Ferrari: 12.93 vs. 11.50; Fan: 16.87 vs. 16.07). However, the SD for the Ferrari was numerically higher

---

(continued on next page)

(2.87 vs. 2.61) on the second assessment, whereas that for the Fan was lower (2.60 vs. 3.67). The only numerical differences that were statistically significant were the difference between the Ferrari and the Fan means, on both occasions. Other numerical differences are used here only to provoke and structure the following discussion.

After training, 8 of 13 raters gave the more obviously creative Fan vehicle a reduced score (4 increased, 1 unchanged), while 6 reduced their rating of the Ferrari (5 increased, 2 unchanged). Our speculation is that the positive judgment "creative" was initially based principally on novelty: The Fan was surprising and therefore judged by several raters to be highly creative, whereas the Ferrari was predictable and therefore initially dismissed as uncreative. After training, the raters who relied on pure novelty gave the Fan a lower score (although still higher than the Ferrari), thus lowering the mean and reducing the variability of scores. The mirror image of this was that several raters now saw the Ferrari's virtues and gave it a higher score, thus increasing the variability of ratings. In other words, raters had become more discerning after training and understood creativity in a more differentiated way, being less influenced by mere surprisingness.

Generalizability of This Scheme

This approach to assessing creativity can be used with a wide variety of tasks. For instance, it can be applied to this book. We have displayed knowledge and made a diagnosis by drawing attention to shortcomings of existing ideas. We have suggested new ways of looking at these problems, thus displaying germinality, and have developed a prescription. These achievements have involved replication, redefinition, combination, and incrementation of existing knowledge and led to redirection, reinitiation, and generation. We judge ourselves to have scored 5 points for Elegance and 3 for Generalizability (including germinality). Thus, we perhaps immodestly award our own product 18 points. Regardless of whether this is too generous, the evaluation of our own book using Table 11.3 gives an example of the application of our scheme to a different kind of product than the engineering example involving the wheeled vehicle models (i.e., an example of the approach's Generalizability).

If we turn now to the assignment on the work of Sir Walter Scott from the 1904 English examination discussed earlier, it is also possible to use Tables 11.2 and 11.3 to assess the new version of the assignment ("Make an evaluation of the historical accuracy of Sir Walter Scott's historical novels"), in contrast with the original version ("List three examples of anachronisms in *Ivanhoe*"). The new version set an open problem, invited discussion of gaps in knowledge or conflicting opinion (i.e., it did not overspecify the problem), encouraged students to define the precise problem, and focused attention in a general way on an issue that could be generalized to other writers (i.e., it encouraged finding a good problem). Thus, it would be judged to be a good assignment in the area of Problem Finding. In addition, it involved a task without a set answer, opened up the possibility of multiple or even conflicting answers (i.e., it did not overspecify the solution), offered students an opportunity to go as far as they dared, and encouraged them to define for themselves the criteria of a satisfactory answer (i.e., it encouraged solution recognition). Thus, it would also score well in the area of Finding Solutions.

By contrast, the traditional statement of the problem met none of the criteria listed in Tables 11.2 and 11.3, although it is not apparent from the actual wording of the assignment what literature was set to support students' preparation for the exam. Tables 11.2 and 11.3 offer guidelines with which it would have been possible to explain in a systematic way to protesting teachers and parents where the strengths and weaknesses of the two types of assignment lay, although this does not guarantee that they would have preferred the new assignment. Unfortunately, no material is available from 1904 about how answers were evaluated, so that the usefulness of Tables 11.2 and 11.3 for helping the people 100 years ago to assess assignments is not known. Nonetheless, these examples offer grounds for believing that the approaches outlined here can be applied in many disciplines in higher education.

References

Abra, J. (1994). Collaboration in creative work: An initiative for investigation. *Creativity Research Journal, 7,* 1–20.

Ajzen, I. (1991). The theory of planned behavior. *Organizational Behavior and Human Performance, 50,* 179–211.

Albert, R. S., & Runco, M. A. (1989). Independence and the creative potential of gifted and exceptionally gifted boys. *Journal of Youth and Adolescence, 18,* 221–230.

Alliance of Artists' Communities. (1996). *American creativity at risk: Restoring creativity as a priority in public policy, cultural philanthropy, and education.* Portland, OR: Author.

Altshuller, G. S. (1988). *Creativity as an exact science.* New York: Gordon & Breach.

Amabile, T. M. (1983). Social psychology of creativity: A componential conceptualization. *Journal of Personality and Social Psychology, 45,* 357–376.

Amabile, T. M. (1996). *Creativity in context.* Boulder, CO: Westview.

Amabile, T. M., Goldfarb, P., & Brackfield, S. C. (1990). Social influences on creativity: Evaluation, coaction, surveillance. *Creativity Research Journal, 3,* 6–21.

Amabile, T. M., & Gryskiewicz, N. D. (1989). The creative environment scales: Work environment inventory. *Creativity Research Journal, 2,* 231–254.

Amabile, T. M., & Tighe, E. (1993). Questions of creativity. In J. Brockman (Ed.), *Creativity* (pp. 7–27). New York: Simon & Schuster.

Anderson, C. C. & Cropley, A. J. (1966). Some correlates of originality. *Australian Journal of Psychology, 18,* 218–227.

Anderson, J. R. (1976). *Language, memory and thought.* Hillsdale, NJ: Lawrence Erlbaum Associates.

Anderson, N., & West, M. (1994). *The Team Climate Inventory: Manual and Users' Guide.* Windsor: NFER-Nelson.

Andreasen, N. C. (1987). Creativity and mental illness: Prevalence rates in writers and their first degree relatives. *American Journal of Psychiatry, 144,* 1288–1292.

Anthony, E. J. (1987). Risk, vulnerability and resilience: An overview. In E. J. Anthony & B. J. Cohen (Eds.), *The invulnerable child* (pp. 3–48). New York: Guilford.

Austin, J. H. (1978). *Chase, chance, and creativity.* New York: Columbia University Press.

Australian Bureau of Statistics. (2003). *Innovation in Australian business.* Accessed May 8, 2006, at www.abs.gov.au.

Bacon, F. (1899). *Advancement of learning and Novum Organum* [1605]. New York: The Colonial Press.

Bacon, F. (1909). *Essays, civil and moral and The New Atlantis* [1627]. New York: Collier.

Baer, J. (1998). The case for domain specificity of creativity. *Creativity Research Journal*, *11*, 173–178.

Bailin, S. (1988). *Achieving extraordinary ends: An essay on creativity*. Dordrecht: Kluwer.

Bandura, A. (1962). Social learning through imitation. In M. R. E. Jones (Ed.), *Nebraska Symposium on Motivation* (pp. 211–269). Lincoln: University of Nebraska Press.

Barron, F. X. (1969). *Creative person and creative process*. New York: Holt, Rinehart & Winston.

Barron, F. X. (1972). *Artists in the making*. New York: Seminar.

Barron, F. X., & Harrington, D. M. (1981). Creativity, intelligence and personality. *Annual Review of Psychology*, *32*, 439–476.

Basadur, M., & Hausdorf, P. A. (1996). Measuring divergent thinking attitudes related to creative problem solving and innovation management. *Creativity Research Journal*, *9*, 21–32.

Berlyne, D. E. (1962). *Conflict, arousal and curiosity*. New York: McGraw-Hill.

Besemer, S. P. (1998). Creative product analysis matrix: Testing the model structure and a comparison among products—three novel chairs. *Creativity Research Journal*, *11*, 333–346.

Besemer, S. P., & O'Quin, K. (1987). Creative product analysis: Testing a model by developing a judging instrument. In S. G. Isaksen (Ed.), *Frontiers of creativity research: Beyond the basics* (pp. 367–389). Buffalo, NY: Bearly.

Besemer, S. P., & O'Quin, K. (1999). Confirming the three-factor creative product analysis matrix model in an American sample. *Creativity Research Journal*, *12*, 287–296.

Biermann, K.-R. (1985). Über Stigmata der Kreativität bei Mathematikern des 17. bis 19. Jahrhunderts [On indicators of creativity in mathematicians of the seventeenth to nineteenth centuries]; *Rostocker Mathematik Kolloquium* [Rostock Mathematics Colloquium], *27*, 5–22.

Biggs, J. B. (2003). *Teaching for quality learning at university* (2nd ed.). Buckingham: Open University Press.

Bloom, B. S. (1985). *Developing talent in young people*. New York: Ballantine.

Boden, M. A. (1994a). Introduction. In M. A. Boden (Ed.), *Dimensions of creativity*. Cambridge, MA: MIT Press.

Boden, M. A. (1994b). What is creativity? In M. A. Boden (Ed.), *Dimensions of creativity* (pp. 75–118). Cambridge, MA: MIT Press.

Boden, M. (1995). Creativity and unpredictability. *Constructions of the Mind*, 4(2). Updated 4 June 1995.

Brophy, J. (1987, October). Synthesis of research on strategies for motivating students to learn. *Educational Leadership*, pp. 40–48.

Brophy, D. R. (1998). Understanding, measuring and enhancing individual creative problem-solving efforts. *Creativity Research Journal*, *11*, 123–150.

Bruner, J. S. (1962). The conditions of creativity. In H. Gruber, G. Terrell, & M. Wertheimer (Eds.), *Contemporary approaches to cognition* (pp. 1–30). New York: Atherton.

Bruner, J. S. (1964). The course of cognitive growth. *American Psychologist*, *19*, 1–15.

Bruner, J. S. (1975). Child development: Play is serious business. *Psychology Today*, *8*, 80–83.

Burkhardt, H. (1985). *Gleichheitswahn Parteienwahn* [Sameness psychosis]. Tübingen: Hohenrain.

Butler, D. L., & Kline, M. A. (1998). Good versus creative solutions: A comparison of brainstorming, hierarchical, and perspective-changing heuristics. *Creativity Research Journal, 11*, 325–331.

Buzan, A. (2003). *The mind map book*. New York: Dutton.

Byrd, R. E. (1986). *Creativity and risk-taking*. San Diego, CA: Pfeiffer International Publishers.

Campbell, D. T. (1960). Blind variation and selective survival as a general strategy in knowledge processes. In M. C. Yovits & S. Cameron (Eds.), *Self-organizing systems* (pp. 205–231). New York: Pergamon.

Cattell, R. B., & Butcher, H. J. (1968). *The prediction of achievement and creativity*. New York: Bobbs-Merrill.

Cattell, R. B., & Drevdahl, J. E. (1955). A comparison of the personality profile of eminent researchers with that of eminent teachers and administrators, and of the general public. *British Journal of Psychology, 46*, 248–261.

Colangelo, N., Kerr, B., Huesman, R., Hallowell, N., & Gaeth, J. (1992). The Iowa Inventiveness Inventory: Toward a measure of mechanical inventiveness. *Creativity Research Journal, 5*, 157–164.

Coleridge, S. T. (1912). *The Poems of Samuel Taylor Coleridge* [1798]. Oxford: Oxford University Press.

Cooper, C., Altman, W., & Garner, A. (2002). *Inventing for business success*. New York: Texere.

Cox, C. M. (1926). *Genetic studies of genius: The early mental traits of three hundred geniuses*. Palo Alto, CA: Stanford University Press.

Cropley, A. J. (1967a). *Creativity*. London: Longman.

Cropley, A. J. (1967b). Divergent thinking and science specialists. *Nature, 215*, 671–672.

Cropley, A. J. (1972). Creativity test scores under timed and untimed conditions. *Australian Journal of Psychology, 24*, 31–36.

Cropley, A. J. (1990). Creativity and mental health in everyday life. *Creativity Research Journal, 3*, 167–178.

Cropley, A. J. (1992a). Glück und Kreativität: Förderung von Aufgeschlossenheit für den zündenden Gedanken [Luck and creativity: Fostering openness for the spark of inspiration]. In K Urban (Ed.), *Begabungen entwickeln, erkennen und fördern* [Developing, recognizing and fostering gifts] (pp. 216–221). Hannover, Germany: University of Hannover, Faculty of Education.

Cropley, A. J. (1992b). *More ways than one. Fostering creativity in the classroom*. Norwood, NJ: Ablex.

Cropley, A. J. (1997a). Fostering creativity in the classroom: General principles. In M. A. Runco (Ed.), *The creativity research handbook* (pp. 83–114). Cresskill, NJ: Hampton.

Cropley, A. J. (1997b). Creativity: A bundle of paradoxes. *Gifted and Talented International, 12*, 8–14.

Cropley, A. J. (1999). Creativity and cognition: Producing effective novelty. *Roeper Review, 21*, 253–260.

Cropley, A. J. (2001). *Creativity in education and learning*. London: Kogan Page.

Cropley, A. J. (2002). Creativity and innovation: Men's business or women's work? *Baltic Journal of Psychology, 3*, 77–88.

Cropley, A. J. (2005). *Creativity and problem-solving: Implications for classroom assessment* (24th Vernon-Wall Lecture, Glasgow, 6 November 2004). Leicester: British Psychological Society.

Cropley, A. J. (2006). In praise of convergent thinking. *Creativity Research Journal, 18,* 391–404.

Cropley, A. J., & Sikand, J. S. (1973). Creativity and schizophrenia. *Journal of Consulting and Clinical Psychology, 40,* 462–468.

Cropley, A. J., & Urban, K. K. (2000). Programs and strategies for nurturing creativity. In K. A. Heller, F. J. Mönks, R. J. Sternberg, & R. F. Subotnik (Eds.), *International handbook of giftedness and talent* (pp. 481–494). Oxford: Pergamon.

Cropley, D. H. (2003). A case for compulsory teaching accreditation of engineering faculty. *IEEE Transactions in Education, 46,* 406–408.

Cropley, D. H. (2005). Eleven principles of creativity and terrorism. *Science, Engineering & Technology Summit on Counter-Terrorism Technology.* Fourth Homeland Security Summit and Homeland Exposition, Canberra.

Cropley, D. H., & Cropley, A. J. (2000). Fostering creativity in engineering undergraduates. *High Ability Studies, 11,* 207–219.

Cropley, D. H., & Cropley, A. J. (2005). Engineering creativity: A systems concept of functional creativity. In J. C. Kaufman & J. Baer (Eds.), *Faces of the muse: How people think, work and act creatively in diverse domains* (pp. 169–185). Hillsdale, NJ: Lawrence Erlbaum Associates.

Cropley, D. H., Kaufman, J. C., & Cropley, A. J. (2008). Malevolent creativity: A functional model of creativity in terrorism and crime. *Creativity Research Journal, 20,* 105–115.

Crozier, W. R. (1999). Age and individual differences in artistic productivity: Trends within a sample of British novelists. *Creativity Research Journal, 12,* 197–204.

Csikszentmihalyi, M. (1988). Society, culture, and person: A system view of creativity. In R. J. Sternberg (Ed.), *The nature of creativity* (pp. 325–339). New York: Cambridge University Press.

Csikszentmihalyi, M. (1996). *Creativity: Flow and the psychology of discovery and invention.* New York: Harper Collins.

Csikszentmihalyi, M. (1999). Implications of a systems perspective for the study of creativity. In R. J. Sternberg (Ed.), *Handbook of creativity* (pp. 313–335). Cambridge: Cambridge University Press.

Csikszentmihalyi, M., Rathunde, K., & Whalen, S. (1993). *Talented teenagers.* New York: Cambridge University Press.

Dacey, J. S. (1989). *Fundamentals of creative thinking.* Lexington, MA: Lexington Press.

Dasgupta, S. (2004). Is creativity a Darwinian process? *Creativity Research Journal, 16,* 403–414.

de Bono, E. (1993). *Water logic.* New York: Viking Penguin.

Dellas, M., & Gaier, E. L. (1970). Identification of creativity: The individual. *Psychological Bulletin, 73,* 55–73.

Dennis W. (1973). *Children of the crèche.* New York: Appleton-Century-Crofts.

Descartes, R. (1991[1644]. *Principles of Philosophy* (V. R. Miller & R. P. Miller, Trans.). Boston: Kluwer.

Diaz de Chumaceiro, C. L. (1999). Research on career paths: Serendipity and its analog. *Creativity Research Journal, 12,* 227–229.

Dillon, J. T. (1982). Problem finding and solving, *Journal of Creative Behavior, 16,* 97–111.

Doolittle, J. H. (1990). *Creative Reasoning Test.* Pacific Grove, CA: Midwest Publications/Critical Thinking Press.

Dow, G. T., & Mayer, R. E. (2004). Teaching students to solve insight problems: Evidence for domain specificity in creativity training. *Creativity Research Journal, 16,* 389–402.

Drevdahl, J. E., & Cattell, R. B. (1958). Personality and creativity—artists and writers. *Journal of Clinical Psychology, 14,* 107–111.

Dudeck, S. Z., & Hall, W. B. (1991). Personality consistency: Eminent architects 25 years later. *Creativity Research Journal, 4,* 213–231.

Edwards, S. M. (2000–2001). The technology paradox: Efficiency versus creativity. *Creativity Research Journal, 13,* 221–228.

Eiduson, B. T. (1958). Artist and non-artist: A comparative study. *Journal of Personality, 26,* 13–28.

Eisenberger, R., & Armeli, S. (1997). Can salient reward increase creative performance without reducing intrinsic creative interest? *Journal of Personality and Social Psychology, 72,* 652–663.

Eisenman, R. (1999). Creative prisoners: Do they exist? *Creativity Research Journal, 12,* 205–210.

Ekvall, G. (1996). Organizational climate for creativity and innovation. *European Journal of Work and Organizational Psychology, 5*(1), 105–123.

Ekvall, G. (1999). Creative climate. In M. A. Runco & S. R. Pritzker (Eds.), *Encyclopedia of creativity* (Vol. 1, pp. 403–412). San Diego: Academic Press.

Ericsson, K. A., & Lehmann, A. C. (1999). Expertise. In M. A. Runco & S. R. Pritzker (Eds.), *Encyclopedia of creativity* (Vol. 1, pp. 695–707). San Diego: Academic Press.

Ericsson, K. A., & Smith, J. (1991) *Toward a general theory of expertise: Prospects and limits.* Cambridge: Cambridge University Press.

Eysenck, H. J. (1940). The general factor in aesthetic judgments. *British Journal of Psychology, 31,* 94–102.

Eysenck, H. J. (1997). Creativity and personality. In M. A. Runco (Ed.), *The creativity research handbook* (Vol. 1, pp. 41–66). Cresskill, NJ: Hampton.

Facaoaru, C. (1985). *Kreativität in Wissenschaft und Technik* [Creativity in science and technology]. Bern: Huber.

Fagot, B. I., & Leinbach, M. D. (1993). Gender role development in young children: From discrimination to labeling. *Developmental Review, 13,* 205–224.

Farisha, B. (1978). Mental imagery and creativity. Review and speculation. *Journal of Mental Imagery, 2,* 209–238.

Fasko, D. (2000–2001). Education and creativity. *Creativity Research Journal, 13,* 317–328.

Feldhusen, J. F. (1988). *The Purdue Creative Thinking Program* (3rd ed.). Lafayette, IN: Gifted Education Resource Institute.

Feldhusen, J. F. (1995). Creativity: A knowledge base, metacognitive skills, and personality factors. *Journal of Creative Behavior, 29,* 255–268.

Finke, R. A., Ward, T. B., & Smith, S. M. (1992). *Creative cognition.* Boston, MA: MIT Press.

Flavell, J. H. (1976). Metacognitive aspects of problem solving. In L. B. Resnick (Ed.), *The nature of intelligence* (pp. 231–236). Hillsdale, NJ: Lawrence Erlbaum Associates.

Florida, R. (2002). *The rise of the creative class.* New York: Basic Books.

Frängsmyr, T. (Ed.). (1997). *Les Prix Nobel. The Nobel Prizes 1996*. Stockholm: Nobel Foundation.

Fromm, E. (1980). *Greatness and limitations of Freud's thought*. New York: New American History.

Gardner, H. (1993). *Creating minds*. New York: Basic Books.

Gautier, T. (1998). *Mademoiselle de Maupin* [1836]. Paris: Editions Bibliopolis.

Getzels, J. A., & Jackson, P. W. (1962). *Creativity and intelligence*. New York: Wiley.

Getzels, J. W., & Csikszentmihalyi, M. (1976). *The creative vision: A longitudinal study of problem finding in art*. New York: Wiley.

Ghiselin, B. (1955). *The creative process*. New York: Mentor.

Glover, J. A., Ronning, R. R., & Reynolds, C. R. (1989). (Eds.). *Handbook of creativity*. New York: Plenum.

Glück, J., Ernst, R., & Unger, F. (2002). How creatives define creativity: Definitions reflect different types of creativity. *Creativity Research Journal, 14*, 55–67.

Goertzel, M. C., Goertzel, V., & Goertzel, T. C. (1978). *300 eminent personalities*. San Francisco: Jossey-Bass.

Gordon, W. J. (1961). *Synectics*. New York: Harper.

Götz, K. O. (1985). *Visual Aesthetic Sensitivity Test* (VAST) (4th ed.). Düsseldorf: Concept Verlag.

Götz, K. O., & Götz, K. (1979). Personality characteristics of professional artists. *Perceptual and Motor Skills, 49*, 327–334.

Gough, H. G. (1979). A creative personality scale for the adjective check list. *Journal of Personality and Social Psychology; 37*, 1398–1405.

Graham, B., Sawyers, J., & DeBord, K. B. (1989). Teachers' creativity, playfulness, and style of interaction. *Creativity Research Journal, 2*, 41–50.

Gribov, I. A. (1989). Psychological and educational conditions of development of creative self-expression of students and teachers. *Voprosy—Psikhologii, 2*, 75–82.

Gruber, H. E. (1993). Creativity in the moral domain: Ought implies can implies create. *Creativity Research Journal, 6*, 3–15.

Gruber, H. E., & Davis, S. N. (1988). Inching our way up Mount Olympus: The evolving-systems approach to creative thinking. In R. J. Sternberg (Ed.), *The nature of creativity* (pp. 243–270). New York: Cambridge University Press.

Grudin, R. (1990). *The grace of great things: Creativity and innovation*. New York: Ticknor and Fields.

Guilford, J. P. (1950). Creativity. *American Psychologist, 5*, 444–454.

Guilford, J. P. (1959). Traits of creativity. In H. H. Anderson (Ed.), *Creativity and its cultivation* (pp. 142–161). New York: Harper.

Guilford, J. P. (1976). *Creativity Tests for Children*. Orange, CA: Sheridan Psychological Services.

Hadamard, J. (1945). *The psychology of invention in the mathematical field*. New York: Dover.

Harrington, D. M. (1999). Conditions and settings/environment. In M. A. Runco & S. R. Pritzker (Eds.), *Encyclopedia of creativity* (Vol. 1, pp. 323–340). San Diego: Academic Press.

Hassenstein, M. (1988). *Bausteine zu einer Naturgeschichte der Intelligenz* [Building blocks for a natural history of creativity]. Stuttgart: Deutsche Verlags-Anstalt.

Hausman, C. R. (1984). *A discourse on novelty and creation*. Albany: State University of New York Press.

Heinelt, G. (1974). *Kreative Lehrer/kreative Schüler* [Creative teachers/creative students]. Freiburg: Herder.

Helson, R. (1983). Creative mathematicians. In R. S. Albert (Ed.), *Genius and eminence: The social psychology of creativity and exceptional achievement* (pp. 311–330). Elmsford, NY: Pergamon.

Helson, R. (1996). In search of the creative personality. *Creativity Research Journal, 9,* 295–306.

Helson, R. (1999). A longitudinal study of creative personality in women. *Creativity Research Journal, 12,* 89–102.

Henle, M. (1974). The cognitive approach: The snail beneath the shell. In S. Rosner & L. E. Aber (Eds.), *Essays in creativity* (pp. 23–44). Croton on Hudson, NY: North River Press.

Hennessey, B. A. (1994). The consensual assessment technique: An examination of the relationships between ratings of product and process creativity. *Creativity Research Journal, 7,* 193–208.

Hennessey, B. A., & Amabile, T. (1999). Consensual assessment. In M. A. Runco & S. R. Pritzker (Eds.), *Encyclopedia of creativity* (pp. 347–359). San Diego: Academic Press.

Heron, W. (1957, January) The pathology of boredom. *Scientific American,* pp. 52–56.

Herrmann, W. (1987). *Auswirkungen verschiedener Fussballtrainingsstile auf Leistungsmotivation* [Effects of different styles for coaching football on motivation]. Unpublished master's thesis, University of Hamburg.

Higgins, J. M. (1994). *101 creative problem solving techniques—The handbook of new ideas for business.* Winter Park, FL: The New Management Publishing Company.

Hoffman, M. L. (1971). Identification and conscience development. *Child Development, 42,* 1071–1082.

Howieson, N. (1984, August 12–17). *Is Western Australia neglecting the creative potential of its youth?* Paper presented at the annual conference of the Australian Psychological Society, Perth, Australia.

Hruby, G. G. (1999). Review of Jensen, E. (1998). Teaching with the brain in mind. *Roeper Review, 21,* 326–327.

Huczynski, W. (1983). *Encyclopedia of management development methods.* Aldershot: Gower.

Hudson, L. (1968). *Contrary imaginations.* London: Methuen.

Isaksen, S. G., Dorval, K. B., & Treffinger, D. J. (1994). *Creative approaches to problem solving.* Dubuque, IA: Kendall-Hunt.

Isaksen, S. G., Lauer, K. J., Ekvall, G., & Britz, A. (2000–2001). Perceptions of the best and worst climates for creativity: Preliminary validation evidence for the Situational Outlook Questionnaire. *Creativity Research Journal, 13,* 171–184.

Isen, A. M., Daubman, K. A., & Nowicki, G. P. (1987). Positive affect facilitates creative problem solving. *Journal of Personality and Social Psychology, 52,* 1122–1131.

Jackson, P. W., & Messick, S. (1965). The person, the product, and the response: Conceptual problems in the assessment of creativity. *Journal of Personality, 33,* 309–329.

James, K., Clark, K., & Cropanzano, R. (1999). Positive and negative creativity in groups, institutions and organizations: A model and theoretical extension. *Creativity Research Journal, 12,* 211–226.

Jamison, K. R. (1993). *Touched with fire: Depressive illness and the artistic temperament.* New York: The Free Press.

Jay, E. S., & Perkins, D. N. (1997). Problem finding: The search for mechanisms. In M. A. Runco (Ed.), *The creativity research handbook* (Vol. 1, pp. 257–294). Cresskill, NJ: Hampton.

Johnson, D. L. (1979). *The Creativity Checklist.* Wood Dale, IL: Stoelting.

Josephson, M. (1959). *Edison: A biography.* New York: Wiley.

Joussemet, M., & Koestner, R. (1999). Effect of expected rewards on children's creativity. *Creativity Research Journal, 12,* 231–240.

Kasof, J. (1997). Creativity and breadth of attention. *Creativity Research Journal, 10,* 303–315.

Katz, D., & Kahn, R. L. (1978). *The social psychology of organizations* (2nd ed.). New York: Wiley.

Kaufman, J. C., & Baer, J. (2002). I bask in dreams of suicide: Mental illness, poetry, and women. *Review of General Psychology, 6,* 271–286.

Kim, K. H. (2006). Can we trust creativity tests? A review of the Torrance Tests of Creative Thinking (TTCT). *Creativity Research Journal, 18,* 3–14.

King, N. (1992). Modeling the innovation process: An empirical comparison of approaches. *Journal of Occupational and Organizational Psychology, 65,* 89–100.

Kinney, D. K., Richards, R., Lowing, P. A., LeBlanc, D., Zimbalist, M. E., & Harlan, P. (2000–2001). Creativity in offspring of schizophrenic and control parents: An adoption study. *Creativity Research Journal, 13,* 17–26.

Kirton, M. (1989). *Adaptors and innovators: Styles of creativity and problem solving.* London: Routledge.

Kitto, J., Lok, D., & Rudowicz, E. (1994.) Measuring creative thinking: An activity-based approach. *Creativity Research Journal, 7,* 59–69.

Knapper, C. K., & Cropley, A. J. (2000). *Lifelong learning and higher education.* London: Kogan Page.

Köstler, A. (1964). *The act of creation.* London: Hutchinson.

Kogan, N. (1983). Stylistic variation in childhood and adolescence: Creativity, metaphor, and cognitive styles. In P. Mussen (Ed.), *Handbook of child psychology* (Vol. 3, pp. 631–706). New York: Wiley.

Kohlberg, L. A. (1966). A cognitive-developmental analysis of childhood sex role concepts and attitudes. In E. E. Maccoby (Ed.), *The development of sex differences* (pp. 179–204). Palo Alto, CA: Stanford University Press.

Krystal, H. (1988). On some roots of creativity. *Psychiatric Clinics of North America, 11,* 475–491.

Larey, T. S., & Paulus, P. B. (1999). Group preference and convergent tendencies in small groups: A content analysis of group brainstorming performance. *Creativity Research Journal, 12,* 175–184.

Lehman, H. C. (1953). *Age and achievement.* Princeton, NJ: Princeton University Press.

Lindauer, M. S. (1993). The span of creativity among long-lived historical artists. *Creativity Research Journal, 6,* 221–240.

Lipman-Blumen, J. (1991). *Individual and organizational achieving styles: A handbook for researchers and human resource professionals* (4th ed.). Claremont, CA: Achieving Styles Institute.

Lipman-Blumen, J. (1996). *Women in corporate leadership: Reviewing a decade's research.* Wellesley, MA: Wellesley College Center for Research on Women.

Litwin, G., & Stringer, R. (1968). *Motivation and organizational climate*. Boston: Harvard University Press.

Lonergan, D. C., Scott, G. M., & Mumford, M. D. (2004). Evaluative aspects of creative thought: Effects on appraisal and revision standards. *Creativity Research Journal, 16*, 231–246.

Lubart, T. (2000–2001). Models of the creative process: Past, present and future. *Creativity Research Journal, 13*, 295–308.

Ludwig, A. M. (1998). Method and madness in the arts and sciences. *Creativity Research Journal, 11*, 93–101.

Maccoby, E. E., & Jacklin, C. N. (1974). *The psychology of sex differences*. Stanford: Stanford University Press.

MacKinnon, D. W. (1978). *In search of human effectiveness: Identifying and developing creativity*. Buffalo, NY: Creative Education Foundation.

MacKinnon, D. W. (1983). Creative architects. In R. S. Albert (Ed.), *Genius and eminence: The social psychology of creativity and exceptional achievement* (pp. 291–301). Elmsford, NY: Pergamon.

Mansfield, R. S., Busse, T. V., & Krepelka, E. J. (1978). The effectiveness of creativity training. *Review of Educational Research, 48*, 517–536.

March, J. G. (1991). Exploration and exploitation in organizational learning. *Organization Science, 2*(1), 71–87.

Martinson, O. (1995). Cognitive styles and experience in solving insight problems: Replication and extension. *Creativity Research Journal, 8*, 291–298.

Maslow, A. H. (1973). Creativity in self-actualizing people. In A. Rothenberg & C. R. Hausman (Eds.), *The creative question* (pp. 86–92). Durham, NC: Duke University Press.

Mathisen, G. E., & Einarsen, S. (2004). A review of instruments assessing creative and innovative environments within organizations. *Creativity Research Journal, 16*, 119–140.

Marvszewski, T., & Noscal, C. S. (Eds.). (1995). *Creative information processing*. Delft: Eburon.

May, R. (1976). *The courage to create*. New York: Bantam.

McCrae, R. R. (1987). Creativity, divergent thinking and openness to experience. *Journal of Personality and Social Psychology, 52*, 1258–1265.

McLaren, R. B. (1993). The dark side of creativity. *Creativity Research Journal, 6*, 137–144.

McMullan, W. E. (1978). Creative individuals: Paradoxical personages. *Journal of Creative Behavior, 10*, 265–275.

Mednick, S. A. (1962). The associative basis of creativity. *Psychological Review, 69*, 220–232.

Meeker, M. (1985). *Structure of Intellect Learning Abilities Test*. Los Angeles, CA: Western Psychological Services.

Michael, W. B., & Colson, K. R. (1979). The development and validation of a life experience inventory for the identification of creative electrical engineers. *Educational and Psychological Measurement, 39*, 463–470.

Michalko, M. (1996). *Thinkertoys*. Berkeley, CA: Ten Speed Press.

Michalko, M. (1998). *Cracking creativity*. Berkeley, CA: Ten Speed Press.

Milgram, R. M., & Hong, E. (1999). Creative out-of-school activities in intellectually gifted adolescents as predictors of their life accomplishments in young adults: A longitudinal study. *Creativity Research Journal, 12*, 77–88.

Miller, A. I. (1992). Scientific creativity: A comparative study of Henri Poincaré and Albert Einstein. *Creativity Research Journal, 5,* 385–418.

Millward, L. J., & Freeman, H. (2002). Role expectations as constraints to innovation: The case of female managers. *Creativity Research Journal, 14,* 93–110.

Morgan, D. N. (1953). Creativity today. *Journal of Aesthetics, 12,* 1–24.

Morning Herald (1904). Adelaide University examinations (15 October, 1904, p. 17).

Motamedi, K. (1982). Extending the concept of creativity. *Journal of Creative Behavior, 16,* 75–88.

Moustakis, C. E. (1977). *Creative life.* New York: Van Nostrand.

Mumford, M. D., Baughman, W. A., Threlfall, K. V., Supinski, E. P., & Costanza, D. P. (1996). Process-based measures of creative problem-solving skills: I. Problem construction. *Creativity Research Journal, 9,* 63–76.

Mumford, M. D., Marks, M. A., Connelly, M. S., Zaccaro, S. J., & Johnson, J. F. (1998). Domain-based scoring of divergent-thinking tests: Validation evidence in an occupational sample. *Creativity Research Journal, 11,* 151–163.

Mumford, M. D., & Moertl, P. (2003). Cases of social innovation: Lessons from two innovations in the 20th century. *Creativity Research Journal, 13,* 261–266.

Mumford, M. D., Supinski, E. P., Baughman, W. A., Costanza, D. P., & Threlfall, K. V. (1997). Process-based measures of creative problem-solving skills: IV. Category combination. *Creativity Research Journal, 10,* 59–71.

Myers-Briggs, I., & McCaulley, M. H. (1992). *Manual: A guide to the development and use of the Myers–Briggs Type Indicator.* Palo Alto, CA: Consulting Psychologists Press.

Nardi, K., & Martindale, C. (1981). *Creativity and preference for tones varying in dissonance and intensity.* Paper presented at Eastern Psychological Association Convention, New York.

Necka, E. (1986). On the nature of creative talent. In A. J. Cropley, K. K. Urban, H. Wagner, & W. H. Wieczerkowski (Eds.), *Giftedness: A continuing worldwide challenge* (pp. 131–140). New York: Trillium.

Neff, G. (1975). Kreativität und Gruppe [Creativity and the group]. In G. Neff (Ed.), *Kreativität in Schule und Gesellschaft* [Creativity in school and society] (pp. 17–29). Ravensburg: Otto Maier.

Newell, A., Shaw, J. C., & Simon, H. A. (1962). The processes of creative thinking. In H. E. Gruber, G. Terrell, & M. Wertheimer (Eds.), *Contemporary approaches to creative thinking* (pp. 63–119). New York: Atherton.

Nichols, J. G. (1972). Creativity in the person who will never produce anything original and useful. The concept of creativity as a normally distributed trait. *American Psychologist, 27,* 717–727.

Nobel Foundation. (1967). *Nobel lectures, Physics 1901–1927.* Amsterdam: Elsevier.

O'Conner, J. J., & Robertson E. F. (2003). *Jules Henri Poincaré.* Access from www-history. mcs.st-andrews.ac.uk/Mathematicians/Poincare.html

Odena, O (2001, September 13–15). *How do secondary school music teachers view creativity? A report on educators' views of teaching composing skills.* Paper presented at the annual conference of the British Educational Research Association, University of Leeds, England.

Oldham, G. M., & Cummings, A. (1996). Employee creativity: Personal and contextual factors at work. *Academy of Management Journal, 39,* 607–634.

Olken, H. (1964, December). Creativity training for engineers—its past, present and future. *International Association for Engineering Education Transactions in Education*, pp. 149–161.

Olson, M. (1982). *The rise and decline of nations*. New Haven, CT: Yale University Press.

Osborn, A. F. (1953). *Applied imagination*. New York: Scribner's.

Park, J., & Jang, K. (2005). Analysis of the actual scientific inquiries of physicists. Accessed September 17, 2006, from www.arxiv.org/abs/physics/0506191.

Parloff, M. B., Datta, L., Kleman, M., & Handlon, J. H. (1968). Personality characteristics which differentiate creative male adolescents and adults. *Journal of Personality, 36*, 530–552.

Parnes, S. J. (1981). *Magic of your mind*. Buffalo, NY: Creative Education Foundation.

Paulus, P. B. (1999). Group creativity. In M. A. Runco & S. R. Pritzker (Eds.), *Encyclopedia of creativity* (pp. 779–784). San Diego, CA: Academic Press.

Perkins, D. N. (1981). *The mind's best work*. Cambridge, MA: Harvard University Press.

Petersen, S. (1989). *Motivation von Laienautoren* [Motivation of hobby authors]. Unpublished master's thesis, University of Hamburg, Germany.

Peterson, H. (Ed.). (1954). *A treasury of the world's great speeches*. Danbury, CT: Grolier.

Pilzer, P. Z. (1991). *Unlimited wealth: The theory and practice of economic alchemy*; New York: Crown.

Planck, M. K. E. L. (1901). On the law of distribution of energy. *Annalen der Physik* [Annual Review of Physics], *4*, 553.

Plucker, J. A. (1998). Beware of simple conclusions: The case for content generality of creativity. *Creativity Research Journal, 11*, 179–182.

Plucker, J. A. (1999). Is the proof in the pudding? Reanalysis of Torrance's (1958 to present) longitudinal data. *Creativity Research Journal, 12*, 103–114.

Poincaré, J. H. (2003[1908]). *Science and method*. Mineola, NY: Courier Dover.

Powell, G. N. (1993). *Women and men in management* (2nd ed.). Newbury Park, CA: Sage.

Prindle, E. J. (1906). The art of inventing. *Transactions of the American Institute for Engineering Education, 25*, 519–547.

Proctor, R. M. J., & Burnett, P. C. (2004). Measuring cognitive and dispositional characteristics of creativity in elementary students. *Creativity Research Journal, 16*, 421–429.

Puccio, G. J. (1999). Teams. In M. A. Runco & S. R. Pritzker (Eds.), *Encyclopedia of creativity* (pp. 640–649). San Diego, CA: Academic Press.

Puccio, G. J., Treffinger, D. J., & Talbot, R. J. (1995). Exploratory examination of the relationship between creativity styles and creative products. *Creativity Research Journal, 8*, 157–152.

Rabinowitz, M., & Glaser, R. (1985). Cognitive structure and process in highly competent performance. In F. D. Horowitz & M. O'Brien (Eds.), *The gifted and talented: Developmental perspectives* (pp. 75–98). Washington, DC: American Psychological Association.

Rechtin, E., & Maier, M. (1997). *The art of systems architecting*. Boca Raton, FL: CRC Press.

Reid, A., & Petocz, P. (2004). Learning domains and the process of creativity. *Australian Educational Researcher, 31*, 45–61.

Renzulli, J. S. (1986). The three-ring conception of giftedness: A developmental model for creative productivity. In R. J. Sternberg & J. E. Davidson (Eds.), *Conceptions of giftedness* (pp. 53–92). Cambridge: Cambridge University Press.

Resnick, L. B. (1987). *Education and learning to think.* Washington, DC: National Academy Press.

Rhodes, M. (1961). An analysis of creativity. *Phi Delta Kappan, 42*, 305–310.

Richards, R., Kinney, D. K., Bennet, M., & Merzel, A. P. C. (1988). Assessing everyday creativity: Characteristics of the Lifetime Creativity Scales and validation with three large samples. *Journal of Personality and Social Psychology, 54*, 476–485.

Rickards, T. J. (1993). Creativity from a business school perspective: Past, present and future. In S. G. Isaksen, M. C. Murdock, R. L. Firestien, & D. J. Treffinger (Eds.), *Nurturing and developing creativity: The emergence of a discipline* (pp. 155–176). Norwood, NJ: Ablex.

Rickards, T. J. (1999). Brainstorming. In M. A. Runco & S. R. Pritzker (Eds.), *Encyclopedia of creativity* (Vol. 1, pp. 219–227). San Diego: Academic Press.

Roe, A. (1953). A psychological study of eminent psychologists and anthropologists, and a comparison with biological and physical scientists. *Psychological Monographs: General and Applied, 67*(352).

Rogers, C. R. (1961). *On becoming a person.* Boston: Houghton-Mifflin.

Root-Bernstein, R. S. (1989). *Discovery.* New York: Cambridge University Press.

Root-Bernstein, R. S., Bernstein, M., & Garnier, H. (1993). Identification of scientists making long-term high-impact contributions, with notes on their methods of working. *Creativity Research Journal, 6*, 329–343.

Ross, L., & Nisbett, R. (1991). *The person and the situation: Perspectives of social psychology.* New York: McGraw-Hill.

Rossman, J. (1931). *The psychology of the inventor: A study of the patentee.* Washington: Inventors' Publishing Company.

Rothenberg, A. (1983). Psychopathology and creative cognition: A comparison of hospitalized patients, Nobel laureates and controls. *Archives of General Psychiatry, 40*, 937–942.

Rothenberg, A. (1988). Creativity and the homospatial process: Experimental studies. *Psychiatric Clinics of North America, 11*, 443–460.

Rothman, A. (1982). Genius and biographers: The fictionalization of Evariste Galois. *American Mathematical Monthly, 89*(2), 84–106.

Runco, M. A. (1993). Creative morality: Intentional and unconventional. *Creativity Research Journal, 6*, 17–28.

Runco, M. A. (Ed.). (2003). *Critical creative processes.* Cresskill, NJ: Hampton.

Runco, M. A., & Charles, R. E. (1997). Developmental trends in creative potential and creative performance. In M. A. Runco (Ed.), *The creativity research handbook* (Vol. 1, pp. 115–152). Cresskill, NJ: Hampton.

Runco, M. A., & Nemiro, J. (2003). Creativity in the moral domain: Integration and implications. *Creativity Research Journal, 15*, 91–105.

Runco, M. A., Plucker, J. A., & Lim, W. (2000–2001). Development and psychometric integrity of a measure of ideational behavior. *Creativity Research Journal, 13*, 393–400.

Savransky, S. D. (2000). *Engineering of creativity.* Boca Raton, FL: CRC Press.

Sawyer, R. K. (1999). Improvisation. In M. A. Runco & S. R. Pritzker (Eds.), *Encyclopedia of creativity* (Vol. 2, pp. 31–38). San Diego, CA: Academic Press.

Schein, V. E. (1994). Managerial sex typing: A persistent and pervasive barrier to women's opportunities. In M. J. Davidson & R. J. Burke (Eds.), *Women in management: Current research issues* (pp. 65–84). London: Chapman.

Schuldberg, D. (2000–2001). Six sub-clinical spectrum traits in normal creativity. *Creativity Research Journal, 13*, 5–16.

Schwebel, M. (1993). Moral creativity as artistic transformation. *Creativity Research Journal, 6*, 65–81.

Scott, G., Leritz, L. E., & Mumford, M. D. (2004). The effectiveness of creativity training: A quantitative review. *Creativity Research Journal, 16*, 361–388.

Scott, S. G., & Bruce, R. A. (1994). Determinants of innovative behaviour: A path model of individual innovation in the workplace. *Academy of Management Journal, 37*, 580–607.

Scott, T. E. (1999). Knowledge. In M. A. Runco & S. R. Pritzker (Eds.), *Encyclopedia of creativity* (Vol. 2, pp. 119–129). San Diego, CA: Academic Press.

Seger, C. A. (1994). Implicit learning. *Psychological Bulletin, 115*, 163–196.

Semmer, E. (1870). Resultate der Injektion von Pilzsporen und Pilzhefen in's Bluth der Thiere [Effects of injecting fungus spores into the blood of animals]. *Virchows Archiv, 50*, 158–160.

Shaughnessy, M. F., & Manz, A. F. (1991). Personological research on creativity in the performing and fine arts. *European Journal for High Ability, 2*, 91–101.

Shaw, M. P. (1989). The Eureka process: A structure for the creative experience in science and engineering. *Creativity Research Journal, 2*, 286–298.

Siegel, S. M., & Kaemmerer, W. F. (1978). Measuring the perceived support for innovation in organizations. *Journal of Applied Psychology, 63*, 553–562.

Simon, H. A. (1989). The scientist as a problem solver. In D. Klahr & K. Kotovsky (Eds.), *Complex information processing* (pp. 375–398). Hillsdale, NJ: Lawrence Erlbaum Associates.

Simonton, D. K. (1988a). *Scientific genius: A psychology of science*. New York: Cambridge University Press.

Simonton, D. K. (1988b). Age and outstanding achievement: What do we know after a century of research? *Psychological Bulletin, 104*, 251–267.

Simonton, D. K. (1994). *Greatness: Who makes history and why?* New York: Guilford.

Simonton, D. K. (1997). Historiometric studies of creative genius. In M. A. Runco (Ed.), *The creativity research handbook* (Vol. 1, pp. 3–28). Cresskill, NJ: Hampton.

Simonton, D. K. (1998). Masterpieces in music: Historiometric inquiries. *Creativity Research Journal, 11*, 103–110.

Simonton, D. K. (1999). *Origins of genius: Darwinian perspectives of creativity*. New York: Oxford University Press.

Snyder, A., Mitchell, J., Bossomaier, T., & Pallier, G. (2004). The creativity quotient: An objective scoring of ideational fluency. *Creativity Research Journal, 16*, 415–420.

Sosa, R., & Gero, J. S. (2003). Design and change: A model of situated creativity. In C. Bento, A. Cardosa, & J. S. Gero (Eds.), *Approaches to creativity in artificial intelligence and cognitive science* (pp. 25–34). Acapulco: IJCAI03.

Sternberg, R. J. (1985). *Beyond IQ: A triarchic theory of human intelligence.* New York: Cambridge University Press.

Sternberg, R. J. (1999). A propulsion model of types of creative contributions. *Review of General Psychology, 3*(2), 83–100.

Sternberg, R. J. (2003). *Wisdom, intelligence, and creativity synthesized.* New York: Cambridge University Press.

Sternberg, R. J. (2006). The nature of creativity. *Creativity Research Journal, 18,* 87–98.

Sternberg, R. J., & Davidson, J. E. (1999). Intuition. In M. A. Runco & S. R. Pritzker (Eds.), *Encyclopedia of creativity* (Vol. 2, pp. 57–69). San Diego: Academic Press.

Sternberg, R. J., & Lubart, T. I. (1995). *Defying the crowd: Cultivating creativity in a culture of conformity.* New York: The Free Press.

Sternberg, R. J., & Lubart, T. I. (1999). The concept of creativity: Prospects and paradigms. In R. J. Sternberg (Ed.), *Handbook of creativity* (pp. 3–15). Cambridge: Cambridge University Press.

Stigler, J. W., & Hiebert, J. (1997). Understanding and improving mathematics instruction: An overview of the TIMSS Video Study. *Phi Delta Kappan, 79*(1), 14–21.

Sweetland, R. C., & Keyser, D. J. (1991). *A comprehensive reference for assessment in psychology, education and business.* Austin, TX: Pro-Ed.

Tardiff, T. Z., & Sternberg, R. J. (1988). What do we know about creativity? In R. J. Sternberg (Ed.), *The nature of creativity* (pp. 429–440). New York: Cambridge University Press.

Taylor, I. A. (1975). An emerging view of creative actions. In I. A. Taylor & J. W. Getzels (Eds.), *Perspectives in creativity* (pp. 297–325). Chicago: Aldine.

Thanksgiving for innovation. (2002, September 21). *Economist Technology Quarterly,* pp. 13–14.

Tilbury, D., Reid, A., & Podger, D. (2003). *Action research for university staff: Changing curricula and graduate skills towards sustainability, Stage 1 Report.* Canberra: Environment Australia.

Torrance, E. P. (1965). *The Minnesota studies of creative thinking: Widening horizons in creativity.* New York: Wiley.

Torrance, E. P. (1966). *The Torrance Tests of Creative Thinking—Norms, technical manual.* Princeton, NJ: Personnel Press.

Torrance, E. P. (1972). Can we teach children to think creatively? *The Journal of Creative Behavior, 6,* 114–143.

Torrance, E. P. (1979). *The search for Satori and creativity.* Buffalo, NY: Creative Education Foundation.

Torrance, E. P. (1992, January/February). A national climate for creativity and invention. *Gifted Child Today,* pp. 10–14.

Torrance, E. P. (1998). *Torrance Test of Creative Thinking: Norms and technical manual.* Bensenville, IL: Scholastic Testing Services.

Torrance, E. P., & Safter, H. T. (1999). *Making the creative leap beyond.* Buffalo, NY: Creative Education Foundation Press.

Treffinger, D. J. (1985). Review of Torrance Tests of Creative Thinking. In J. V. Mitchell (Ed.), *Ninth Mental Measurements Yearbook* (pp. 1632–1634). Lincoln: University of Nebraska Press.

Treffinger, D. J. (1995). Creative problem solving: Overview and educational implications. *Educational Psychology Review, 7,* 301–312.

Treffinger, D. J., Isaksen, S. G., & Dorval, K. B. (1995). *Creative problem solving: An introduction*. Sarasota, FL: Center for Creative Learning.

Treffinger, D. J., Isaksen, S. G., & Firestien, R. L. (1983). Theoretical perspectives on creative learning and its facilitation. *Journal of Creative Behavior, 17*, 9–17.

Treffinger, D. J., Sortore, M. R., & Cross, J. A. (1993). Programs and strategies for nurturing creativity. In K. Heller, F. J. Mönks, & A. H. Passow (Eds.), *International handbook for research on giftedness and talent* (pp. 555–567). Oxford: Pergamon.

Urban K. K. (1997). Modeling creativity: The convergence of divergence or the art of balancing. In J. Chan, R. Li, & J. Spinks (Eds.), *Maximizing potential: Lengthening and strengthening our stride* (pp. 39–50). Hong Kong: University of Hong Kong Social Sciences Research Centre.

Urban, K. K., & Jellen, H. G. (1996). *Test for Creative Thinking–Drawing Production (TCT–DP)*. Lisse, Netherlands: Swets & Zeitlinger.

van der Heijden, B. I. J. M. (2000). The development and psychometric evaluation of a multi-dimensional measurement instrument of professional expertise. *High Ability Studies, 11*, 9–39.

VanGundy, A. B. (1984). *Managing group creativity: A modular approach to problem solving*. New York: American Management Association.

Vielot, J. (2001). Accessed from www.ijee.dit.ie/forum/forum1.html

Vosburg, S. K. (1998). Mood and quantity and quality of ideas. *Creativity Research Journal, 11*, 315–324.

Walberg, H. J., & Stariha, W. E. (1992). Productive human capital: Learning, creativity and eminence. *Creativity Research Journal, 5*, 323–340.

Walk, C. L. (1996). *Management and leadership. MBTI applications: A decade of research on the Myers–Briggs Type Indicator*. Palo Alto, CA: Consulting Psychology Press.

Wallach, M. A. (1985). Creativity testing and giftedness. In F. D. Horowitz & M. O'Brien (Eds.), *The gifted and talented: Developmental perspectives* (pp. 99–123). Washington, DC: American Psychological Association.

Wallach, M. M., & Kogan, N. (1965). *Modes of thinking in young children*. New York: Holt, Rinehart & Winston.

Wallas, G. (1926). *The art of thought*. New York: Harcourt Brace.

Ward, T. B., Saunders, K. N., & Dodds, R. A. (1999). Creative cognition in gifted adolescents. *Roeper Review, 21*, 260–266.

Weeks, D. J., & Ward, K. (1988). *Eccentrics: The scientific investigation*. Stirling: Stirling University Press.

Weisberg, R. W. (2004). On structure in the process: A quantitative case-study of the creation of Picasso's Guernica. *Empirical Studies in the Arts, 22*, 23–54.

Welsh, G. S. (1975). *Creativity and intelligence: A personality approach*. Chapel Hill, NC: Institute for Research in Social Science.

West, M. A., & Richards, T. (1999). Innovation. In M. A. Runco & S. R. Pritzker (Eds.), *Encyclopedia of creativity* (pp. 45–55). San Diego, CA: Academic Press.

Zuckerman, M. (1969). Theoretical formulations. In J. Zubek (Ed.), *Sensory deprivation: Fifteen years of research* (pp. 407–432). New York: Appleton-Century-Crofts.

Author Index

Abra, J., 168, *275*
Ajzen, I., 111, *275*
Albert, R. S., 103, 104, *275*
Alliance of Artists' Communities, 6, *275*
Altman, W., 6, *277*
Altshuller, G. S., 79, 222, 251, *275*
Amabile, T. M., 29–30, 112, 141, 152, 178, 197, 198(t), 208, 242, 254, 262, *275*
Anderson, C. C., 141, *275*
Anderson, J. R., 56, *275*
Anderson, N., 199(t), 200, *275*
Andreason, N. C., 97, *275*
Anthony, E. J., 98, *275*
Armeli, S., 13, 119, 204, 272, 245, 262, *279*
Austin, J. H., 45, *275*
Australian Bureau of Statistics, 2, *275*

Bacon, F., 124, *275*
Baer, J., 27, 209, *276*
Baer, J., 96, *282*
Bailin, S., 28, 72, 75, *276*
Bandura, A., 161, 164, *276*
Barron, F. X., 11, 97, 102, 103, 104, *276*
Basadur, M., 104, 116, 194, *276*
Baughman, W. A., 192, 193, 250, 252, *284*
Bennet, M., 208, *286*
Berlyne, D. E., 105, 135, *276*
Bernstein, M., 90, 146, *286*
Besemer, S. P., 179, 254, *276*
Biermann, K.-R., 110, *276*
Biggs, J. B., 15, *276*

Bloom, B. S., 157, *276*
Boden, M. A., 48, 75, 123, 250, *276*
Bossomaier, T., 189, *287*
Brackfield, S. C., 141, *275*
Britz, A., 190(t), 200, *281*
Brophy, J., 69, 159, *276*
Bruce, R. A., 163, *287*
Bruner, J. S., 53, 54, 105, 127, 254, *276*
Burkhardt, H., 105, 123, 142, *276*
Burnett, P. C., 181, 182, *285*
Busse, T. V., 224, *283*
Butcher, H. J., 30, 102, *277*
Butler, D. L., 219, *277*
Buzan, A., 219, *277*
Byrd, R. E., 195, *277*

Campbell, D. T., 40, 44, *277*
Cattell, R. B., 30, 101, 102, *277, 279*
Charles, R. E., 100, *286*
Clark, K., 161, *281*
Colangelo, N., 194, *277*
Coleridge, S. T., 74, *277*
Colson, K. R., 183, *283*
Connelly, M. S., 185, 186, *284*
Cooper, C., 6, *277*
Costanza, D. P., 192, 193, 250, 252, *284*
Cox, C. M., 110, *277*
Cropanzano, R., 161, *281*
Cropley, A. J., 1, 2, 6, 7, 11, 25, 30, 35, 45, 67, 69, 76, 85–86, 97, 98, 102, 103(n1), 105, 113, 141, 125, 161, 162, 165, 180, 183, 186, 187, 188, 191, 192, 201, 205, 208, 214, 216, 224, 227, 256, *275, 277, 278, 282*

Cropley, D. H., 2, 6, 11, 25, 35, 76, 103(n1), 113, 125, 126, 191, 192, 205, 224, 227, 256, 278
Cross, J. A., 25, 215, 224, 289
Crozier, W. R., 156, 278
Csikszentmihalyi, M., 44, 75, 88, 117, 127, 156, 183, 215, 253, 278, 280
Cummings, A., 8, 176, 284

Dacey, J. S., 103, 278
Dasgupta, S., 44, 88, 278
Datta, L., 104, 285
Daubman, K. A., 105, 281
Davidson, J. E., 40, 44, 288
Davis, S. N., 118, 280
de Bono, E., 50, 222, 223, 278
DeBord, K. B., 105, 280
Dellas, M., 103, 104, 106, 278
Dennis, W., 135, 278
Descartes, R., 124, 278
Diaz de Chumaceiro, C. L., 45, 278
Dillon, J. T., 252, 279
Dodds, R. A., 85, 289
Doolittle, J. H., 193, 252, 279
Dorval, K. B., 222, 289
Dow, G. T., 208, 224, 279
Drevhahl, J. E., 101, 277, 279
Dudeck, S. Z., 146, 279

Edwards, S. M., 207, 279
Eiduson, B. T., 101, 279
Einarsen, S., 155, 197, 283
Eisenberger, R., 13, 119, 204, 272, 245, 262, 279
Eisenman, R., 125, 279
Ekvall, G., 158, 198(t), 200, 279, 281
Ericsson, K. A., 74, 90, 279
Ernst, R., 132, 280
Eysenck, H., 103, 114, 279

Facaoaru, C., 86, 102, 110, 279
Fagot, B. I., 165, 279
Farisha, B., 103, 279
Fasko, D., 6, 279
Feldhusen, J. F., 75, 220, 279
Finke, R. A., 79, 85, 279
Firestien, R. L., 103, 289

Flavell, J. H., 59, 279
Florida, R., 3, 9, 279
Frängsmyr, T., 44, 168, 280
Freeman, H., 130, 163, 284
Fromm, E., 141, 280

Gaeth, J., 194, 277
Gaier, E. L., 103, 104, 106, 278
Gardner, H., 74, 89, 280
Garner, A., 6, 277
Garnier, H., 90, 146, 286
Gautier, T., 24, 280
Gero, J. S., 135, 138, 151, 253, 287
Getzels, J. A., 67, 105, 253, 280
Ghiselin, B., 70, 255, 280
Glaser, R., 250, 285
Glover, J. A., 86, 280
Glück, J., 132, 280
Goertzel, M. C., 110, 280
Goertzel, T. C., 110, 280
Goertzel, V., 110, 280
Goldfarb, P., 141, 275
Gordon, W. J., 221, 280
Götz, K., 101, 280
Götz, K. O., 101, 114, 280
Gough, H. G., 105, 280
Graham, B., 105, 280
Gribov, I. A., 124, 142, 280
Gruber, H. E., 118, 124, 280
Grudin, R., 31, 280
Gryskiewicz, N. D., 198, 198(t), 275
Guilford, J. P., 7, 190, 249, 280

Hadamard, J., 46, 280
Hall, W. B., 146, 279
Hallowell, N., 194, 277
Handlon, J. H., 104, 285
Harlan, P., 97, 282
Harrington, D. M., 103, 104, 133, 153, 166, 276, 280
Hassenstein, M., 85, 100, 280
Hausdorf, P. A., 104, 116, 194, 276
Hausman, C. R., 72, 280
Heinelt, G., 30, 104, 281
Helson, R., 95, 98, 102, 177, 181, 234, 281
Henle, M., 111, 281

Hennessey, B. A., 178, 180, 263, *281*
Heron, W., 105, 135, *281*
Herrmann, W., 130, *281*
Hiebert, J., 16, *288*
Higgins, J. M., 8, 30, *281*
Hoffman, M. L., 164, *281*
Hong, E., 177, 183, *283*
Hruby, G. G., 223, *281*
Huczynski, W., 215, *281*
Hudson, L., 85, 86, *281*
Huesman, R., 194, 277

Isaksen, S. G., 103, 198(t), 200, 222, *281*,
   289
Isen, A. M., 105, *281*

Jacklin, C. N., 163, *283*
Jackson, P. W., 67, 105, 179, *280*, *281*
James, K., 161, *281*
Jamison, K. R., 97, 109, *281*
Jang, K., 111, *285*
Jay, E. S., 252, *282*
Jellen, H. G., 191, 234, *289*
Johnson, D. I., 194, *282*
Johnson, J. F., 185, 186, *284*
Josephson, M., 74, *282*
Joussemet, M., 262, *282*

Kaemmerer, W. F., 198(t), 200, *287*
Kahn, R. I., 9, *282*
Kasof, J., 190, *282*
Katz, D., 9, *282*
Kaufman, J. C., 2, 25, 35, 76, 96, 103(n1),
   125, *278*, *282*
Kerr, B., 194, 277
Keyser, D. J., 185, *288*
Kim, K. H., 185, *282*
King, N., 25, *282*
Kinney, D. K., 97, 208, *282*, *286*
Kirton, M., 197, *282*
Kitto, J., 181, *282*
Kleman, M., 104, *285*
Kline, M. A., 219, 277
Knapper, C. K., 1, *282*
Koestner, R., 262, *282*
Kogan, N., 190, 191, *282*, *289*
Kohlberg, L. A., 165, *282*

Köstler, A., 56, *282*
Krepelka, E. J., 224, *283*
Krystal, 98, *282*

Larey, T. S., 167, *282*
Lauer, K. J., 198(t), 200, *281*
LeBlanc, D., 97, *282*
Lehman, H. C., 145, *282*
Lehmann, A. C., 74, *279*
Leinbach, M. D., 165, *279*
Leritz, L. E., 215, 224, 225, 226, 243, 244,
   287
Lewin, G., 157–158, *283*
Lim, W., 192, *286*
Lindauer, M. S., 145, *282*
Lipmen-Blumen, J., 163, 164, 166, 176,
   199(t), 201, *282*
Lok, D., 181, *282*
Lonergan, D. C., 80, *283*
Lowing, P. A., 97, *282*
Lubart, T. I., 74, 75, 85, 123, *283*,
   288
Ludwig, A. M., 27, 99, 210, *283*

Maccoby, E. E., 163, *283*
MacKinnon, D. W., 28, 101, 102, *283*
Maier, M., 127, *285*
Mansfield, R. S., 224, *283*
Manz, A. E., 114, *287*
March, J. G., 79, *283*
Marks, M. A., 185, 186, *284*
Martindale, C., 114, *284*
Martinson, O., 56, *283*
Marvzewski, T., 251, *283*
Maslow, A. H., 98, 123, *283*
Mathisen, G. E., 155, 197, *283*
May, R., 98, *283*
Mayer, R. E., 208, 224, *279*
McCaulley, M. H., 196, *284*
McCrae, R. R., 105, *283*
McLaren, R. B., 125, *283*
McMullan, W. E., 116, 117, *283*
Mednick, S. A., 51, 169, *283*
Meeker, M., 190, *283*
Merzel, A. P. C., 208, *286*
Messici, S., 179, *281*
Michael, W. B., 183, *283*

Michalko, M., 217, 223, *283*
Milgram, R. M., 177, 183, *283*
Miller, A. I., 31, 56, 111, *284*
Millward, L. J., 130, 163, *284*
Mitchell, J., 189, *287*
Moertl, P., 111, 156–157, 158, *284*
Morning Herald, 259, *284*
Motamedi, K., 103, *284*
Moustakis, C. E., 123, *284*
Mumford, M. D., 80, 111, 156–157, 158, 185, 186, 192, 193, 215, 224, 225, 226, 243, 244, 250, 252, *283, 284, 287*
Myers-Briggs, I., 196, *284*

Nardi, K., 114, *284*
Necka, E., 118, *284*
Neff, G., 104, *284*
Nemiro, J., 124, *286*
Newell, A., 250, *284*
Nichols, J. G., 102, 208, *284*
Nisbett, R., 152, *286*
Nobel Foundation, 70, *284*
Noscal, C. S., 251, *283*
Nowicki, G. P., 105, *281*

O'Connor, J. J., 67, *284*
O'Quin, K., 179, 254, *276*
Odena, O., 246, *284*
Oldham, G. M., 8, 176, *284*
Olken, H., 40, 60, 207, *285*
Olson, M., 9, *285*
Osborn, A. F., 216, 217, *285*

Pallier, G., 189, *287*
Park, J., 111, *285*
Parloff, M. B., 104, *285*
Parnes, S. J., 222, *285*
Paulus, B., 166, 167, *285*
Paulus, P. B., 167, *282*
Perkins, D. N., 110, 252, *282, 285*
Petersen, S., 157, *285*
Peterson, H., 69, *285*
Petocz, P., 204, *285*
Pilzer, P. Z., 8, *285*
Planck, M. K. E. L., 112, *285*

Plucker, J. A., 27, 177, 186, 192, 209, *285, 286*
Podger, D., 6, *288*
Poincaré, J. H., 60, 254, *285*
Powell, G. N., 163, *285*
Prindle, E. J., 86, 101, *285*
Proctor, R. M. J., 181, 182, *285*
Puccio, G. J., 167, *285*

Rabinowitz, M., 250, *285*
Rathunde, K., 183, *278*
Rechtin, E., 127, *285*
Reid, A., 6, 204, *285, 288*
Renzulli, J. S., 85, *286*
Reynolds, C. R., 86, *280*
Rhodes, M., 11, *286*
Richards, R., 97, 208, *282, 286*
Rickards, T. J., 59, 69, 155, 159, *286, 289*
Robertson, E. F., 67, *284*
Roe, A., 102, *285*
Rogers, C. R., 98, *285*
Ronning, R. R., 86, *280*
Root-Bernstein, R. S., 90, 146, *286*
Ross, L., 152, *286*
Rossman, J., 75, 101, *286*
Rothenberg, A., 49, *286*
Rothman, A., 36, *286*
Rudowicz, E., 181, *282*
Runco, M. A., 80, 100, 103, 104, 124, 192, *275, 286*

Safter, H. T., 106, 156, *288*
Saunders, K. N., 85, *289*
Savransky, S. D., 78, 222, 251, *286*
Sawyer, R. K., 77, *287*
Sawyers, J., 105, *280*
Schein, V. E., 163, *287*
Schuldberg, D., 98, 109, 128, *287*
Schwebel, M., 124, *287*
Scott, G., 80, 163, 215, 224, 225, 226, 243, 244, *283, 287*
Scott, T. E., 74, *287*
Seger, C. A., 68, *287*
Semmer, E., 71, 90, *287*
Shaughnessy, M. E., 114, *287*

Shaw, J. C., 250, *284*
Shaw, M. P., 116, 118, 138, *287*
Siegel, S. M., 198(t), 200, *287*
Sikand, J. S., 97, *278*
Simon, H. A., 59, 250, *284*, *287*
Simonton, D. K., 44, 91, 132, 133, 145, *287*
Smith, J., 90, *279*
Smith, S. M., 79, 85, *279*
Snyder, A., 189, *287*
Sortore, M., 25, 215, 224, *289*
Sosa, R., 135, 138, 151, 253, *287*
Stariha, W. E., 124, *289*
Sternberg, R. J., 40, 44, 75, 78, 85, 123, 124, 130, 182, 251, 253, *288*
Stigler, J. W., 16, *288*
Stringer, R., 157–158, *283*
Supinski, E. P., 192, 193, 250, 252, *284*
Sweetland, R. C., 185, *288*

Talbot, R. J., 197, *285*
Tardiff, T. Z., 253, *288*
Taylor, I. A., 179, 254, *288*
Threlfall, K. V., 192, 193, 250, 252, *284*
Tighe, E., 29–30, 254, *275*
Tilbury, D., 6, *288*
Torrance, E. P., 88, 106, 156, 185, 186, 187, 217, 224, 252, *288*

Treffinger, D. J., 25, 103, 197, 215, 222, 224, *285*, *288*, *289*

Unger, F., 132, *280*
Urnan, K. K., 166, 191, 224, 234, *289*

van der Heijden, B. I. J. M., 90, *289*
VanGundy, A. B., 166, 167, *289*
Vielot, J., 23(n1), 24, *289*
Vosberg, S. K., 180, 191, 263, *289*

Walberg, H. J., 124, *289*
Walk, C. L., 196, *289*
Wallach, M. A., 224, *289*
Wallach, M. M., 190, *289*
Wallas, G., 12, 46, *289*
Ward, K., 96, *289*
Ward, T. B., 79, 85, *279*, *289*
Weeks, D. J., 96, *289*
Weisberg, R., 74, *289*
Welsh, G. S., 114, *289*
West, M., 155, 199(t), 200, *275*, *289*
Whalen, S., 183, *278*

Zaccaro, S. J., 185, 186, *284*
Zimbalist, M. E., 97, *282*
Zuckerman, M., 135, *289*

Subject Index

accommodation, 56–57
age and creativity, 145–146
aleatoric music, 44
assessment
    accuracy of, 258
    consensual assessment, 178
    creativity-facilitating, 263–265
    Cropley Solution Diagnosis Scale, 271
    evaluating assignments, 261–263
    in higher education, 237, 249
    knowledge and, 251, 260–261, 264–270
    in music, 246
    non-custodial, 204–205
    of creativity of solutions, 263–273
    problem finding and, 252
    self-assessment, 50, 57, 60, 98, 116, 133,
        156, 157, 181, 195, 196
    setting assignments, 260–261
assignments
    effects of evaluation, 262–263
    evaluating, 261–263
    grading of, 178
    in higher education, 256
    knowledge and, 260
    setting, 260–261
    underdefined, 260–261
assimilation, 56–57

blocks
    creativity training and, 212–217
    external encouragement, 112–113
    gender roles as, 213
    groups, 167
    personal properties, 182–183

personality, 108–109
problem definition and, 256
social motivation and, 136
teams and, 168
broad networks, 56
business
    lack of effective novelty, 8–10

case studies
    a remote associate, 52
    assessment of creativity in education,
        266–273
    creativity as an environmental norm,
        108
    creativity that shakes deeply held
        beliefs, 140
    defining the problem in a creative-
        facilitating way, 252
    effective novelty that goes too far, 130
    incidental learning, 68
    latent creativity, 36
    le plus ca change, le plus c'est la meme
        chose, 259
    negative consequences of well-
        intentioned creativity, 125
    novelty that others cannot understand,
        144
    personality and creativity, 100–101
    preference for overdefined problems,
        258–259
    problem discovery and creativity, 112
    raw talent is not enough, 84
    resistance to change, 9
    socially challenging creativity, 131

case studies *(continued)*
  the Cropley solution diagnosis scale
    (CSDS), 271–272
  the prepared mind, 70
  the relationship between novelty and
    effectiveness in creative products, 35
  the role of knowledge and routine in a
    highly creative activity, 77
  the unprepared mind, 71
  transferring knowledge from one field
    to another, 72
  two constrasting ways of teaching
    mathematics, 16
  unusual coding of a familiar object, 55
case study of creativity in education
  analysis, 242–243
  assignments, 235–237
  creativity counseling, 234–235
  instruction 229ff
  evaluative phase, 237–238
  generalisation to other classes and dis-
    ciplines, 243–246
  outcomes, 238–242
  principles for fostering creativity in the
    classroom, 247
change
  blind, 10
  competition as a driver of, 2
  disastrous, 82–83, 89
  emerging technologies, 2
  evolutionary, 24, 32, 142–143
  innovation and, 1–2
  need for, 1–2
  organisational, 2, 8–9
  processes of, 78
  resistance to, 9
  revolutionary, 24, 32, 142–143
  steps in, 9–10
  techniques, 216–217
  tolerable, 105, 130
characteristics
  needed for creativity, 162
  test-defined, 205
climate
  institutional, 157–158
cognitive styles, 57–58
  meta-cognition, 59–60

competition
  driver of change, 2
communication
  innovation and, 160
complexity
  preference for, 114–116
  tolerance for, 115
conventional thinking
  creativity and, 67–93
convergent
  thinking, 7–8, 11, 47–49
convergent thinking
  contribution to creativity, 82
  importance in effective novelty, 80–81
  interaction with divergent thinking,
    79–87
counseling, 205, 228–231, 234–235,
    237–239, 242, 245–246
creative
  characteristics, 152
  leadership, 159–161
  people, 3–5
  potential in people, 181–188
  products, x, 18, 29
  profile, 118
  social definition of what is, 126–127
  social definition of who is, 128–129
  solutions, 254–255
  types, 195–197
creative behavior
  social influence on content, 133–134
creativity
  acknowledged, 3, 86, 96, 97, 101, 106,
    107, 110, 116, 145, 191, 194
  aesthetic, 7, 27, 30, 76–77, 102
  age and, 145–146
  amount of, 130
  artistic, 7, 25
  as a system, 23, 25–26, 34ff, 118–119,
    137–138
  as a system, 25–27
  aspects (three), ix
  aspects identified through tests,
    202–203
  assessment and, 249–273
  blind combination, 43–45
  chance-configuration model, 44–45

characteristics needed for, 162
cognitive factors, 10, 26, 117, 139
cognitive styles and, 57–59
conventional thinking and, 67–93
counseling, 205, 228–231, 234–235,
    237–239, 242, 245–246
criteria for products, 29–31
criteria of, 34, 36–38
dark side, 125
deliberate challenge, 24
deviance and, 126
diagnosing, 175–205
differentiated model of, 11–14, 19–20
differentiated model of, 176
divergent thinking, 8
domain-specificity of, 208–209
effect of the problem on, 256–258
effectiveness and, 25, 30
effectiveness of training for, 224–226
effects of evaluation on, 262–263
effortful, 67–72
effortless, 43–46, 68–70, 86
eliminating blockers to, 213–215
emotions in, 116
encouragement of, 7–8
engineering and, 3, 6, 14, 27, 33, 79,
    101, 210, 216, 228–229, 233–234,
    244
ethical aspects of, 124–126
evaluation and, 262
evaluation of relevance and effective-
    ness, 25–27
"fast-food," 15
-facilitating engineering class, 227–228
feelings in, 116
fostering in individual people, 212–216
fostering, 13, 207–212
functional, 14, 27, 36, 38, 52, 100, 102,
    106, 178–180
gender and, 162–166
generality of, 209–210
generation of effective novelty, 25–27
generation of variability, 27
groups and, 166–169
guidelines for assessment, 263
hard work and, 70–71
importance of, 24–25

in different domains, 210–212
in different fields, 27–28
in education, 6–8
in higher education, 7–8, 14
in science, 14, 27, 37, 101, 102, 124,
    208, 210ff
institutional environment and, 151–173
intention to bring about change, 24
interpersonal factors in, 25–26
intrapersonal factors in, 95–122, 25–26
intuition, 46
joy of creating, 116, 208, 231
kind of, 130–133
knowledge and, 72–79
lack of encouragement of, 6–7
lack of, 6
latent functional, 36–37
life history and, 183–184
luck, 45
malevolent, 2, 125–126
mechanisms of suppression/support,
    137–146
mental illness, 96–99
mood disturbance and, 97–98
motivation, 110–117
need to diagnose, 175–178
noncognitive factors, 11, 26, 108, 116,
    118, 177, 216
occupational, 101–102
organisations and, 151–158
paradoxes of, x, 38, 75, 95, 102
people and, 3–5
personality and, 100–110, 115
physical environment, 25
pre-requisite for, 2, 182
principles for fostering, 247
principles of, 180
problem-solving and, 249–255
production of novelty, 27
products, 28–41, 178–181
prosperity, 2–3, 228
pseudo-, 29–30, 110, 125, 139
quasi-, 29–30, 139
quotient, 188–197
relevance as a prerequisite of, 30
schizophrenia and, 96–97
skill deficiencies, 6

creativity *(continued)*
  social approach to, 123–126
  social determination of, 129
  social dimensions of, 126–134
  social environment and, 25, 123–150
  social mechanisms, 140–143
  social motivation, 135–137
  socially assigned roles and, 145–146
  source of organisational change, 2
  "spinach," 15
  sputnik shock, 7–8
  surprise and, 127
  teamwork, 168
  techniques for facilitating, 216–223
  test-defined characteristics, 205
  time and, 75–76
  usefulness and, 24–25
  value of, 13–14
  Vielot's conundrum, 23–24, 37–38
  war and, 125
  what is, 23–28

diagnosing creativity, 175–205
  goodness of fit, 176
  solution scale, 180–181
  the need for a multi-faceted approach
    to, 177–178
divergent thinking 8, 11, 47–49, 69–70
  interaction with convergent thinking,
    79–87
  measuring, 184–186
  scoring tests of, 186–188

education
  existing approaches to problem-setting
    in, 257–258
  lack of encouragement of creativity in,
    6–7
effective novelty
  generation of, 2
  introduction of, 2, 28
  lack of production of, 8–10
  production of, 26
  social environment and, 127–129, 137,
    138

effectiveness, 11, 18, 25, 30, 32, 34, 39,
  62–63, 178, 180, 202–203, 264
elegance, 11, 18, 31–32, 34, 39, 62–63,
  125, 178, 180, 203, 265
  external, 180
  internal, 180
emotions
  in creativity, 98, 99, 109, 116, 119, 162,
    165, 166
engineering and creativity, 3, 6, 14, 27,
  33, 79, 101, 210, 216, 228–229,
  233–234, 244
environment
  assisters and resisters, 156–157
  business, 8
  congenial, xi, 153–156, 158
  creativity and, 11, 129, 133, 137, 151,
    152
  effectiveness and, 127, 137, 138
  institutional climate, 157–158
  press, ix, 11, 13, 19, 20, 146
  social, 25, 107, 116, 129, 133, 134, 139,
    145
evaluation
  need for, 1–21
  of assignments, 261–263
evolutionary epistemology, 44
expertise, 90–91
exploration of novelty, 4, 9, 26–27, 46–47,
  51–59, 79–83, 100 107, 151, 160,
  209

feelings, 120
  in creativity, 95, 98, 116–120
fostering creativity 207–212
  eliminating blockers, 213–215
  in individual people, 212–216
  in the classroom, 247
functional creativity 14, 27, 36, 38, 52,
  100, 102, 106, 178–180

gender
  creativity and, 162–166
  male and female stereotypes, 163–165
  roles, 165, 201, 213

generalizability, 11, 18, 32, 34, 39, 62–63,
    125, 178, 180, 203, 265
generation
    of effective novelty, 2, 9
    of variability, 4, 9, 26–27, 46–47, 51–59,
        79–83, 100 107, 151, 160, 209
goodness of fit, 176
groups
    creativity and, 166–169
    ideal composition of, 168
    learning in, 236
    roles in, 167

higher education
    assignments in, 256
    lack of creativity in, 6–8
    learning in, 15
    place of creativity in, 7

interaction of convergent and divergent
        thinking
    phase approach, 86–87
    pre-requisite models, 84–85
    style models, 85–86
    superordinate ability approach, 85
innovation
    call for, 1–5
    change and, 1–2
    communication and, 160
    creativity and, 2–3
    definition, 2, 27, 87
    economic growth and, 8
    educational problem of, 6
    existing knowledge and, 72–74
    extended-phase model of, 87–91
    innovation-friendly behavior, 40, 41
    knowledge and, 26
    management for, 158–161
    motivation and, 111
    need for, 1–2
    openness for, 34
    organizations and, 157
    prosperity, 8
    psychological factors associated with,
        162

pyramid, 26
scale, 200
system of interacting factors, 26
wrong way approach and, 60–61
instruction
    contents of, 233, 245
    creativity facilitating, 228ff
    evaluation of, 237
    goals of, 229, 233–234
    methods, 245, 247
intrapersonal factors
    creativity and, 25–26
    creativity-facilitating traits, 103–104
intuition, 43, 46, 68–69

knowledge
    acquisition of general and specific, 26
    basis of creativity, 75
    conditional, 15–18
    creative problem-solving and, 251
    creativity and, 13, 38, 45, 49, 56–57,
        60, 69–71, 72–79, 82, 91, 138, 141,
        176, 180, 208, 210, 212, 256
    declarative, 15–18
    functioning, 15–18
    groups and, 166, 167, 221
    innovation and, 26, 87, 169
    intuition and, 46–47, 68
    kinds of, 15
    knowledge base, 90, 182, 251
    motivation and, 111–112, 114
    phases and, 117
    prerequisite for creativity, 182
    problems caused by, 87–89
    problem-solving and, 249–251
    procedural, 15–18
    professional, 16
    tacit, 68
    university, 16

leadership
    creative, 159–161
    gender and, 166
    in higher education, 161
    in organizations, 200–201

leadership *(continued)*
  innovation and, 26
  originality and, 186
  strategies, 21, 41, 71, 93, 122, 172
  test of, 190
learning verbs, 16–17
loops, 79, 118, 138
luck and creativity, 26, 43, 45, 61, 69–71, 80, 81–83, 156, 177, 251

management
  for innovation, 26, 80, 87, 111, 132, 146, 158–161
  gender and, 163–165
  goodness of fit and, 176
  scientific, 137
master and apprentice, 13–14
measuring
  divergent thinking, 184–186
mental illness/health
  creativity, 96–99, 129, 130
meta-cognition, 59–61
  barriers, 60–61
mind, 46, 52, 61, 75, 104, 111, 127, 152, 158
  blocks in the, 213–214
  prepared, 69–71
  unprepared, 71–72
mood disturbance and creativity, 97–98
motivation, ix, 120, 202–203
  assisters and, 157
  biological aspects, 135
  blocks and, 213
  cognitive, 111
  creativity and, 10, 11, 25, 26, 28, 38, 45, 85, 102, 110–117, 118, 154
  extrinsic, 112–114, 228, 242, 262
  gender and, 164
  individual differences in, 115
  innovation and, 111, 162
  instruction and, 228–229, 233, 234, 245, 247
  interaction with personality, 119, 182
  intrinsic, 112–114, 117
  knowledge and, 111–112, 114
  organizations and, 158

  paradoxes of, 116–117
  prerequisite for creativity, 182
  problem awareness and, 136
  social as pects of, 124, 135–137, 146
  test-defined, 195, 197, 205
  training creativity and, 224–226

novelty, 11, 18, 32, 34, 39, 62–63, 125, 178, 180, 202, 264
  ability to generate useful, 24–25
  as part of system, 119
  attitude to, 243
  blind combinations and, 44–45, 68
  blocks, 113
  change and, 2
  coding and, 54–55
  cognitive styler and, 57–59
  creativity training and, 242
  criterion of creativity, 11, 29–30
  decay, 76
  divergent and convergent thinking in, 81
  effective, 2–5, 13, 18, 20, 25–28, 35, 36
  exploration of, 81–83, 146, 209
  generalizable, 31
  intuition and, 46
  knowledge and, 89–90
  luck and, 45
  need for, 1–2, 9
  networks and, 56
  normal distribution, 188
  organizations and, 9, 197, 200
  orthodox, 130, 132
  paradox, 119, 175
  personality and, 106, 109
  phases and, 38–39, 86–87, 95, 119
  product vs. processs oriented, 132
  production of, 46–51, 78, 79–81
  radical, 130, 132, 133, 136, 171
  rejecting, 113
  relevant and effective, 25
  remote associates and, 51–52, 221
  society's ability to tolerate, 77, 104, 129, 138–140, 142
  steps in, 9
  surprise and, 127

TCT-DP and, 191–192
teams and, 168
thinking, 43–65

openness
importance of, 104–105
of a society, 143–145
organizations
assessing creativity of, 197–201
broad understanding of, 153
challenges to, 8–10
components of, 153
creativity-facilitating aspects of,
197–201
goodness of fit, 176
openness in, 9–10
site of creativity, 151–158
tests of conditions in, 197–201
orthodoxy
production of, 51

packages
for fostering creativity, 207–226
paradoxes, x, 38, 75, 95, 102
novelty paradox, 75
paradoxical personality, 116–117,
165–166
person, 11–13, 20, 120
creative potential in, 181–188
creative types, 195–197
creativity technicians, 5
diagnosing creativity of, 175–205
finding creative, 2–5
fostering creativity in individual,
212–216
producers, 3–5
secretary, 5
thought leaders, 3–5
personal properties
as a prerequisite for creativity, 182
special, 194–195
personality, 120, 202–203
compelling cause, 107–108
creative, 95–99
dynamics of, 106–110
facilitator/blocker, 108–109

method for studying, 100–102
paradoxical, 116–117, 165–166
play and humour, 105–106
results of studies, 102–106
test-defined characteristics of, 205
traits favourable to creativity, 103–104
unacclaimed behaviour, 102
personality and creativity
cause-effect relationship, 106–107
common-cause explanation, 109–110
dynamics of, 106–110
phases, 11–13, 20, 86–88, 170–171, 202
phase model, 86–89, 117
activation, 12, 20, 39, 62, 89, 92, 120,
148, 170, 202, 250
communication, 12, 20, 39, 63, 89, 92,
121, 148, 171, 203, 250
extended, 12–13
generation, 12, 20, 39, 62, 89, 92, 120,
148, 170, 202, 250
illumination, 12, 20, 39, 63, 87, 89, 92,
120, 148, 170, 203, 250
incubation, 12, 87
innovation and, 87
motivation and, 117
phases and, 250
preparation, 12, 20, 39, 62, 89, 92, 120,
148, 170, 202, 250
validation, 12, 20, 39, 63, 89, 92, 121,
148, 171, 203, 250
verification, 12, 20, 39, 63, 87, 89, 92,
121, 148, 170, 203, 250
Wallas, 12, 46, 86–87, 222
potential
psychological dimensions of creative,
181–183
press, 11–13, 20, 148, 170–171, 202–203
problem, 11–13, 20
awareness, 136, 253–254
definition, 256
finding, 252–253
setting, 257–258
problem-solving
aspects of, 249–250
assessment and creativity, 249–273
components of creative, 251–254

problem-solving *(continued)*
 creativity and, 249–255
 phases and, 250
 tests based on, 192–194
procedures
 popular and commercial, 223
process, 11–13, 20, 92, 120, 148, 170–171, 202–203
processes
 of divergent and convergent thinking, 81
products, 11–13, 20, 120, 148, 170–171, 202–203
 creativity of, 18, 28–37
 diagnosing creativity of, 175–205
 dimensions of creative, 178, 180
 domain relevance of creative, 33–34
 elegant, 31–33
 fields, 29
 hierarchy of creative, 31–33
 innovative, 31–33
 original, 31–33
 routine, 31–33
 scales for assessing, 178–180
 situation relevance of, 33–34
 specifying creativity of, 178–181
programs
 for fostering creativity, 207–226
 formal training, 220–223
pseudo-, 29–30, 110, 125

quasicreativity, 30, 32, 76, 80, 108, 139, 260

relevance, 11, 18, 34, 39, 62–63, 178, 180, 202, 264
remote associates, 51–52, 221
risk
 change and, 10, 81–83
 gender and, 163–164
 groups and, 166, 168
 play and, 105–106
 socialization and, 212–213
 willingness to take, 27, 69, 99, 103, 109, 111, 114, 132, 138, 154, 156, 162, 195, 197, 205, 208, 212

roles, 140, 145, 146
 in organizations, 151, 153, 160–161, 169
 models, 161

scales
 Cropley solution diagnosis, 180–181
 for assessing the creativity of products, 178–180
schizophrenia and creativity, 96–97
scientific creativity, 27, 101, 102, 124, 208, 210ff
 motivation and, 111
self-assessment, 50, 57, 60, 98, 116, 133, 156, 157, 181, 195, 196
social
 approach to creativity, 123–126
 definition of what is creative, 126–127
 definition of who is creative, 128–129
 determination of creativity, 129
 dimensions of creativity, 126–134
 influence on content of behaviour, 133–134
 mechanisms and creativity, 140–143
 nature of impulse, 135–137
social environment
 changing standards, 127–128
society
 ability to tolerate novelty, 138–140
 openness of, 143–145
solution
 elegant, 265
 generalizable, 265
 original, 264
 routine, 264
solutions
 creative, 254–255
 creativity as first step, 2–3
 defining creative, 255
 guidelines for assessment of, 263–273
Sydney Opera House, 33, 138, 254
system
 creativity as a, 34–36, 137–138

teams/teamwork, 168
techniques, 15, 17, 26, 29, 210, 214, 215–216, 220

brainstorming, 24, 167–168, 217–218
CPS, 222–223
creativity facilitating, 210, 214
hierarchical method, 219
imagery training, 217
KJ method, 217–218
mind maps, 217, 219, 220
morphological analysis, 217–218
NM method, 217
specific creativity-facilitating, 216–223
synectics, 217, 221
TRIZ, 79, 222
technology
change and, 2
tests
creativity quotient, 188–189
CRT, 193–194
divergent thinking, 184–186
identifying creativity, 202–203
KAI, 197
life history, 183–184
MBTI, 196
MMPI, 97
of products, 178–181
organisational conditions, 197–201
personal properties, 194–195
problem-solving, 192–194
RAT, 189–190
scoring, 186–188
TCT-DP, 191–192, 205, 229, 234, 235, 238, 239, 242
TTCT, 177, 185, 186, 191, 194, 224
types, 195–196
thinking
concentration on uncreative forms of, 7–8

conventional, 67–93
convergent and divergent, 48
convergent, 68–69
divergent, 47–49
generation of variability, 51–59
heterospatial, 50
homospatial, 50
interaction of convergent and divergent, 79–87
janusian, 49–50
meta-cognition, 59–61
novelty, 43–65
prerequisite for creativity, 182
tests of creative, 189–191
training
characteristics of good, 226
effectiveness of, 224–226
formal programs, 220–223
value of, 224–226

understanding
deep, 16
extended abstract, 16–18
levels of, 15–18
multistructural, 16–18
prestructural, 16–18
relational, 16–18
surface, 16
unistructural, 16–18
unusual categories, 53–55

variability
generation and exploration of, 4, 9, 26–27, 46–47, 51–59, 79–83, 100 107, 151, 160, 209